CAREER OPPORTUNITIES IN COMPUTERS AND CYBERSPACE

Second Edition

CAREER OPPORTUNITIES IN COMPUTERS AND CYBERSPACE

Second Edition

Harry Henderson

Checkmark Books®
An imprint of Facts On File, Inc.

latest ed 2/06

Career Opportunities in Computers and Cyberspace, Second Edition

Copyright © 1999, 2004 by Harry Henderson

Checkmark Books
An imprint of Facts On File, Inc.
132 West 31st Street
New York NY 10001

Library of Congress Cataloging-in-Publication Data
Henderson, Harry, 1951–
    Career opportunities in computers and cyberspace / Harry Henderson.—2nd ed.
      p. cm.
    Includes bibliographical references and index.
    ISBN 0-8160-5094-5 (alk. paper)—ISBN 0-8160-5095-3 (pb.: alk. paper)
    1. Computer industry—Vocational guidance. 2. Internet—Vocational guidance. I. Title.

    QA76.25.H46 2004
    004′.023—dc21   2003053142

Checkmark Books are available at special discounts when purchased in bulk quantities for businesses, associations, institutions, or sales promotions. Please call our Special Sales Department in New York at (212) 967-8800 or (800) 322-8755.

You can find Facts On File on the World Wide Web at http://www.factsonfile.com

Cover design by Nora Wertz

Printed in the United States of America

VB Hermitage 10 9 8 7 6 5 4 3 2 1

This book is printed on acid-free paper.

CONTENTS

FOREWORD
Challenge and Opportunity

In 1999, when the first edition of this book was published, it seemed as though the computer industry and in particular the Internet and World Wide Web would continue their remarkable growth indefinitely. Plenty of career opportunities would thus be available to students graduating from high school and college in the years to come, and there would also be good opportunities for older workers to seek more promising careers.

As readers of this second edition will certainly know, things did not quite work out that way. The computer industry, particularly the high-flying "dot-com" (Internet) businesses, entered a downturn in 2001. Hundreds of dot-coms went out of business. While there have been some notable successes, such as the giant bookstore Amazon.com and the remarkably robust auction service eBay, the reality of selling goods and services has proved to be much more difficult than just opening up a website and waiting for customers to flock in.

Even the "core" of the computer industry—the manufacture of computer chips, PCs, and business software—has seen a slowdown. With the economy as a whole becoming stagnant, many businesses postponed their purchases of additional PCs or the upgrading of existing systems. The general economy has also been hurt by the uncertainty brought about by terrorist attacks, the challenges of wars and lengthy foreign entanglements, and the loss of confidence in business leaders resulting from the Enron and other corporate accounting scandals. As of late 2003 the economy showed signs of recovery, but was still a long way from its pre-downturn peak.

With all that said, there are some important things that readers seeking computer-related careers need to keep in perspective. First, while the rate of growth of the computer industry has at least temporarily slowed, the PC, local networks, and the Internet are definitely here to stay. Computers have forever changed the ways in which people carry out business, education, government, and home life.

Keep in mind that for a student looking at future careers (and even for an older worker looking at a career change), it is not the economic conditions of this year or even the next couple of years that matter most. Stock markets and economies recover from downturns. New markets and technologies continue to open up. In deciding how to study and plan for a career, readers need to focus not so much on what is in demand today but on what is most likely to be in demand in the next three, five, or 10 years.

Change comes swiftly. By the end of the 1980s the personal computer had moved from a kit for experimenters to an essential tool for every office. During the 1990s the World Wide Web went from the research laboratory into millions of businesses and schools. While the current decade may not have such a single compelling technological revolution, there are a number of important emerging technologies that offer exciting career possibilities. These areas include:

- Health care, including pharmaceuticals and hospital services. (This is particularly true, because the vast baby boom generation is getting older and will need more medical services while enjoying a longer lifespan than ever before.)
- Biotechnology, genetics, and related fields such as bioinformatics. The "database" that is life's DNA code is being unlocked and analyzed using new software and techniques, and this long-term effort promises to bring effective new treatments for many serious diseases.
- "Data mining," or the discovery and analysis of patterns hidden within the data being processed in business and science. Companies are using data mining techniques to better understand (and market to) their customers. Government agencies are beginning to use the same techniques in law enforcement and the fight against terrorism.
- "Information Architecture" or the use of XML (Extensible Markup Language) and other facilities for making information on the Web more useful by making relevant data easier to find.
- The creation of programs called "bots" or "Intelligent Agents." Using artificial intelligence techniques, these programs can "understand" much more than simple commands. They represent the next generation of Web search tools, as well as offering help with everything from shopping to health care questions.
- Powerful new kinds of computer systems, including those that harness large numbers of processors and "distributed" systems, which allow many computers to cooperate to solve a problem.
- Mobile and wireless communications devices and networks, leading to "pervasive computing" where people are continuously linked to one another and to information sources regardless of geographical location.

- New security technology to fight terrorism, including "biometrics" (such as face recognition) and analysis and profiling of behavior. Of course these applications also bring genuine concerns about privacy and civil liberties.
- Long-term research that might lead to a breakthrough as important as the transistor and integrated circuit. This may lead to computing on a molecular scale (nanotechnology) or even "quantum computing," which might be able to use the mysterious inner properties of matter to infinitely expand computing power.

Meanwhile, opportunities will still be available in more conventional areas. The computer industry depends on talented programmers, multimedia developers, and writers to create the next generation of products for the office, science and engineering, and educational applications. Businesses will continue to want to use the Web to advertise and sell products. Opportunities in e-commerce are likely to be less grandiose than the business plans of the late 1990s, but thousands of small businesses are selling goods on-line, whether through their own websites or via on-line store services and auction sites such as eBay.

People will also be needed to design, manufacture, sell, and service PCs and other computer products and to install conventional, satellite, and wireless networks. Teachers will be needed to train computer users within corporations and vocational schools or to teach computer science classes at universities. As the list of jobs covered in this book demonstrates, computers play an important role in many kinds of work, each an opportunity for the individual who is motivated and willing to properly prepare.

In this world of uncertainty, challenge, and continuing opportunity there are some general approaches that can help anyone begin a rewarding career in the computer field:

- If you are still in high school, explore widely and consider a variety of possible interests. Don't get "tunnel vision" by focusing too soon on a narrow area.
- Use the resources available at school and on-line to learn more about the careers in this book—and perhaps others that are just beginning to emerge.
- Use the book's Introduction and the Cross-Training sections in the various entries to identify key "clusters" of skills. By focusing on skills rather than specific jobs you can prepare yourself for several related careers, increasing your chances of finding a good position.
- Remember that if you are in high school or early college, the world in which you are preparing to work will likely be different in important ways from today's world. Try to be prepared, work systematically to gain experience, but stay flexible!
- If you are an older worker, look for ways to explore new skills and interests, even if you seem secure in your current job. The earlier you start to prepare, the easier it will be to make the transition to a new career if you find it necessary or desirable.

Today's world may be more challenging and less certain, but within difficulty and uncertainty wait many new opportunities for individuals who are prepared to take advantage of them. I hope this book will help you discover and explore a variety of such opportunities, and help you take the first steps down the road in preparing for an exciting future.

INTRODUCTION
Jobs in Information Technology

Computers and computer skills are used in just about every job or profession today. No organization, whether in business, science, government, education, or entertainment, can get along without them. After all, even baseball managers are using laptops in the dugout for keeping track of hits and pitches.

Two basic criteria were used for selecting the employment opportunities highlighted in this book. The first includes jobs that are directly involved in the computer industry—developing, marketing, advertising, selling, and supporting software and hardware. The second extends to jobs that are not limited to the computer industry, but that rely heavily on information technology and continue to be transformed by that technology. Examples include manufacturing, office work, journalism, librarianship, and various specialty occupations.

The jobs described in this book are broken down into 10 categories. These categories reflect the fact that jobs tend to come in related groups that share a "cluster" of skills, objectives, and working conditions. For example, while systems, applications, and scientific programmers write programs for different purposes and tend to use different features of the computer system, the process they are engaged in—software development—draws on a common set of skills, such as problem analysis, organization of data and functions, and the writing and testing of computer code.

This introduction briefly introduces each of the 10 categories and brings out some of the common features and skills of each set of jobs. You can use it as a guide in browsing for job descriptions that might match your interests and aptitudes.

Programming and Software Development

Software development is a process that starts with the analysis of a need for managing or processing information such as organizing data into a database or graphically displaying scientific measurements. Software developers must turn this analysis into specifications for creating the software. The description of what data is to be processed and how to process it becomes the blueprint for writing the program code. The code must be written, tested, and refined until it works reliably and meets the need.

There are two major venues for software development. Commercial software developers create software to be used by businesses, other organizations, and consumers. They do market research to identify needs that could be met by a new product, and then develop such a product for sale. In-house software developers in corporations or other organizations outside the computer industry respond to requests from managers and professionals within the organization to create programming that meets their specific needs.

In addition to regular employment prospects within or outside the software industry, there are many opportunities for programmers and analysts to work as freelance consultants. Some of the hottest areas in programming today include data analysis ("data mining"), genetics, bioinformatics and other scientific programming, distributed computing (using multiple processors or networked computers), and security applications.

The skills cluster for software development includes problem analysis, program design, structuring data and procedures (routines), attention to detail, and ability to improvise and adapt.

Information Systems Operation and Management

Complex computer systems and networks must be constantly maintained and adapted to changing needs. Workers in this category operate, test, manage, or otherwise support an information system. The skills can be divided into operational (running equipment, carrying out monitoring procedures, and organizing data) and management (supervising and planning). The jobs range from the clerical (computer operators and archivists) to systems administrators, upper management, and executive positions.

In general, these positions require the ability to master complex procedures and perform them consistently, pay constant attention to details, and deal with unexpected problems. Some positions also require considerable interpersonal communication skills or management ability.

Training and Support

Because modern software and operating systems are complex and full of features and options, users must be trained and helped to solve any problems with the operation of the software or hardware. Trainers provide systematic instruction in the use of the systems and software, while support representatives deal with particular problems or questions. These jobs combine technical knowledge and problem-solving skills with the ability to teach, explain, and communicate.

General Networking

These positions deal with the ever-growing networking and telecommunications connections that link computers within an organization or between the organization and the outside world. Skills employed range from engineering and design to operation and management. Workers in this field must master complex details and procedures, and continually assess the options and tradeoffs offered by new technology. In particular, they must develop ways to integrate emerging technology such as wireless Internet and multifunction mobile telephones.

Web and Internet

The Internet has radically changed the networking environment since the mid-1990s. Although the dot-com boom of the late 1990s became something of a bust in the early 2000s, the Internet continues to reshape education, government, commerce, and society as a whole. Internet work includes providing connectivity and services and the design, development, and management of webpages and websites. There are also a growing number of traditional professions such as journalism, advertising, and marketing that are appearing in new forms on the net. Graphics and design skills, along with writing and marketing ability, are the keys to utilizing this new medium.

Graphics and Multimedia

Closely related to multimedia Web design is the use of computer graphics, animation, and sound for educational and game programs, whether stand-alone or networked. Traditional artistic and writing skills are adapted to the new interactive media. Specialists in creating and manipulating graphic images, animation programming, sound production, and narration must coordinate their efforts under the guidance of directors or producers in order to create a successful product. The various jobs in this category offer opportunities to be a designer, creator, or manager—or sometimes all three!

Manufacturing

Most people are familiar with the use of computers in business and education, but many don't realize how much computers and automation have changed the traditional manufacturing industries. Specialists in this field use skills ranging from designing and drawing to programming robot machinery and embedded computers. Technicians help engineers implement and test their designs, and keep the machines running smoothly. This field offers an exciting mix of theory and practical mechanical knowledge, and the challenge of turning ideas into physical reality.

Computer Industry Specialists

This job category covers people who work in the business side of the computer hardware and software industry. They configure, advertise, market, and sell products. They deal with the public and media, or analyze industry trends. Skills shared by these specialities include understanding of customer needs and industry trends, the ability to communicate with the public, and plain old-fashioned sales technique.

Computer-Related Office Positions

This category looks outside the computer industry at other business activities in which computers are extensively used. Some of these positions are modern versions of traditional clerical jobs such as typing and filing. Others involve knowledge of more advanced software used to create documents, publications, maps, and other products. Several more specialized positions use mathematical and analytical skill. In addition to mastering the appropriate computer skills, the individual is challenged to use the technological tools to meet the organization's overall objectives.

Academic Information Science Professions

The final category deals with the people who work with the science of information management. This includes professors who teach courses in software design, programming, and information management and who perform basic research in information science. Librarians and library workers are also included, for two reasons. First, computers are now used extensively in library reference and cataloging work. Second, librarians have always played a key role in the organization of information and in making it accessible to people from diverse backgrounds.

Skills and interests in this area range from pure research and teaching to organizing information and making it accessible to a wide variety of people. Communication skills are a very important component of this process.

HOW TO USE THIS BOOK

The job descriptions in this book provide an overview and discussion of more than 85 positions involving computers and information processing. They are divided into 10 categories. Each entry is organized as follows.

Career Profile

The entry begins with a section that briefly summarizes key aspects of the position.

Duties: This describes the essential purpose of the position.

Alternate Title(s): This lists other titles for this position that may be found in employment ads. Some titles may indicate closely related positions or more specialized positions.

Salary Range: This is an *approximate* indication of what an individual may expect to earn in this position as of early 2003. Generally this reflects a range from entry-level to moderately experienced. Highly experienced individuals or those with highly specialized skills may make considerably more. The salary range is best used as an indication of the relative value of the position compared to others, and should not be relied on too much.

Employment Prospects: This is a rating ranging from poor to excellent, with most falling in the fair to good category of how easy or hard it is to get an entry-level position.

Advancement Prospects: This is a general indication of how easy or hard it is to move up the career ladder from this position.

Prerequisites:

Education or Training: This covers the level of education or training likely to be required by prospective employers, such as high school graduate, two-year college (associate degree), four-year college (B.A. or B.S. degree), or graduate degree (M.S. or Ph.D.).

Experience: This lists the type of work experience that employers prefer applicants to have.

Special Skills and Personality Traits: This provides a brief indication of the work skills that are most essential to this position, and the personality traits most likely to lead to success.

Career Ladder

This section indicates the location of the position within a typical career path, such as junior programmer, programmer/analyst, systems analyst, and project manager. Not all positions listed in the career ladder are discussed separately in this book. Smaller organizations may not have a formal career ladder, and may combine responsibilities from several positions. Large organizations may have many grades or steps within each level of the ladder.

Position Description

This is generally the longest part of the Career Profile. It describes in detail the tasks associated with the position, the typical workplace, and how the position relates to other positions. Bulleted lists are often used to summarize important tasks or considerations.

Salaries

This section discusses the factors that determine how much money a person will earn in this position. These factors include:

- the educational qualifications and experience of the individual at the time of hiring—higher education and more experience generally bring a higher starting salary
- whether the individual has particular skills that are in high demand
- whether the employer is in the private, academic, or government sector (government jobs in particular often pay somewhat less than jobs in the private sector, but may offer more job security)
- the size of the hiring firm (big firms may pay more, but smaller firms may offer better opportunities for quick advancement)
- the number of workers competing for openings (which can be influenced by educational trends and geographical concentration)
- economic growth and wage inflation

You can refine this analysis by consulting the latest salary surveys on the World Wide Web (see Appendix I).

Employment Prospects

This section treats many of the above factors from the point of view of how they affect an applicant's chance of being hired. Technological changes have reduced demand for some positions (such as data entry clerks). On the other hand, the growing complexity of information systems has driven up demand for positions such as systems analyst. The discussion also includes trends that may influence future demand for the position and ways in which applicants might improve their prospects.

Advancement Prospects

This discusses how hard it is to move up the career ladder from this position, and the typical paths to advancement (such as through greater specialization, going freelance, or going into management).

Education and Training

The educational qualifications given in the Career Profile summary are expanded, including recommended courses or subject areas. Additional training or industry certification is included where appropriate.

Experience, Skills, and Personality Traits

Experience and demonstrable skills are often as important as education. This section summarizes intellectual and social skills that are most important for being successful in this position. There is also some indication of the kind of personality most suited for the work, but this should be taken only as a suggestion, since people and jobs are too complicated to pigeonhole.

Cross-Training

An important factor in career success in the Information Age is the ability to identify one's skills and interests and then find several related positions that might suit them. The Cross-Training section lists several interests that you might have in addition to those needed for the position being discussed. Corresponding positions are given for each interest. For example, someone who is interested in programming but also in testing software might want to look at the Quality Assurance Specialist profile.

By comparing such related career profiles you may be able to identify ways in which you can build up one or two skills that are applicable to several job descriptions. This "cross-training" can be used to prepare an individual for several different positions simultaneously, improving the chances for employment.

Unions and Associations

Some positions in this book may be unionized. Most, however, are considered professional or specialist positions and have professional organizations devoted to them. This section characterizes the kinds of organizations that a person in this position may wish to join, and gives a few examples. Appendix II lists many more organizations broken down into categories.

Tips for Entry

This final section gives a series of suggestions that can help an individual prepare for entry into the position. The first suggestions are geared to high school or college students who are still choosing which courses, internships, or work-study opportunities to take. Later suggestions give pointers for gaining work experience for the résumé and, eventually, entry-level positions.

Other Resources in This Book

The appendixes that follow the job descriptions describe additional resources that can help with career research and job hunting. Appendix I distills tips and techniques for using the World Wide Web to find job opportunities. The importance of learning to use on-line resources cannot be overemphasized. The other appendixes feature selected professional and industry organizations, periodicals, and books.

PROGRAMMING AND SOFTWARE DEVELOPMENT

PROGRAMMER, ENTRY-LEVEL

CAREER PROFILE

Duties: Writes or revises programs that instruct computers to perform tasks; tests and documents programs; usually works under the supervision of a senior programmer

Alternate Title(s): Assistant Programmer; Junior Programmer

Salary Range: $35,000 to $50,000 (more at higher levels)

Employment Prospects: Good

Advancement Prospects: Good

Prerequisites:

Education or Training—Four-year college in most cases; degree in computer science preferable; courses in application area (business or science) and technical writing helpful

Experience—Some background in business or science, as well as having written programs at school or home that can demonstrate proficiency

Special Skills and Personality Traits—Analytical and organizational ability; attention to detail; self-motivation and ability to work with minimal supervision

CAREER LADDER

| Lead Programmer/Project Manager |

| Systems Analyst or Software Engineer |

| Programmer or Programmer/Analyst |

| Junior (Entry-Level) Programmer |

Position Description

Computers have become a widespread and indispensable part of our daily lives. Without them, businesses could not manage their operations, airplanes could not land safely, and doctors would find it much harder to diagnose illness. The automatic teller and debit card machines used in daily commerce are part of a vast computer network. The dazzling special effects seen on the movie screen are created using special computer software. Even such ordinary objects as microwave ovens, VCRs, telephone answering machines, and cars depend on computer processors to control their operation.

Each of these devices can do nothing without a programmer having first created a sequence of instructions, or program, to control its operation. Programmers write their machine instructions in special languages such as C++, Java, and BASIC. The instructions specify how data will be obtained, organized, processed, and displayed. A special program called a compiler converts the instructions from key words and statements into low-level instructions called machine codes that tell the computer processor precisely

how to move each tiny piece of data inside the computer and how to perform calculations.

Most students today have been exposed to computer programming by taking school courses in languages such as BASIC and C++. Some students have gained additional experience by writing programs for their home computers.

Business Programmers, however, must work in a more structured environment. They often work together to create or revise lengthy programs. Some programs may obtain data from databases and create reports needed by managers to control the operation of the business. Other programs may keep track of inventory or perform transactions such as the buying or selling of products. Programs must often be modified to account for changes in the way business is done or revised to work with newer versions of the computer's operating system.

An Entry-Level Programmer works under the supervision of senior programmers or managers. Tasks for a beginning programmer might include the following:

- writing short "utility" programs to perform simple tasks
- writing a specified part of a large program

- finding and fixing "bugs" in existing programs
- making specified changes in a program ("program maintenance")
- testing "beta" or preliminary versions of programs
- writing or organizing program documentation (comments in the code or notes to be passed on to Technical Writers)

The Entry-Level Programmer will often work using detailed specifications provided by a senior programmer or analyst. In large information systems or data processing departments the beginning programmer will probably have to methodically work his or her way up the career ladder to more senior programming positions. In a smaller business, however, the beginning Programmer may soon be given greater responsibilities and more interesting challenges.

Salaries
Programming is one of the more highly paid professions available to recent college graduates. Salaries vary considerably, with pay being highest in major metropolitan areas and areas with a high concentration of technology companies (such as "Silicon Valley," south of San Francisco). An Entry-Level Programmer in a large corporate setting might expect to start at about $40,000 to $45,000 annually, although this will vary with the local cost of living. Salaries paid by federal or other governments are somewhat lower. Independent contractors performing basic programming tasks can receive from about $40 to $75 per hour.

Employment Prospects
While the average demand for Programmers continues to grow somewhat faster than the average for other kinds of work, increasing specialization and other changes in the industry have made it somewhat harder to find entry-level positions. Many positions have specific requirements for experience with particular languages, databases, and operating systems. People with a willingness to travel to areas with major corporate headquarters and/or many software development companies can improve their chances of obtaining employment.

Two trends that will tend to reduce the demand for Entry-Level Programmers are the increasing automation of low-level programming tasks (allowing nonprogrammers to develop database reports, for example) and the growing number of Programmers in other countries who can compete effectively with American Programmers in bidding for contracts.

On the other hand, emerging new technologies such as genetic engineering, mobile multimedia communications, or new kinds of Internet-based transaction systems can create a host of new opportunities for the well-prepared individual.

Advancement Prospects
Programmers working in large corporate settings generally experience greater job security but a slower rate of advancement. Programmers in small or "startup" companies may find themselves on a fast track to greater responsibilities and pay (and perhaps valuable stock options). Since the majority of startup businesses fail, however, there is little job security in such a career path, as was shown in the dot-com collapse of 2000–2002.

Programmers can improve their chances for advancement by keeping in touch with the latest developments in the field and developing expertise in languages, programming tools, and operating systems that are in high demand.

Education and Training
Until fairly recently education (beyond high school or basic college) was not a major consideration for many employers in this field. Increasingly, however, employers are using education as a "filter" to determine which candidates are likely to have the required skills for developing increasingly complex software products. Four years of college should be considered minimum for most positions, with a major in computer science, information systems, or a similar field preferred.

Still, there are some opportunities for people who do not have four years of college. For example, people who have strong real-world business experience may be able to combine it with some courses in programming at a local junior college and gain an entry-level programming position. Trade (vocational) schools offer training that can lead to an entry-level position. Such programs should be examined carefully, however, to ensure that the programming languages and other skills offered are those actually in demand in the marketplace.

Courses in mathematics, graphic design, and writing (composition) may prove helpful in preparation for the various aspects of modern software development. Persons interested in becoming business applications programmers should also take courses in business operations, management, accounting, and related fields. Similarly, persons with some background in science or medicine could pick up some programming skills and become attractive candidates for applications programming jobs in fields such as biotechnology or health care.

Earning industry certifications such as the MCSE (Microsoft Certified System Engineer) can also be useful, in that they help assure employers that candidates for entry-level programming jobs have sufficient understanding of the operating or network system to be used for the application.

It is still possible to break into programming with a minimum of formal qualifications. This is more likely with smaller business and Internet startups than with major corporations.

Experience, Skills, and Personality Traits

It is often said that the only way to become a writer is to write. This is also true of programming: Skill is developed by writing, testing, and improving a variety of different kinds of programs, either in school or on one's own. The combination of computer science theory and practical applications builds a foundation of skills that will be useful in the job market. Some of these skills include the ability to:

- break a problem into separate, manageable parts
- translate user specifications into appropriate objects (representations) to be constructed in the programming language
- take advantage of existing software as "building blocks" for new applications
- visualize a variety of possible solutions to a problem
- methodically test program code and ensure its reliability
- work well with other people on the software development team
- work under deadline pressure

Cross-Training for Entry-Level Programmers

Interests	Related Job Descriptions
science or engineering	Scientific or Engineering Programmer; Statistician; Bioinformatics Specialist
testing software operation	Quality Assurance Specialist
automating business operations	Systems Analyst; Database Analyst
databases	Database Analyst; Data Miner
creating software documentation	Technical Writer or Editor
self-employment	Systems Consultant

Unions and Associations

While some Programmers may belong to labor unions, most are considered to be professionals. Professional organizations for Programmers include the Association for Computing Machinery and the Institute for the Certification of Computer Professionals.

Tips for Entry

1. Take courses in both computer science/programming and business operations. Courses in writing (composition) can help you both with job applications and the documenting of program code on the job. Technical writing is a good cross-training possibility.
2. Use school projects and internship, work-study, or volunteer opportunities to gain actual programming experience that you can list on job applications.
3. Read technical journals. Become familiar with the Internet and use it as a resource for learning programming tools and techniques and also for finding employment opportunities.

SOFTWARE ENGINEER

CAREER PROFILE

Duties: Designs and writes complex computer programs as part of a software development team; applies principles of computer science to solving practical problems

Alternate Title(s): Programmer/Analyst; Programmer; Software Developer

Salary Range: $60,000 to $80,000 or more

Employment Prospects: Good

Advancement Prospects: Good

Prerequisites:

Education or Training—Minimum of four-year college degree with major in computer science; graduate degree preferred for senior positions; knowledge of science, engineering, or business depending on the type of programming to be done

Experience—Several years of programming experience, appropriate certification or training in operating systems, networks, or related areas

Special Skills and Personality Traits—Design, visualization, and problem-solving skills; ability to break down tasks into manageable pieces; ability to supervise junior members of the software development team; able to work long hours under pressure

CAREER LADDER

```
┌─────────────────────────────────┐
│   Manager, Information Systems   │
└─────────────────────────────────┘

┌─────────────────────────────────┐
│        Project Manager          │
└─────────────────────────────────┘

┌─────────────────────────────────┐
│ Lead Programmer/Systems Analyst │
└─────────────────────────────────┘

┌─────────────────────────────────┐
│     Software Engineer or        │
│      Programmer/Analyst         │
└─────────────────────────────────┘
```

Position Description

The traditional job title for a person who plays a major role in designing software for a corporation's internal use is programmer/analyst. This title implies a combination of design and programming skills.

In companies that develop software products for the general public, the term "software engineer" has become more prevalent. It reflects the movement in computer science toward seeing software development as a rigorous discipline similar to traditional forms of engineering. Much of the material in this entry applies to both titles.

Designing modern commercial and scientific software is a complex task that is usually broken down into several stages:

- determining the needs of the intended users of the program, sometimes with the aid of interviews or surveys
- writing a set of specifications that describe what data will be used by the program, how it will be collected and verified, the user interface to control the program, and the results (calculations or reports) to be produced from the data
- designing the overall structure of the program, including the major modules or objects and their relationships
- writing and testing the code for the modules
- testing and revising the program as a whole, including getting feedback from users
- maintaining the program by providing fixes and updates as users' needs change
- providing documentation for the program and help screens or other aids for users

The Software Engineer (or programmer/analyst) will often do both design work and program code writing.

Software developers are often under intense pressure to deliver projects on time. While this is true for developers of "in-house" systems for business, it is even more the case for companies whose product is software itself. A late product may well mean loss of business to a competitor, or worse. The lifestyle of software developers can feature 60- to 70-hour weeks. Poor nutrition and lack of exercise are potential dangers of what can be an intellectually exhilarating profession.

While programming is traditionally not considered to be a "people-oriented" activity, the best software designers are those who combine design skills, mastery of technical detail, and the ability to identify with the needs of the people who will use the software. Good people skills can also help a programmer move into management positions such as Lead Programmer or MIS Director.

Salaries

Salaries for intermediate-level programmers, programmer/analysts, or Software Engineers start around $60,000 but can be much higher for people whose particular skills are in high demand. Commercial software development companies tend to pay more than companies developing in-house software for their own use.

Employment Prospects

Software Engineers are expected to continue to be in high demand in the computer industry, the corporate world in general, government, and other agencies. Because of the complexity of the skills required, there is less threat from the automation of programming tasks. Competition from high-quality foreign workers may eventually depress salaries and opportunities for American Software Engineers. However, the effects of the industry downturn that began in 2000 are likely to be temporary.

Jobs in commercial software development are concentrated geographically in areas such as Silicon Valley in California, the Northwest, and the East Coast. Telecommuting and the desire to cut costs is resulting in more opportunities outside those areas.

Advancement Prospects

Having top-quality skills that are in high demand plus a proven track record lets one just about "write his or her own ticket." Some people with top skills prefer to work as independent contractors (see the entry for "Systems Consultant"). Within the corporate environment, a typical advancement track starts with becoming a senior programmer (or programmer/analyst), then lead programmer for projects, and finally, manager or director of the software development unit.

Education and Training

The basic educational requirement is a four-year college program in computer science with related studies in mathematics, engineering, or business operations. A graduate degree is recommended for senior positions. Specialized training and certification in networks or operating systems (Novell, Windows XP, Unix, etc.) may be required by companies, depending on the platform (type of computer) for which they are developing software.

Experience, Skills, and Personality Traits

Candidates for intermediate-level systems analyst/Software Engineer positions are generally expected to have several years of programming experience involving work of increasing complexity. Major skills include:

- object analysis and design
- languages such as C++, Java, or Visual Basic, as well as specialized programming interfaces and tools
- knowledge of the internal workings of operating systems such as MS Windows XP or Unix
- writing skills for creating specifications and program documentation
- knowledge or experience in the areas for which software is being developed (science, business, government, etc.)

Cross-Training for Software Engineers

Interests	Related Job Descriptions
designing operating systems and device drivers	Systems Programmer
databases	Database Analyst; Data Miner
configuring business computer systems	Systems Integrator
consulting for computer problems	Systems Consultant
teaching program design	Professor, Computer Science

Unions and Associations

Software Engineers belong to professional organizations such as the Association for Computing Machinery (ACM) or Institute of Electrical and Electronics Engineers (IEEE).

Tips for Entry

1. If you don't have much programming experience, try for an entry-level programming job or internship to build up your résumé.
2. Try to get experience in designing programs, not just coding or testing them.
3. Note the skills that are in high demand in classified ads and Internet job postings. Seek courses or certification programs to keep skills up to date.
4. Consider smaller or start-up firms where you are likely to be given more advanced responsibilities.

USER INTERFACE DESIGNER

CAREER PROFILE

Duties: Designs the menus, icons, and other features that people will use to interact with a computer program or operating system

Alternate Title(s): Human Factors Specialist

Salary Range: $40,000 to $60,000 or more, depending on experience

Employment Prospects: Fair

Advancement Prospects: Fair to good

Prerequisites:

Education or Training—Four-year college degree (not necessarily in computer science), courses in programming and operating systems; psychology, graphical arts, semiotics (signs and symbols), industrial design, and business operations helpful

Experience—Some companies will hire people with a comprehensive background but limited experience. Internships or undergraduate projects can be used to create a portfolio of sample work to show employers

Special Skills and Personality Traits—Understanding of and empathy with computer users; artistic sense of composition (how graphical elements fit together); comfortable with complex systems and operating procedures; imagination

CAREER LADDER

```
┌─────────────────────────────────────┐
│   Manager, User Interface Design     │
└─────────────────────────────────────┘

┌─────────────────────────────────────┐
│     Lead Designer or Consultant,     │
│        User Interface Design         │
└─────────────────────────────────────┘

┌─────────────────────────────────────┐
│       User Interface Designer        │
└─────────────────────────────────────┘

┌─────────────────────────────────────┐
│    Trainee, User Interface Design    │
└─────────────────────────────────────┘
```

Position Description

The first computer programs processed batches of data with little or no user control. During the 1970s, programs were usually controlled by users typing in commands at the terminal. In the 1980s, however, new operating systems from Apple, Microsoft, Sun Microsystems, and others featured a "graphical user interface."

A "GUI" generally employs a mouse or other pointing device with which the user points to and selects menu items or other objects on the screen. The objects represent resources such as files or programs, or activities such as saving data, changing the screen display, printing, and so on. The symbols or "icons" that represent programs and data files are designed to be identifiable and appropriate to the object they represent. For example, the icon for a word processing program may look like a sheet of paper with writing on it, while the icon for a communications program may show a telephone.

The designer seeks to provide ways to manipulate data that more nearly mirror the things people do with real-world objects. For example, a file can be moved by dragging its icon from one folder to another, or deleted by dragging it into a "trash can" icon.

Design principles suggest that a good user interface should be:

- intuitive—that is, users should be able to figure it out with little explanation or training
- consistent—programs using the same operating system should provide the same basic techniques so that learning a new program becomes easier
- ergonomic—unnecessary or awkward keystrokes or mouse movements should be avoided

Modern operating systems such as MS Windows provide many built-in features that regular programmers can use to provide basic menus, dialog boxes, and other parts of their program's interface. A separate User Interface Designer is usually not employed for simple programs that have few options or that will be used only by a few people. Major commercial software projects such as word processors and graphics programs usually include a user interface specialist on the design team. This specialist may be a programmer who has taken a special interest in user interfaces, or a technically knowledgeable nonprogrammer with a background in fields such as psychology, graphic arts, or human factors research.

As part of the design team, the User Interface Designer must work closely with the program designers and programmers. The designer will take the program specifications developed by the system analyst or lead programmer and design the screen objects and procedures that provide access to the specified features. To be successful, the interface designer must, even if not a programmer, be familiar with the technical capabilities of the operating system and computer hardware to be used.

Salaries

Salaries are quite variable, reflecting different job descriptions. Large developers of operating systems or commercial software tend to pay salaries in the upper end of the range. Freelance design consultants can make an hourly rate of $50 to $125 depending on their experience and the size of the project.

Employment Prospects

While software developers often emphasize the importance of having a good user interface, the field of user interface design is only gradually being defined. Many programmers or analysts are given interface design as part of their programming tasks. A designer who also has strong general programming skills won't be dependent on the availability of specialized design positions. While it is more difficult to become established as a designer than as a general programmer, employment prospects are generally good for experienced designers. Since operating system and major application developers tend to be concentrated in a few areas such as Silicon Valley, relocation may be necessary. (While some work can be done by phone link, major projects require much face-to-face discussion with other members of the development team.)

Advancement Prospects

There are two main paths to advancement. Within a corporate ladder, a User Interface Designer can become a lead designer or manager. The alternative path is to become a consultant with a growing reputation and track record that leads to larger (and better paid) roles.

Education and Training

User interface design is an area where the liberal arts graduate may actually have an advantage over the more narrowly trained "techie." This is because interface design requires understanding of many seemingly unrelated fields; psychology, learning theory, business operation, and graphic design, as well as computer science. Like technical writing, interface design may be a good "crossover field" for liberal arts majors faced with the need to find a creative and reasonably well-paid job.

Experience, Skills, and Personality Traits

User interface design is more of an art than a science. There is no substitute for actual experience in putting together program specifications and design elements to create an integrated whole. Since writing on-line help screens may be part of the job, good writing skills are also very important. The ideal personality for this position combines creativity with discipline under deadline pressures, and the ability to understand the points of view of other programmers and of computer users.

Cross-Training for User Interface Designers

Interests	Related Job Descriptions
writing	Technical Writer
designing for business operations	Systems Analyst
hardware and operating systems	Systems Programmer; Systems Integrator
use of graphics and symbols	Art Director (Computer Graphics); Multimedia Developer

Unions and Associations

A User Interface Designer may belong to a variety of organizations reflecting different aspects of the field such as:

- computer science and engineering (Association for Computing Machinery, Institute of Electrical and Electronics Engineers)
- graphics and design (SIGGRAPH, the Graphics Special Interest Group of the ACM)
- user communications (Society for Technical Communications)

Tips for Entry

1. As an undergraduate, take a broad variety of courses such as psychology, graphics design, writing (composition), programming languages, and computer science.

2. If you already have a liberal arts degree, round out your background by taking the above courses as necessary at your community college.

3. Study the interface and help screens for a variety of software. Note strong and weak points from your perspective as a user.

4. Use tools such as Visual Basic and Help Authoring systems to practice creating user interfaces and on-line help displays.

5. Look for companies that are beginning major software projects and may be hiring designer trainees.

DATABASE ANALYST

CAREER PROFILE

Duties: Designs and creates programs used to collect, maintain, and analyze data needed by business, government, or other institutions; adapts programs to changing business needs

Alternate Title(s): Database Specialist

Salary Range: $65,000 to $85,000

Employment Prospects: Good

Advancement Prospects: Good

Prerequisites:

Education or Training—Four-year college degree (major related to information technology preferred); additional business degree a plus

Experience—Moderate programming experience focused on databases and report creation

Special Skills and Personality Traits—Ability to translate business requirements into information design; programming and familiarity with major database languages and products; ability to work with managers and other professionals

CAREER LADDER

```
┌─────────────────────────────────┐
│  Manager, Information Systems    │
└─────────────────────────────────┘

┌─────────────────────────────────┐
│    Database Administrator        │
└─────────────────────────────────┘

┌─────────────────────────────────┐
│      Database Analyst            │
└─────────────────────────────────┘

┌─────────────────────────────────┐
│  Trainee, Database Operations    │
└─────────────────────────────────┘
```

Position Description

Database work is the "bread and butter" of the Information Age. Every business needs to keep track of large amounts of data such as customer information and accounts, medical and insurance records, or inventory. The Database Analyst is responsible for:

- designing databases for each type of information the business uses
- making changes in systems to reflect changes in business practices, new standards, or regulations
- providing the reports that managers and analysts need to use information effectively

Up through the 1970s, most large businesses maintained their databases on large mainframe computers programmed using languages such as COBOL or RPG. Today, however, most data is accessed from networks of personal computers and stored in file or database servers. Special database systems such as Oracle, Informix, and Microsoft Access make it easier to create more "user friendly" data reports.

The Database Analyst is like a specialized systems analyst and has a similar approach to designing programs, but with specialization in database applications. He or she must be able to understand the data needs of the company's different departments and work with their managers to design the most usable and efficient forms and reports.

Salaries

Database management is one of the strongest growing areas in corporate information technology. Demand for Database Analysts is high, but employers often require that an applicant have experience in the precise database products or languages being used in the company. If an individual who needs to get up to speed is hired, his or her salary may be considerably lower than for someone who can be productive right away.

Employment Prospects

Because databases are so central to all modern enterprises, steady growth in demand for Database Analysts can be expected. Because most positions demand knowledge of particular database software and operating systems, it is important to keep skills up to date in order to have the best job choices. Recently there has been considerable interest in using statistical and pattern-matching tools to extract new information from existing databases. This process, called data mining, is discussed in the next entry. Data mining may be a logical skill set for a Database Analyst who wants more challenging and perhaps higher-paid positions.

Advancement Prospects

Advancement comes through gaining specialized skills and going into consulting, or entering the managerial track and becoming the database administrator for a whole company or department.

Education and Training

An undergraduate college degree is usually required. Because database programming emphasizes the practical aspects of computer science, a major such as information systems or even a business major (with programming and operating systems courses) may be preferable to a straight computer science major.

Experience, Skills, and Personality Traits

Database work emphasizes the ability to understand the structure and relationships among different items of information, as well as the workflow and procedures used by the people who carry out business functions. Experience in a variety of business settings can thus be quite helpful. As a software developer, the Database Analyst needs to be able to work smoothly with other programmers as well as documentation and training specialists. Persistence, attention to detail, and the ability to work under pressure round out the skill set for the Database Analyst.

Cross-Training for Database Analysts

Interests	Related Job Descriptions
designing general business programs	Systems Analyst
designing data systems for networks or the World Wide Web	Networking Consultant; Webmaster
finding patterns in information	Data Miner
teaching database theory	Professor, Computer Science

Unions and Associations

Like other software developers, Database Analysts may belong to the Association for Computing Machinery, participating in special interest groups (SIGs) devoted to database issues. Individuals with an interest in business or management may also want to join groups involved with MIS (Management Information Systems) issues.

Tips for Entry

1. Think about the information needs of businesses where you have worked (perhaps in a summer or work-study job). How would you design databases to meet those needs?
2. Use your home PC to become familiar with moderately complex database design programs such as Microsoft Access or FileMaker.
3. If you're still in college, take advantage of courses in popular database languages and systems, as well as taking courses in business administration, information science, or related fields.
4. If you've already graduated from college, consider taking courses at community colleges to round out your background.
5. Try to gain volunteer or paid experience helping local nonprofit groups with their database needs. They will be grateful for the help, and you will gain a good line for your résumé when you look for an entry-level position.

DATA MINER

CAREER PROFILE

Duties: Analyzes databases in business, government, or scientific applications in order to extract additional information or to find useful patterns

Alternate Title(s): Database Analyst (Specialized)

Salary Range: $60,000 to $80,000 or more

Employment Prospects: Good to excellent

Advancement Prospects: Good

Prerequisites:

   Education or Training—Generally requires an advanced (graduate) degree in computer science or computational mathematics; additional degrees or training in statistics and scientific areas such as biology or physical science is helpful

   Experience—Familiarity with major database and statistical packages; experience with statistical and database applications in a particular area such as biology (biostatistics), physical science, economics, or marketing

   Special Skills and Personality Traits—Successful data miners combine strong analytical skills, attention to detail, and the intuitive ability to discern patterns and possible relationships and their significance

CAREER LADDER

```
┌─────────────────────────────────────┐
│  Laboratory Director or Executive    │
│   (in data-mining corporation)       │
└─────────────────────────────────────┘

┌─────────────────────────────────────┐
│  Senior Consultant or Project Leader │
└─────────────────────────────────────┘

┌─────────────────────────────────────┐
│       Data Mining Specialist         │
└─────────────────────────────────────┘

┌─────────────────────────────────────┐
│ Database Analyst or Junior Specialist│
└─────────────────────────────────────┘
```

Position Description

During the 1990s researchers in a variety of fields began to realize that the huge amount of data being collected from scientific experiments, social science surveys, and business transactions represented an untapped information resource with great potential. Although a given data item might have originally been collected for a simple, limited purpose (such as measuring a local temperature or recording a customer's purchases), statistical and pattern-matching tools can often be used to extract new information that can be applied for different purposes. For example:

- Customer purchase data can be correlated to create profiles of typical types of customers to be targeted in marketing efforts.
- Tax returns can be analyzed to find patterns that correlate to various types of fraud, and a profile can be developed for identifying and auditing suspect returns.

- Data from manufacturing processes can be analyzed to find sources of flaws or inefficiencies in the manufacturing process.
- Data from the human genome or from molecular structure can be analyzed for purposes such as identifying possible effective drugs for a particular condition (see the entry for Bioinformatics Specialist for more about this type of application).

Data mining begins with formulating a problem or objective and selecting suitable databases to be examined. The data must be "cleaned" to remove erroneous or incomplete records. The Data Miner can then apply a variety of tools and algorithms that draw on a variety of fields such as statistics, pattern recognition, expert systems, or other forms of artificial intelligence. Many such tools are now available "off the shelf," but Data Miners may need to write their own software for advanced applications.

Because of the huge size of many of the databases involved, a preliminary assessment is often done using a small portion of the data. If useful patterns are identified, the procedure can then be repeated with larger samples to see whether the tentative results hold up.

Data mining is increasingly used in e-commerce settings. For example, an on-line store might examine customers' purchases of books, CDs, software, and other products to see whether a customer's purchases in one area might predict the customer's willingness to buy products in other areas. If it turned out, for example, that purchasers of Harry Potter books who were between the ages of 12 and 16 also bought fantasy computer games, future teenage purchasers of Potter books might be offered a 10 percent discount on their next computer game.

Data mining has thus been embraced by many e-commerce companies, such as Amazon.com, as a way to leverage their large customer databases and increase sales. Applying data mining techniques to customer surveys, complaints, or requests for support can also lead to creating company policies that are more likely to retain or enhance customer loyalty, which is often vital to the continuing success of a business. (This effort is often called customer relationship management or CRM.)

Two recent developments have further highlighted the potential of data mining. One is the successful deciphering of the human genetic code. The gene code is essentially a huge database of human characteristics, and that database can be mined to find possible relationships between genes and diseases, perhaps leading to new treatment strategies.

On a more controversial note, the attacks of September 11, 2001, and the subsequent "war on terror" have led to government proposals such as Total Information Awareness (TIA), later renamed Terrorist Information Awareness, which would combine information about individuals from many separate sources and use data mining techniques to try to identify potential terrorists. Data mining is also used for security and risk assessments in industries such as banking that are vulnerable to criminal attack.

Data Miners have the potential for an interesting and challenging career, but the growing use of data mining by corporations and government agencies also raises privacy and civil liberties concerns. The development and application of ethical standards and regulations for data mining will be part of the challenge of this exciting new profession.

Salaries

Because of the set of advanced skills needed and the growing demand for data mining applications, specialists in this field can command high salaries. Although persons with limited experience may fall into the lower database analyst salary range ($60,000 or so), Data Miners with significant experience in particular applications (such as e-commerce) can easily exceed $100,000 in annual salaries.

Employment Prospects

The growing demand for data mining skills has meant that this field has not suffered as much as other areas from the recent dot-com downturn. E-commerce firms and traditional businesses such as banks, insurance companies, and health care providers are all trying to use data mining to devise marketing programs to reach new customers while keeping existing customers satisfied. However, Data Miners working with e-commerce firms that are unable to find sufficient revenue may lose their jobs along with other employees.

Individuals starting a career in data mining should realize that employment may be relatively short-term (perhaps for a single large project). Becoming an independent consultant may also be an attractive possibility, especially for persons with advanced skills.

Advancement Prospects

The data mining field is still new and relatively open-ended. Whether an employee or independent contractor, the data mining specialist has great potential for advancement if he or she gains (and keeps honing) skills in using the new and emerging tools in the field. Advancement can be through gaining increasing responsibility as a manager or executive involved with data mining programs, or through gaining skills that are in high demand and that bring higher salaries or fees.

Education and Training

Data mining is a demanding, multidisciplinary field. Students interested in this field should take introductory programming or computer science classes in high school and, if available, courses in statistics and advanced mathematics. In college a solid degree in computer science is recommended, including courses in programming, database design, algorithms, computational mathematics, and artificial intelligence. Courses specifically in data mining are also starting to be offered.

Students should also take coursework (or perhaps a second degree) in fields where they would like to apply their data mining skills. For example, Data Miners in the life sciences field might take biology, including biostatistics or bioinformatics, while those interested in commercial applications should take economics, business administration, marketing, and related courses.

It is expected that degrees and professional certifications in data mining will become available (and desirable) in the coming years.

Experience, Skills, and Personality Traits

Although data mining as a profession is gradually becoming more formalized, it is probably not a field for people who want a clear path to always be laid out in front of them. New techniques and applications are constantly being developed. On the one hand, the successful Data Miner must have the discipline to master challenging techniques and applications; on the other hand, he or she must also possess the flexibility and imagination to unlock the potential hidden in the vast resources of databases.

Employers and clients generally have specific objectives or problems that they want solved by the Data Miner, but it is often necessary to clarify them before beginning a new project. Communications skills and the ability to work well with other professionals are thus important, in addition to analytical skills.

Cross-Training for Data Miners

Interests	Related Job Descriptions
science	Scientific or Engineering Programmer
life sciences, medicine	Bioinformatics Specialist
statistics	Statistician
problem-solving	Systems Analyst, Systems Consultant
database design	Database Analyst; Database Administrator; Software Engineer
artificial intelligence	Artificial Intelligence Programmer
information structure	Professor, Computer Science; Reference or Special Librarian

Unions and Associations

Data Miners generally do not belong to labor unions. They will typically join professional organizations in the computer field, such as the Association for Computing Machinery (ACM) and the Institute of Electrical and Electronics Engineers (IEEE), as well as organizations relating to application areas such as science or marketing.

Tips for Entry

1. Use high school and the first few years of college to take a broad range of computer, math, science, and/or business-related courses. This will help you decide on particular areas or applications for data mining.
2. Read articles or books on data mining. Consider doing a school science project that applies data mining techniques to a problem in an area such as city planning or ecology.
3. In college look for internships or summer jobs (such as with a research laboratory or a marketing company) that will give you an opportunity to work with database systems and analytical tools.

SYSTEMS PROGRAMMER

CAREER PROFILE

Duties: Designs and writes programs that interface with a computer's low-level operating system, such as device drivers and utilities

Alternate Title(s): Software Tools Designer

Salary Range: $40,000 to $75,000

Employment Prospects: Fair

Advancement Prospects: Good

Prerequisites:

Education or Training—Four-year or graduate degree in computer science

Experience—Several years of training in basic system and software configuration, testing, and program maintenance; detailed familiarity with major operating systems and their application programming interfaces (APIs)

Special Skills and Personality Traits—Understanding of computer architecture and operating principles; attention to detail; concentration; ability to communicate with applications programmers

CAREER LADDER

```
┌─────────────────────────────────────┐
│   Lead Programmer or Project Manager,│
│        Systems Development           │
└─────────────────────────────────────┘

┌─────────────────────────────────────┐
│     Senior Systems Programmer        │
└─────────────────────────────────────┘

┌─────────────────────────────────────┐
│        Systems Programmer            │
└─────────────────────────────────────┘

┌─────────────────────────────────────┐
│     Trainee, Systems Programming     │
└─────────────────────────────────────┘
```

Position Description

Most programmers write applications programs—software designed to help users with common tasks (such as writing or drawing), solve particular problems in business or science, or automate information processing in an organization. Applications programmers usually concentrate on defining the objects and functions of the program in languages such as BASIC, C++, or Java, or use special database development systems.

Ultimately, however, any program's basic functions depend on the computer's operating system. A command in C++ to save or read a file, for example, is linked by the language compiler to a set of "library routines" (often called an API, or "applications programming interface"). The API is the bridge between the higher-level commands of the application program and the internal workings of the operating system. But who is responsible for the operating system itself? The Systems Programmer—the person who builds the tools other programmers use.

Some Systems Programmers work directly on operating systems development for companies like Microsoft (Windows XP) or companies like Sun Microsystems that have particular versions of the UNIX operating system. Other Systems Programmers write "drivers"—the special programs that allow the operating system to control printers, monitors, and other peripheral devices. Still others specialize in creating "software tools"—the compilers, editors, and other program development aids used by applications programmers to write code.

Systems Programmers are intimately familiar with the hundreds of functions provided in each operating system's programming interface. They must constantly keep up with bugs, fixes, and revisions distributed by operating system and software vendors. C and C++ are the most common languages for systems programming.

Salaries

Salaries with mainframe or microcomputer operating system companies (IBM, Microsoft, Sun, etc.) tend toward the higher end of the range, especially for programmers who are helping design and develop operating systems. Writers of software tools and drivers make somewhat less.

Employment Prospects

The decline in mainframe computing has reduced opportunities involving traditional mainframe operating systems such as MVS. This may affect older programmers. On the other hand, the rapid growth in networking and the Internet as well as the steady demand for experts in MS Windows and Unix/Linux programming will keep demand for Systems Programmers strong.

Because most systems programming jobs are the computer industry itself, jobs tend to be concentrated in places like Silicon Valley, the Pacific Northwest, or the Eastern seaboard. Individuals may have to relocate periodically. Frequent changes in the computer market make job security a problem, but individuals with good skills and flexibility can thrive.

Advancement Prospects

Companies that sell operating systems and program development systems focus on systems programming and will have the most clearly defined career ladder. A Systems Programmer who deals with operating systems issues for an applications software company may have limited advancement prospects. As with other specialities, becoming an independent consultant is a possibility.

Education and Training

Systems programming is the most "techie" part of programming, so a solid four-year (or preferably, graduate) degree in computer science is generally required. Coursework should reflect an emphasis on operating systems principles, compiler design, and related subjects. While some companies write "cross platform" software designed to run on a variety of computer systems, others specialize only in Windows or UNIX-based software. Employers are often looking for specific areas of expertise, such as writing Windows hardware drivers or UNIX network features.

Experience, Skills, and Personality Traits

Gaining practical experience (even while still in school) is very helpful. An internship or trainee position will provide an opportunity to learn the basics of installing and configuring the operating system software, device drivers, and systems components that support database operations. After gaining basic experience, the trainee can begin to participate in writing, modifying, and testing drivers and new versions of system software.

The Systems Programmer needs to master a tremendous amount of detail while keeping in touch with the overall structure of the operating system and its relationship to the programs that use it. He or she also needs good communication and documentation skills in order to be able to answer questions from other programmers or users.

Cross-Training for Systems Programmers

Skills or Interests	Related Job Descriptions
designing computer languages and operating systems	Professor, Computer Science
designing control programs for hardware devices	Embedded Systems Designer
designing interfaces	User Interface Designer

Unions and Associations

Since Systems Programmers are concerned with computer science and software engineering principles, they are likely to belong to organizations such as the Association for Computing Machinery (ACM) and the Institute for Electronic and Electrical Engineers (IEEE) and their affiliated special interest groups.

Tips for Entry

1. Focus on one operating system that interests you the most and use internships to gain practical experience in installation and configuration of the system as well as knowledge of key internal features. At the same time, try to learn enough about other major operating systems so that you can be a plausible candidate for an entry-level position involving them.
2. Subscribe to technical journals that focus on your target operating system(s).
3. Look for ads with keywords such as "drivers" or "API" that indicate system-level work.

SCIENTIFIC OR ENGINEERING PROGRAMMER

CAREER PROFILE

Duties: Writes programs that simulate natural phenomena or analyze experimental results, or apply scientific or engineering principles to research or manufacturing

Alternate Title(s): Software Engineer (scientific or engineering applications)

Salary Range: $50,000 to $75,000

Employment Prospects: Good

Advancement Prospects: Fair

Prerequisites:

Education or Training—Minimum four-year college degree (strong science and/or math background); graduate study preferred

Experience—Two or more years of experience in scientific or engineering work involving computers

Special Skills and Personality Traits—Ability to visualize physical phenomena and processes; use of scientific method; programming in languages such as Fortran or C/C++; comfortable with hands-on use of instruments

CAREER LADDER

```
┌─────────────────────────────────┐
│       Manager, Laboratory        │
│   or Factory Computing Center    │
└─────────────────────────────────┘

┌─────────────────────────────────┐
│   Senior Programmer or Analyst   │
│ (scientific or engineering applications) │
└─────────────────────────────────┘

┌─────────────────────────────────┐
│     Programmer (scientific       │
│   or engineering applications)   │
└─────────────────────────────────┘

┌─────────────────────────────────┐
│  Trainee or Entry-Level Programmer │
│ (scientific or engineering applications) │
└─────────────────────────────────┘
```

Position Description

Because scientific and engineering work depend on a precise and comprehensive system of mathematical formulas, computers are a vital tool for turning math into usable results. The Scientific Programmer can turn the computer into a versatile piece of laboratory equipment or a window into the processes of nature. For example, programs can help scientists and engineers to:

- record and tabulate data from a particle physics experiment
- calculate the stress on an airplane wing
- control the fermentation vats on a biotech production line
- identify key sequences of human DNA
- simulate the behavior of a population of bacteria

The in-house Scientific or Engineering Programmer works closely with scientists and engineers to define the problem and to provide displays or reports that will be most useful to the researchers. Work settings can range from a pure research laboratory to an engineering, design, or manufacturing facility.

Since very tiny numbers can be significant in science and engineering, the programmer must be concerned with accuracy both in the way the instruments obtain data and the way the computer calculates with it. He or she must have a good knowledge of statistical analysis and measurement techniques.

Programs that simulate natural phenomena usually involve many variables whose relationships have to be specified in formulas. There are some fascinating techniques available to simulation programmers. The popular "Monte Carlo technique" employs random numbers and probability to turn a series of simulated events (such as atomic particle interactions) into an overall picture. A technique called cellular automation (found in the Game of Life popularized in *Scientific American* in the 1970s) can be used to create surprisingly complex simulations out of simple behaviors.

Whatever techniques are employed, simulations usually have to be "fine-tuned" by being compared to experimental data. Knowledge of computer graphics and interface design is important for making simulations easier to use.

Scientific Programmers can also find work with companies that produce commercial software for scientists or engineers. Many scientific instruments come with their own built-in computer processor and software that processes the data and makes it available to a connected desktop computer.

Salaries

The best salaries are paid by major firms in fields such as biotech, chemicals, and aviation. Commercial producers of scientific software are next. Small start-up companies generally pay least but may offer stock options.

Employment Prospects

Employment prospects are tied closely to the growth of particular industries. In the 1980s biotech emerged as a "hot" field only to decline as many companies failed to meet investor expectations. Around 2000, however, success in decoding the human genome brought genetic sequence and protein structure analysis into prominence (see the entry for Bioinformatics Specialist). Engineering of biometric (such as face recognition) and other security systems is another hot field in the wake of the recent terrorist attacks. Established industries such as chemicals and plastics tend to have a steady if modest demand.

Advancement Prospects

Advancement tends to be slow but steady in large companies. Start-ups have a higher risk of unemployment but more rapid advancement if the business is successful.

Education and Training

The best undergraduate preparation is either a major in computer science and a minor in a science or engineering field, or the other way around. The Scientific or Engineering Programmer is less focused on features of typical commercial software (such as an elaborate user interface or endless add-on features or options) and more on the use of the computer as a practical tool to solve problems. Accuracy and reliability of the program's results are more important than cosmetic appearances. Software design in this field tends to be more straightforward and less subject to the latest fads in computer science.

Experience, Skills, and Personality Traits

A college student or recent graduate may be able to get a job writing small utility programs for start-ups or other small companies in the science or engineering field. The pay will be modest, but the experience listed on the résumé may well convince later employers that the candidate has demonstrated motivation and willingness to do real work.

Cross-Training for Scientific or Engineering Programmers

Skills or Interests	Related Job Descriptions
teaching	Professor, Computer Science
mechanical engineering, automation	Robotics Engineer
interfacing operating system and hardware	Systems Programmer
life sciences	Bioinformatics Specialist
data analysis	Statistician; Data Miner

Unions and Associations

Programmers in this field are likely to belong to scientific or engineering societies that fit their interests and area of specialization. The Association for Computing Machinery (ACM) and Institute of Electrical and Electronics Engineers (IEEE) have many appropriate special interest groups. The Society for Computer Simulation also offers resources.

Tips for Entry

1. Take introductory or intermediate courses in the area of science or engineering you are most interested in. Try to find out how computers are used in this field of science.

2. Be sure to supplement basic computer science courses with a solid background in math (calculus, statistics, etc.), measurement, and simulation techniques.

3. Look for work-study or summer intern work in scientific laboratories or engineering firms. Find out if these employers need utility programs or other relatively simple software. When you write the program, be sure to keep it (and its documentation) to add to your portfolio for future employment.

BIOINFORMATICS SPECIALIST

CAREER PROFILE

Duties: Organize and manipulate information relating to genetic sequences, molecular structure, and other data relevant to the biological sciences

Alternate Title(s): Biocomputing Specialist; Computational Biologist

Salary Range: $70,000 to $90,000 and up

Employment Prospects: Excellent

Advancement Prospects: Good

Prerequisites:

Education or Training—Advanced (graduate) degree in computer science and degree (or considerable coursework) in biology and related fields

Experience—Should be familiar with database structure, statistical analysis, and pattern recognition techniques as well as genetics and biochemistry

Special Skills and Personality Traits—Ability to work with complex, detailed data and devise systematic algorithms and procedures; strong inference, reasoning, and problem-solving skills; ability to communicate and collaborate with other scientists

CAREER LADDER

Director, Bioinformatics

Senior Bioinformatics Specialist or Scientist

Bioinformatics Specialist or Scientist

Associate Bioinformatics Specialist

Position Description

The decoding of the genetic structure of humans and other living things has provided a vast database of information about the sequences of molecules that determine their characteristics. At the same time, detailed information about the formation of proteins and other complex molecules is beginning to fill in the gap between the genetic blueprint and its physical expressions, including disease. The use of computer-based data management, analysis, and modeling techniques makes this groundbreaking research possible. Many observers have remarked that if the 20th century was the century of physics, the 21st century may belong to biology—powerfully aided by electronics.

Beginning Bioinformatics Specialists help create and maintain databases of information about genetic sequences and molecular structures. To make this information useful to biological and medical researchers, programmers create interfaces for querying this information and for adding new entries to the database.

The more advanced (and more interesting) part of bioinformatics is analyzing genetic sequences and trying to predict what relationship they will have to the structure and function of living things. Searching manually for relevant patterns in the approximately 30,000 genes that make up the human genome might take centuries—it would be like trying to read without knowing the meaning of most of the words. However, fast computers using appropriate algorithms (including pattern recognition and statistical correlation) can identify the most promising sequences for further attention by researchers. The computer can also sift through about 200,000 known protein sequences and identify the most promising ones for a given application. (For a profession that applies similar techniques in other applications, see the Data Miner entry.)

Although it's a true scientific milestone, simply knowing the genes that make up human DNA is only the first step in being able to truly understand living things. The next step is to learn how the information in genes drives the complex chemical interactions that create the molecules that enable living cells to function. Just as computer software can analyze genetic sequences, suitable programs can also examine the sequences of atoms within protein molecules and begin to piece together the steps by which they were created. In turn, protein structures can be related to functions such as cell growth or the immune system. Three-dimensional models of the molecule's possible physical structure can be constructed to help scientists visualize these processes. In turn, molecular models can be used to predict the effects of experimental drugs for cancer, AIDS, or other diseases, or to find new drugs.

The Bioinformatics Specialist is a computer scientist who applies the principles of that field to working with the genetic and molecular data of biology. He or she might work in a university laboratory, an organization such as the Centers for Disease Control, or for a pharmaceutical company.

Entry-level Bioinformatics Specialists will maintain databases of genetic or molecular information and run routine screenings and queries against the database. More experienced specialists or scientists can create new screening tools and other software for analyzing the data, displaying results, or creating dynamic visual models of biochemical processes.

Salaries

The demand and competition for Bioinformatics Specialists puts their pay at the top of the range for scientific researchers. Large pharmaceutical companies tend to offer the highest pay, but academic and government settings may offer more job security. Persons with medical or advanced biology degrees tend to get the highest salaries, ranging to $100,000 and beyond.

Employment Prospects

High demand and heavy investment in pharmaceutical and medical research combined with the relatively small number of individuals who combine advanced computer skills and the relevant scientific background mean that qualified candidates are likely to receive a range of attractive employment offers. Continued growth in employment will depend on the success of the genetics, genetic engineering, and biotech fields as a whole.

Advancement Prospects

There are several possible routes to advancement. Individuals interested in designing or overseeing research projects can gain management experience with a view to eventually becoming project managers, department directors or managers, or executives in biotechnology companies. Those whose primary interest is in research and scientific discovery can still improve their salary and benefits by gaining advanced skills or earning additional degrees (such as an

M.D.). The National Bioinformatics Institute offers a number of certification programs in bioinformatics.

Education and Training

This multidisciplinary field rests on two foundations: computer science and biology. In high school, students should explore programming, computer science, and biology to get an idea of the subject matter and determine their possible interest. In college, students can major in computer science (with emphasis on programming languages, databases, statistics, and computational mathematics) but should also take courses in biology, biochemistry, and related fields. A number of universities are starting to offer specific courses or even degree programs in biotechnology or bioinformatics.

Experience, Skills, and Personality Traits

Research in this fascinating but challenging field requires the discipline to maintain attention to details along with intuition and imagination that enables "finding the forest among the trees" of data. Strong writing skills will help with preparing papers and reports, and good communication skills are needed because most research projects are team efforts. The Bioinformatics Specialist will frequently need to work with computer programmers, system administrators, other research scientists, or clinicians.

Cross-Training for Bioinformatics Specialists

Interests	Related Job Descriptions
databases	Database Analyst
information patterns	Data Miner
statistics	Statistician
programming	Scientific or Engineering Programmer
computer science	Professor, Computer Science

Unions and Associations

Bioinformatics Specialists will generally belong to a variety of professional organizations, both in computer science (such as the Association for Computing Machinery or the Institute of Electrical and Electronics Engineers) and in the life sciences, as well as emerging organizations in bioinformatics such as the National Bioinformatics Institute.

Tips for Entry

1. Read magazines such as *Scientific American* and *Science News* to learn about exciting developments in biotech, genetics, pharmaceuticals, and other areas.
2. During the first four years of college, take courses in database design and analysis, statistics, and arti-

ficial intelligence. Use sample, educational, or "demo" versions to learn about software packages used in bioinformatics.

3. Consider a dual degree in computer science and biology or, if available, a degree specifically in bioinformatics.

4. Look for summer jobs or internships (such as in government or private research laboratories) that offer relevant experience, such as in maintaining genomics databases or performing routine queries or analysis.

ARTIFICIAL INTELLIGENCE PROGRAMMER

CAREER PROFILE

Duties: Applies principles of artificial intelligence to design and implement systems that perform complex tasks such as decision making, pattern recognition, or the operation of robotic systems

Alternate Title(s): Knowledge Engineer; Expert Systems Programmer; Robotics Programmer

Salary Range: from about $40,000 (trainees) to $75,000 for experienced programmers with graduate degrees, $100,000 or more for top experts with doctoral degrees

Employment Prospects: Fair

Advancement Prospects: Fair

Prerequisites:

    Education or Training—Minimum of a four-year college degree (usually in computer science); graduate degree preferred

    Experience—Work (possibly as a graduate student or intern) in laboratory or corporate AI research projects

    Special Skills and Personality Traits—Ability to generalize principles and create complex sets of rules or procedures; concentration; patience and persistence

CAREER LADDER

> **Research Director (AI projects)**

> **Lead or Principal Researcher**

> **Artificial Intelligence Programmer**

> **Artificial Intelligence Intern or Trainee**

Position Description

Truly humanlike computers like Hal in the film *2001: A Space Odyssey* turned out to be beyond the reach of the 20th century. Nevertheless, artificial intelligence (AI) researchers and programmers have created systems that perform tasks such as chess playing that were once thought to require a human mind. Practical applications of artificial intelligence include:

- "expert systems" that apply rules to making decisions, such as scheduling freight shipments, checking credit, or diagnosing disease
- pattern recognition systems that can match faces seen in cameras to those of criminal or terrorist suspects
- "neural network" programs that can learn to perform tasks by constantly reevaluating their performance

Most theoretical work in artificial intelligence takes place in university laboratories such as those at the Massachusetts Institute of Technology (MIT) or the California Institute of Technology (Caltech). Several major corpora-

tions such as Xerox and AT&T have also created research labs that tackle long-range problems that may yield practical benefits only after many years. Practical application work is usually done by start-up corporations that try to take advantage of new discoveries to create new products.

Artificial intelligence is a multidisciplinary field that draws upon not only computer science but also philosophy, linguistics, and even psychology. Since the 1950s AI researchers have tried many approaches to giving computers the ability to think—or at least to act in ways that would be considered thoughtful in people. While some researchers tried to adapt human psychology and reasoning to computer processing, others, called cognitive psychologists, applied computer principles to understanding human thought processes.

Artificial Intelligence Programmers can be pure researchers, creating systems that try to demonstrate the validity of their theories. AI Programmers working for business, however, try to adapt the researchers' ideas to creating systems that can solve practical problems. The two approaches that have brought the most success are expert systems and neural networks.

An expert system is essentially an elaborate set of rules that specify what conclusions are to be drawn (or actions taken) when certain conditions are true. A biology student who works down a classification tree to determine the species of an organism is acting much like a computer with an expert system. Expert systems work best in applications where there are well-known rules that can be applied systematically. The AI Programmer (sometimes called a knowledge engineer) interviews experts such as doctors or mechanics and gets them to describe their thought processes. For example, a doctor might be asked, "What do you look for in order to tell whether someone has pneumonia or just a bad cold?" This expert knowledge is then codified into rules, sometimes in a special computer language called Prolog.

Neural networks take the opposite approach to expert systems. An expert system starts out "knowing" many things that the programmer has told it. A neural network starts out knowing very little. It has many individual parts or "nodes" that all attempt a particular task, such as sorting data or classifying part of a visual image. The system determines which nodes were successful in the task and gives them greater strength or importance. The methods selected by the successful nodes gradually become the way the system as a whole solves the problem, with the system getting better as it "learns" what works best. Neural networks have been used to train robots to recognize objects or faces. Important emerging applications for AI Programmers today include security and law enforcement, where software is being developed to identify patterns that might be associated with criminal or terrorist activity. (See the Data Miner entry for related techniques.) AI is being used in the military to create "smarter" battlefield systems and weapons. The field of robotics is also closely related to AI (see the Robotics Engineer entry). In business, expert systems and neural networks are being used to create automated customer support services and to target product offers using sophisticated customer profiles.

The developing AI Programmer can thus choose from a variety of specialized areas after learning general techniques. Combining theoretical knowledge with practical experience in areas such as engineering or business is a definite plus when competing for more specialized positions.

AI Programmers often use specialized languages (such as LISP and Prolog) and software tools to develop their programs. Besides being good at understanding and applying abstract principles, they must be creative and adaptable when things don't work out. Since managers and investors expect concrete results, the programmer is under pressure to come up with something that works, even if it is not yet elegant.

Salaries

Salaries for AI Programmers depend considerably on the work setting. Academic researchers will earn salaries similar to those paid other scientists or professors. Major corporate projects are likely to pay more, but may be ended if the research gets bogged down or the corporation decides to change its priorities.

Employment Prospects

The popularity of AI seems to go up and down periodically. The last big surge of interest began in the 1980s when expert systems and neural networks became popular. Today AI systems and robots are beginning to enter the mainstream of technology. Having a keen awareness of opportunities and the ability to match skills and interests to employer needs is important in such an abstract field where job descriptions are of limited value.

Advancement Prospects

AI researchers following an academic track will advance in ways similar to other professors—by doing and publishing work that is recognized by one's colleagues, and perhaps eventually gaining tenure. Researchers in corporate projects may be able to advance in-house to senior or management status. Top researchers can turn their reputation into a varied (and often well-paid) career as freelance consultants.

Education and Training

An artificial intelligence specialist needs a four-year program in computer science and preferably a graduate degree. But AI theory also draws on fields normally considered to be part of the liberal arts, such as psychology, linguistics, and even philosophy.

Much AI research is done using specialized computer languages such as LISP or Prolog, although practical products will often be coded in C++ or other more mainstream languages.

Experience, Skills, and Personality Traits

Like science or art, serious AI research is a career for people who have a compelling fascination and interest in it. (When an ordinary person sees an ant crawling on the floor, he or she might step on it. An AI researcher gets down to floor level and begins to ponder how such a tiny creature can navigate around its environment and form successful communities that have flourished for hundreds of millions of years!)

True mastery of the field requires many years of study, although mainstream programmers can certainly add some AI techniques to their toolbox.

Besides patience and curiosity, the AI researcher needs the ability to think in very abstract terms (such as finding patterns of patterns or discovering the rules that other rules follow). The goal is to develop algorithms, or procedures that a computer (or robot) can use to organize knowledge, draw conclusions, or deal with the physical environment.

Cross-Training for Artificial Intelligence Programmers

Interests	Related Job Descriptions
automating knowledge of business operations	Knowledge Engineer (expert systems designer)
building mechanical systems	Robotics Engineer
teaching AI theory	Professor, Computer Science
finding data patterns	Data Miner

Unions and Associations

AI Programmers will belong to many of the same organizations as mainstream software engineers, such as the Associ-

ation for Computing Machinery (ACM). They will also belong to special interest groups devoted to artificial intelligence, and organizations such as the American Association for Artificial Intelligence.

Tips for Entry

1. Get a broad background in the study of intelligence by taking courses in fields such as psychology (cognition), linguistics, anthropology, or philosophy.
2. Study a variety of applications of AI such as game-playing programs, neural networks, expert systems, and robots.
3. Look for a computer science program that has a strong sub-major in artificial intelligence and a leading research lab where you can gain experience as an undergraduate assistant or intern.
4. Keep up with how AI is being used in practical ways by corporations. This will help you get job leads and show prospective employers your knowledge of and interest in their problems.

SYSTEMS ANALYST

CAREER PROFILE

Duties: Determines an organization's needs and designs programs to meet them; supervises lower-level programmers

Alternate Title(s): Systems Consultant; Software Engineer

Salary Range: $55,000 to $75,000

Employment Prospects: Good

Advancement Prospects: Good

Prerequisites:

Education or Training—Undergraduate college degree with course work in programming, systems analysis, other computer science subjects, and courses in business operations

Experience—Several years' experience as an entry-level programmer or programmer/analyst

Special Skills and Personality Traits—Both detail and "big picture" orientation; program design and coding skills; ability to understand people's needs and communicate well with colleagues

CAREER LADDER

```
┌─────────────────────────────────┐
│   Manager, Information Systems   │
└─────────────────────────────────┘

┌─────────────────────────────────┐
│        Project Manager          │
│      (or Lead Programmer)       │
└─────────────────────────────────┘

┌─────────────────────────────────┐
│        Systems Analyst          │
└─────────────────────────────────┘

┌─────────────────────────────────┐
│       Programmer/Analyst        │
│     (or Software Engineer)      │
└─────────────────────────────────┘
```

Position Description

The process of developing software for a business or other organization involves a never-ending cycle of tasks:

- determining the organization's information needs
- writing detailed specifications—the "blueprints" for computer software
- choosing appropriate programming tools and methods
- supervising the writing of the program code
- testing the program and getting feedback from its intended users
- fixing problems and adding requested features

The in-house Systems Analyst is the key person for making sure these tasks are done in a thorough, efficient, and timely way.

While the Systems Analyst must be very familiar with programming techniques, the above list shows that "people skills" are as important as technical skills. The Systems Analyst must be able to relate to the program's users, work well with other programmers, and provide information needed by technical writers and technical support staff.

The program development cycle usually begins with one of the company's managers bringing up a problem. For example, a company may have grown substantially over the past few years. The people in the billing department have become frustrated because their billing software can no longer keep up with the increasing volume. As a result, bills aren't being sent promptly, leading to a reduction of cash flow. Even worse, some orders are getting lost, leading to loss of sales and the departure of disgruntled customers.

The Systems Analyst will probably interview the manager and perhaps even go into the billing department and observe the flow of work. He or she may create flowcharts or other diagrams that summarize the steps involved in processing an order. Next, the Systems Analyst will prepare specifications that describe the data involved with an order, how it will be gathered and stored, the calculations involved in billing (such as taxes and shipping charges), the average and peak volume of orders to be handled, and so on.

The Systems Analyst will then look at available software. If the company's business is like many others, he or she may choose a commercially available billing program and modify it as necessary to meet the company's needs. If the business has special needs, however, the analyst may decide to develop custom software in-house. (Since this is likely to be expensive and time consuming, it is important to make sure this flexibility is really necessary.) The Systems Analyst may also decide that more powerful computer hardware is needed. This may well require a report to higher management that justifies the cost of the equipment in terms of expected cost savings from the efficiency of the new system.

The workflow diagram and specifications are then translated into programming terms. An order record, for example, may be defined as an object in a language such as C++, or as a record in a database language. The various procedures for dealing with this data (such as input, storage, calculation, formatting, and printing) must also be specified.

Once the program is broken down into its logical components, the Systems Analyst (or perhaps the Project Leader) will assign them to various members of the programming team.

As the code is written, the Systems Analyst will probably create procedures for testing the program with sample data. When the program seems to be reasonably solid, a test, or "beta," version may be given to the billing department for them to try out. The beta reports will be used to fix remaining bugs. While all this is going on, documentation writers will be preparing a user manual for the program as well as text for on-line help screens.

Finally, the day comes when the program is finalized and "ready for production." The next day, however, the billing department manager walks in and tells the Systems Analyst, "This new program is great! But I was wondering. Could you . . .?" The cycle never really ends.

Salaries

Salaries are generally higher in larger corporations. Salaries are higher in cities with a major corporate presence, although the cost of living is usually also higher. As usual, experience also brings higher pay.

Employment Prospects

The ever-increasing role of information processing in business, health, education, and science should keep demand high for qualified Systems Analysts. Since these positions are most often found in corporate headquarters, it may be necessary to relocate to a major metropolitan area.

Advancement Prospects

In smaller companies the Systems Analyst may perform all tasks in the development cycle given above. In larger businesses, however, the Systems Analyst may report to a project manager who has overall responsibility. (The term *project manager* is used more often in commercial software development than for in-house development.) A Systems Analyst with a good track record and who has demonstrated strong management skills may become manager of the Information Systems (IS) Department for a small- to medium-size company or for a division of a larger company.

It is important for career advancement that a Systems Analyst keep up with the latest software design tools and methods.

Education and Training

The minimum background requirement is generally a four-year college degree with courses in programming and business administration for business analysts or appropriate scientific or engineering courses for Systems Analysts working with companies in those fields. A degree in computer science with a minor in a business or scientific/engineering area is advantageous and may be required for positions with corporations with complex data-processing needs. Top positions may require graduate degrees.

A college graduate usually begins with a position as entry-level programmer or programmer/analyst to gain the experience necessary to become a Systems Analyst.

Training does not stop once a person begins work. Systems Analysts have to keep up with the latest development in computer hardware, software, and design techniques. Usually the company will pay for the analyst's attendance at conferences, seminars, and training courses provided by software vendors or professional associations.

Experience, Skills, and Personality Traits

The Systems Analyst is part analyst (studying processes), part program designer, and part manager. A good balance of analytical, programming, and communications skills is essential.

Cross-Training for Systems Analysts

Interests	Related Job Descriptions
management	Manager, Information Systems
database design	Database Analyst
self-employment	Systems Consultant
putting together complete computer systems	Systems Integrator

Unions and Associations

Systems Analysts can belong to computer science organizations such as the Association for Computing Machinery (ACM). Since they are concerned with the design of software to meet organizational needs, many Systems Analysts also belong to information management groups such as the Data Processing Management Association or the Association for Systems Management.

Tips for Entry

1. While in college, be sure to supplement computer science courses with courses in business administration and management or science/engineering, depending on the setting in which you want to work as a Systems Analyst.

2. In work-study or internship, look for positions where you can help interview computer users, write or review specifications, or design programs. You may be able to get valuable experience through a placement with a small business or nonprofit organization that cannot afford a full-time professional Systems Analyst.

3. Follow the trade journals and keep track of the latest tools and options for different areas of programming such as databases, inventory or order systems, document management systems, and so on.

4. Try to get a couple of years of solid programming experience. If this includes some program design work, that's a definite plus.

SYSTEMS CONSULTANT

CAREER PROFILE

Duties: Works under contract to install or configure hardware or software, write or customize programs, or otherwise help solve information processing problems for an organization

Alternate Title(s): Software Consultant; Contract Programmer

Salary Range: $45,000 to $75,000 or more (hourly, $75 to $150 or more)

Employment Prospects: Fair

Advancement Prospects: Good

Prerequisites:

Education or Training—Undergraduate degree with emphasis on computer science of information systems preferred; business-related courses helpful

Experience—Experience configuring and customizing business software and computer systems

Special Skills and Personality Traits—Problem solving; mastery of details; flexibility; self-motivation

CAREER LADDER

```
┌─────────────────────────────────────┐
│   Manager, Information Systems       │
└─────────────────────────────────────┘

┌─────────────────────────────────────┐
│   Systems Consultant (experienced)  │
└─────────────────────────────────────┘

┌─────────────────────────────────────┐
│        Systems Consultant           │
│     (part-time or entry-level)      │
└─────────────────────────────────────┘
```

Position Description

The Systems Consultant is similar to the systems analyst in some respects. Both combine the ability to analyze problems, design solutions, and communicate with other professionals. The main difference is that while the systems analyst has a long-term in-house position with a single organization, the Systems Consultant typically offers his or her services on a shorter-term contract basis (perhaps six months to two years) or may work for several clients simultaneously.

The roster of typical tasks tends to be different, too. The Systems Consultant is often more oriented toward selecting, installing, and configuring hardware and software than to designing programs, although the ability to write utility programs (such as batch files, macros, etc.) is helpful.

The Systems Consultant is usually brought in either when an organization is expanding its information processing facilities or when it is experiencing problems getting systems and software to work properly. He or she may be called on to:

- recommend the purchase of hardware or software
- install and configure new hardware (individual PCs or networks) or software

- provide basic training in operation of the system
- write programs (or scripts) that combine different software programs to solve problems. (Most operating systems have some sort of scripting tool, such as Visual Basic for Applications [VBA] for Windows-based systems.)

The Systems Consultant must be able to work with both managers and "frontline" workers, determine their needs, and communicate solutions. He or she must also be able to deal with the occasional touchy situation in office politics, such as a manager who is insecure and unwilling to consider changes.

The Systems Consultant must use the trade press and the World Wide Web to keep up with the latest features and prices for computer products. He or she also develops an extensive file of contacts such as the technical support departments and websites for major software vendors. The consultant is always looking for better tools for diagnosing and fixing common problems.

Salaries

Since the Systems Consultant is self-employed and can perform a wide variety of tasks, it is hard to pin down a salary range. A consultant who can install and configure a system but has little programming or business background will make considerably less than one who has mastered several scripting languages and database systems. Consultants with specialized skills that are in high demand are at the top of the pay scale and can make literally hundreds of dollars an hour.

Employment Prospects

In today's constrained economic climate many businesses seek to save money by hiring just the people they need for a particular project rather than maintaining large payrolls. This has increased the demand for consultants of all types.

Independent contracting has some significant advantages: ever-changing challenges, high hourly pay rates, and the ability to set one's own working hours. However, the freelancer must be self-disciplined, highly motivated, and willing to accept a varying workload and the lack of a secure income. Freelancers must also obtain their own health insurance and keep detailed tax records unless they work for an agency.

Advancement Prospects

If a consultant chooses to continue with independent contracting, advancement is measured in the mastering of valuable skills and the compiling of a track record that can justify demanding higher rates. Some consultants may prefer to cross over into management in order to obtain a secure salary and benefits package.

Education and Training

For an established consultant, potential employers are likely to pay more attention to a history of major contracts and a list of skill areas than to formal education. However, in order to get established, the consultant must win those first few contracts, and a combination of a four-year information systems degree, business courses, and accreditation (such as Microsoft's MCSE or the CNE for Novell Netware Systems) may give the employer enough confidence to hire the beginner.

Experience, Skills, and Personality Traits

Each successfully completed contract becomes part of a consultant's qualifying experience—which is why it is important to get good letters of recommendation from satisfied clients. The ideal skills mix combines problem solving, mastery of the technical details of several operating systems and hardware platforms, and the "people skills" of listening and communication. The consultant needs a personality that combines self-motivation (since he or she will be working without much supervision), flexibility (because each situation will be different), and the ability to deal with the uncertainties of self-employment.

Cross-Training for Systems Consultants

Interests	Related Job Descriptions
designing software in-house	Systems Analyst
managing MIS department	Manager, Information Systems
building compatible systems	Systems Integrator

Unions and Associations

Systems Consultants tend to go for practical organizations that can offer certification rather than the theoretical computer science groups. There are many organizations devoted to software consultants (and to management or business consultants in general). Examples include the Association of Independent Information Professionals, Independent Computer Consultants Association, Institute for the Certification of Computing Professionals, and the Professional and Technical Consultants Association. In addition to professional resources and job leads, many of these organizations may provide benefits such as group insurance plans.

Tips for Entry

1. It's quite possible to ease oneself into consulting, and that's probably the safest way to go. Consider taking small contracts while still in school or while working at a full-time job. You can gain some experience and decide whether independent consulting is really for you.
2. Make sure your background includes a good mix of computer-related courses (programming, networks, etc.) and business-related (management) courses.
3. If you have a particular area of interest, consider working toward becoming a specialized consultant (for example, in science, engineering, or manufacturing). Specialization may limit the number of available jobs, however.
4. Keep a journal or note system that describes the various problems you've faced and solved. If well organized, it can help you tackle similar problems later.
5. If a client is pleased with your work, ask if he or she will recommend you to others. Make sure people who may need your services know how to contact you. Consider putting up a website that describes your background and skills.

PROJECT MANAGER, SOFTWARE DEVELOPMENT

CAREER PROFILE

Duties: Directs all facets of a software development project; assigns tasks, schedules work, and coordinates efforts of developers, testers, and documenters

Alternate Title(s): Lead Programmer

Salary Range: $60,000 to $85,000

Employment Prospects: Fair

Advancement Prospects: Fair

Prerequisites:

Education or Training—Degree (preferably graduate) in computer science and related business or specialty courses

Experience—Several years as a software engineer or programmer/analyst with increasing responsibility for design or management

Special Skills and Personality Traits—Must be able to keep track of many details; supervise and motivate workers; communicate with upper management and the marketing department

CAREER LADDER

```
┌─────────────────────────────────┐
│   Chief Information Officer      │
└─────────────────────────────────┘

┌─────────────────────────────────┐
│   Manager, Information Systems   │
└─────────────────────────────────┘

┌─────────────────────────────────┐
│        Project Manager          │
└─────────────────────────────────┘
```

Position Description

Project Managers usually work for a company that produces commercial computer software. The position combines technical knowledge and management skills. Typical tasks include:

- combining the design work of systems analysts or software engineers (and usually feedback from the marketing department) to create the overall specifications for the software
- assigning and supervising the programmers who write the program code
- representing the software development team in meetings with the company's upper management and other department heads
- dealing with problems in a timely manner so the product is ready to ship on time

(In smaller companies the Project Manager may actually be a product manager responsible for marketing as well as product development. Larger companies have a separate marketing department.)

The Project Manager must be prepared to deal with the many things that can (and often do) go wrong in a development project. Programmers may run into unexpected problems such as conflicts with the operating system or hardware. "Everything takes longer than planned" is a common observation.

The nontechnical challenges are equally important. Major software projects are multimillion-dollar investments that may make or break a company's future. The Project Manager must work with the marketing department to successfully "launch" or introduce the product to the public.

The marketing department closely follows industry trends, commentary in the trade press, and feedback from customers. As a result, it often pressures the software developers to add new features to the product that customers demand, or that they feel will make it more competitive. But adding features can disrupt the development process, create new program bugs, and cause missed deadlines.

The marketing department has to prepare an advertising campaign in advance of the product "launch," and the campaign is geared to that deadline. They thus pressure the developers to ship the product on time. If the product is late, major customers may switch to that of a competitor. If too many deadlines are missed, the company will lose credibility, and customers may no longer wait for new products. This can lead to a downward spiral into bankruptcy as the company has fewer resources available to develop or improve its products.

Because of these considerations, the Project Manager position, while requiring broad technical knowledge and experience with software development, emphasizes the managerial skills.

Salaries

Individuals who manage small projects (such as the most experienced programmer taking on managerial tasks as lead programmer) may make only a little more than the average systems analyst. However, an experienced Project Manager in a major commercial software project is a key person who can command a salary of $75,000 to $100,000 or more. Salaries depend on the person's years of experience, track record, and the size of the company.

Employment Prospects

There are many software engineers who would like to become Project Managers, so positions are not easy to find. Individuals interested in this work need to be methodical in gaining qualifications and experience.

Advancement Prospects

Project Manager can be the transition from the software development team to the company's upper levels of management. The successful Project Manager can move into becoming the overall manager in charge of all software development projects or, eventually, a chief information officer.

Education and Training

A four-year degree in computer science with some business-related courses is minimum; a graduate degree is preferred for this level. The educational background should include a strong emphasis on both the methodology of software development and management theory. The individual needs to be a competent programmer in order to understand what is or is not *technically* possible. The management courses bring understanding of what is *humanly* possible.

Experience, Skills, and Personality Traits

The successful candidate needs to build a reputation as a systems analyst or software engineer, including assisting in management tasks. Necessary skills include problem solving, management of detail, ability to work under heavy pressure, and strong leadership and communications skills. The introverted personality that often enables top programming wizards to concentrate so effectively may become an obstacle to success as a manager.

Cross-Training for Project Managers

Interests	Related Job Descriptions
designing software solutions	Systems Analyst
entering upper management	Manager, Information Systems; Chief Information Officer
managing the marketing effort	Marketing Manager (Computer Products and Services)

Unions and Associations

Project Managers tend to be interested both in technical organizations (such as the Association for Computing Machinery) and organizations focused on business needs (MIS, or Management Information Systems).

Tips for Entry

1. If you are still in college, take management courses in addition to a solid computer science program.
2. After getting an entry-level job as a programmer or programmer/analyst, work toward software engineering skills that go beyond low-level programming tasks.
3. Look for opportunities to assist the Project Manager or systems analysts in coordinating or managing the different aspects of developing software.
4. If possible, spend some time in the marketing department to get a "feel" for their concerns.

INFORMATION SYSTEMS OPERATION AND MANAGEMENT

COMPUTER OPERATOR

CAREER PROFILE

Duties: Performs routine tasks involving the running of programs, collation of output, and the maintenance of the computer system

Alternate Title(s): Data Processing Assistant or Technician

Salary Range: $22,000 to $40,000

Employment Prospects: Poor to fair

Advancement Prospects: Fair

Prerequisites:

Education or Training—High school diploma; vocational school or two-year college preferred

Experience—Familiarity with basic computer operations, perhaps through an internship or work-study job

Special Skills and Personality Traits—Attention to detail; problem-solving ability; willingness to accept tedious or routine work

CAREER LADDER

```
┌─────────────────────────────┐
│   Manager or Supervisor,    │
│    Computer Operations      │
└─────────────────────────────┘

┌─────────────────────────────┐
│ Senior or Lead Computer Operator │
└─────────────────────────────┘

┌─────────────────────────────┐
│      Computer Operator      │
└─────────────────────────────┘

┌─────────────────────────────┐
│   Trainee, Computer Operations  │
└─────────────────────────────┘
```

Position Description

The role and duties of a Computer Operator are evolving as the focus of data processing continues to move away from traditional large mainframe computers to networked PCs and file servers.

In a mainframe installation, the tasks for Computer Operators typically include the following:

- entering commands to run regularly scheduled programs
- monitoring for and fixing common operating system problems
- collecting, collating, and distributing printed output from programs
- loading ("mounting") program and data tapes as needed
- running and filing routine backup tapes
- adjusting printers, replenishing paper and other supplies (sometimes a task for an entry-level "peripheral equipment operator")
- scheduling and managing the overall workflow of the computer center (usually a task for the lead or senior operator or supervising operator)

In PC-based networks individual users rather than Operators often run programs and produce printouts and reports. There are some tasks that still must be performed by an Operator, including:

- maintaining and troubleshooting equipment such as high-performance printers that may be shared by many users
- making sure the file server (a powerful PC with large disk capacity from which users get data and programs) is running properly, has enough disk space, and is accessible through the network
- logging network performance and dealing with routine network maintenance tasks
- installing and configuring software for users
- keeping an inventory of software in use (necessary for following license agreements made with software vendors)

The tasks of the Computer Operator are likely to continue to change as the features of computer equipment evolve, and as more routine tasks (such as backups and system monitoring) are handled by software with less human intervention.

Salaries

Computer Operator is one of the lower-paid positions in information technology, but pay will grow with seniority and the addition of supervisory duties. Government or other highly unionized shops tend to have higher salaries.

Employment Prospects

Employment of Computer Operators is continuing to decline, so competition for existing positions has become tougher. Prospects may be better for candidates who emphasize PC network-related skills.

Advancement Prospects

Computer operations is traditionally a good "stepping stone" to either supervisory positions in operations or for "crossing over" to programmer or systems analyst positions after appropriate training and experience.

Education and Training

A high school diploma with basic computer courses may be sufficient for an entry-level position, but a vocational school or two-year college program emphasizing computer operations is recommended. A person with more education who is seemingly "overqualified" may still consider an Operator position as a way to get essential paid work experience.

Experience, Skills, and Personality Traits

Since this is an entry-level job, formal experience may not be necessary. The candidate should be able to show course work and some hands-on exposure to computer operations. Important skills include the ability to keep up with the flow of work, identify and troubleshoot problems, and work well with other staff members (although night-shift work may be more comfortable for introverts).

Cross-Training for Computer Operators

Interests	Related Job Descriptions
managing computer operations department	Systems Administrator, Supervisor or Manager, Computer Operations
programming	Programmer, Entry-Level
configuring computer systems	Systems Integrator

Unions and Associations

Computer Operator is often considered to be a clerical position, so some Computer Operators (particularly for government agencies, schools, or large businesses) may be members of clerical worker unions.

Tips for Entry

1. If in high school, become familiar with the operation of your school's computer lab. Volunteer to help keep the software, hardware, and network running.
2. Look for local nonprofit agencies or small businesses that might need help running their computer systems.
3. After graduation, look for community college programs or vocational schools that offer degrees or certificates in computer operations. (But make sure the school's program is up to date and that graduates have a high job placement rate. Also consult reference guides that rate schools and seek advice from people you know who have experience in the field.)
4. Be aware that you may have to accept night-shift or other less desirable work to "get your foot in the door."

QUALITY ASSURANCE SPECIALIST

CAREER PROFILE

Duties: Tests and evaluates software programs to make sure they work correctly and meet specifications

Alternate Title(s): Software Tester; Quality Assurance Technician

Salary Range: $30,000 to $50,000 or more, depending on experience

Employment Prospects: Fair

Advancement Prospects: Fair

Prerequisites:

Education or Training—Some companies will train high school graduates with strong computer skills, but a two-year undergraduate degree in a technology-related field is a plus

Experience—Should be familiar with the major operating systems and types of software packages; could "cross over" from a support or help desk job

Special Skills and Personality Traits—Good observation skills and attention to detail; must be thorough and systematic; good written and oral communication skills; a pinch of curiosity helps

CAREER LADDER

```
┌─────────────────────────────────────────┐
│   Senior Quality Assurance Specialist    │
└─────────────────────────────────────────┘

┌─────────────────────────────────────────┐
│      Quality Assurance Specialist        │
└─────────────────────────────────────────┘

┌─────────────────────────────────────────┐
│        Trainee (software testing)        │
└─────────────────────────────────────────┘
```

Position Description

Modern software programs often have a complicated structure with many menus, submenus, and dialog boxes that are used to specify exactly how the program will operate. Since programmers focus mainly on the inner operation of the program's various modules or routines, it is difficult for them to anticipate the many ways in which actual users will want to use the program. Although programmers do test the operation of their routines, they are likely to let some bugs slip through.

The Quality Assurance Specialist is the main line of defense against "buggy" products. He or she systematically tests every menu or other program option and compares what happens to the program's design specifications. Automated test programs can also be used to feed sets of test data into a program and record the output. Each problem found must be carefully documented in the form of a "bug report" that will be resolved by the software engineers.

Experienced Quality Assurance Specialists may take a more active role in program development. They can test early versions of a program, find potential user problems, and suggest ways to improve the user interface.

Salaries

While starting salaries are fairly low for this position, experienced Quality Assurance Specialists can earn more, particularly if they have additional duties such as supervising other testers.

Employment Prospects

There has been some decline in demand for quality assurance testing. Some companies test their software using automated test utility suites run by low-level technicians. Other companies send out preliminary or "beta" versions of the software to selected customers. These "beta testers" are expected to work with the product and report any problems they find to the manufacturer. Beta testing can be very helpful since the more people work with a program from different points of view, the more likely its bugs will be identified.

Automated testing and beta testing are reducing the demand for in-house Quality Assurance Specialists.

Advancement Prospects

An experienced Quality Assurance Specialist in a large firm may have the opportunity to become manager of the testing operation, supervising testers or running a beta test program.

Another possible career route would involve obtaining degrees or credentials in information processing and business that would enable entry into a position as an EDP auditor.

Education and Training

Quality assurance is a good field for someone with some interest in and experience with computers but little formal training. Some companies will train candidates who show enthusiasm and a long-term career interest. Nevertheless, college-level courses in basic computer theory, programming, and software engineering are helpful.

Experience, Skills, and Personality Traits

Quality assurance work requires familiarity with common software and operating systems (such as Windows and UNIX) and an understanding of the practical principles of user interfaces, such as the standard conventions used for displaying menus and dialog boxes. (Even if an option works correctly, the QA Specialist may need to identify ways in which it is nonstandard and thus potentially confusing to the user.)

Skills needed include close observation to spot small discrepancies; problem solving (so possible fixes can be suggested); good writing and communication skills; and the ability to work with programmers and managers. Helpful personality traits include concentration and self-discipline (since much of the work can be tedious).

Cross-Training for Quality Assurance Specialists

Interests	Related Job Descriptions
explaining use of programs	Technical Writer/Trainer
computer games	Playtester
verifying business operations	EDP Auditor
designing user interfaces	User Interface Designer

Unions and Associations

Quality Assurance Specialist falls between clerical and professional work. QA Specialists do not usually belong to labor unions. For career development they can consider joining an organization such as the Quality Assurance Institute or EDP Auditors Association.

Tips for Entry

1. Try to become familiar with different types of software such as word processors, graphics programs, educational programs, and games. Note the different ways in which program functions are organized and how the program interacts with the user.
2. If your present company or school uses a lot of software, they may have a beta testing arrangement with a software company. If so, volunteer to be a beta tester so you can practice your testing skills.
3. Look for game companies that want playtesters. Also, you can test "shareware" programs and correspond with their developers, who often appreciate the feedback.
4. If you haven't done so, take some basic courses in programming so you can learn how user interfaces are designed. Languages like Visual Basic are particularly helpful because they make it easy to experiment with interface ideas.

AUDITOR, ELECTRONIC DATA PROCESSING

CAREER PROFILE

Duties: Closely examines data processing operations to guard against loss through mistakes, carelessness, or fraud; brings problems to the attention of managers or authorities

Alternate Title(s): Information Systems Auditor

Salary Range: $45,000 to $60,000

Employment Prospects: Good

Advancement Prospects: Fair

Prerequisites:

Education or Training—Four-year college degree with major in information systems or accounting; graduate degree and certification in accounting preferred

Experience—Work as an assistant in auditing or accounting

Special Skills and Personality Traits—Systematic thinking; attention to detail; good communications skills; willingness to confront problems or wrongdoing

CAREER LADDER

```
Partner (public accounting firm)
```

```
Senior EDP Auditor
```

```
EDP Auditor
```

```
EDP Auditor/Trainee
```

Position Description

The electronic data processing (EDP) operations of a major business or financial institution are responsible for tracking billions of dollars worth of transactions. EDP Auditors most often work in banks, insurance companies, accounting firms, and other organizations that use a large amount of financial data. Typical duties include:

- verifying that databases and other programs have proper procedures for avoiding errors and ensuring the accuracy of data
- carefully examining the procedures that clerical workers use in working with programs to identify sources of error
- watching for possible computer fraud or other criminal activities, and reporting them to authorities or computer security specialists
- making sure that accounting, banking, or insurance operations comply with government regulations and industry standards
- preparing regular reports for management

The EDP Auditor is part systems analyst, part accountant, and part detective. Because so much depends on the integrity of the information processing system, he or she must be will-

ing to take responsibility for the thoroughness of the audit procedures. If evidence of criminal activity is found, the EDP Auditor may have to deal with computer security specialists and law enforcement officials, or testify in court.

Salaries

Salaries for EDP Auditors depend on experience, the size and complexity of the systems audited, and the nature of the employer. Auditors who work with large accounting firms and reach senior or partnership status will earn the highest salaries.

Employment Prospects

EDP auditing has only recently emerged as a well-defined position. Demand for Auditors is increasing as executives increasingly realize the crucial importance of EDP operations to businesses and their vulnerability to slipshod operations or outright fraud.

Advancement Prospects

Experienced Auditors can advance as manager of an audit department, become consultants, or can even become full partners in accounting firms that value their expertise.

Education and Training

There are two main training paths for EDP Auditors, both of which require minimum four-year college degrees with a graduate degree and certification recommended. Some individuals start out taking courses in programming and information systems and then take courses in accounting and business operations. Others start out as business majors and add solid coursework in the computer field. Some may work for several years as general auditors or accountants and then go back to school to take computer courses. Specific degree programs in EDP (or information systems) auditing are starting to become available. An MBA degree is a solid plus.

Experience, Skills, and Personality Traits

The successful candidate needs experience in both programming and computer operations and accounting or auditing in the business environment. Needed skills include understanding the relationship of parts of a system to one another, mastery of detail, and investigation skills. "People skills" are also important: The auditor must be able to effectively interview people in the workplace, and will sometimes have to confront reluctant managers with problems they may not want to hear about.

Cross-Training for EDP Auditors

Interests	Related Job Descriptions
system design	Systems Analyst
accounting	Certified Public Accountant (with specialty in EDP)
computer security	Computer Security Specialist

Unions and Associations

The Information Systems Audit and Control Association is a professional organization for EDP Auditors. Many auditors also have the designation of certified public accountant (CPA) and belong to accountancy organizations.

Tips for Entry

1. If you are already working as an accountant or general auditor, look for a college program in information systems where you can gain programming and analysis skills.

2. If you are a programmer/analyst or systems analyst, look for training in accounting and business operations.

3. Get a sense of the nature of the work by asking people who are already working EDP Auditors to describe their typical tasks and some of the problems they have encountered. Also contact the Electronic Data Processing Auditors Association (EDPAA) for more information.

4. Focus your job search on government agencies (which have many auditing-related jobs) and accounting firms.

TAPE LIBRARIAN/ARCHIVIST

CAREER PROFILE

Duties: Organizes and maintains the tapes or disks that store a computer installation's data and programs

Alternate Title(s): Archivist; Records Specialist

Salary Range: $20,000 to $30,000

Employment Prospects: Poor

Advancement Prospects: Fair

Prerequisites:

Education or Training—Minimum of a high school diploma with some course work in data processing; positions at some facilities (such as libraries) may require an undergraduate degree and/or training in library science

Experience—Clerical experiences such as filing, classification, or maintenance of supplies is helpful

Special Skills and Personality Traits—Should be careful and methodical about following procedures

CAREER LADDER

```
┌─────────────────────────────────────┐
│  Manager, Tape Library or Archive    │
└─────────────────────────────────────┘

┌─────────────────────────────────────┐
│      Tape Librarian/Archivist        │
└─────────────────────────────────────┘

┌─────────────────────────────────────┐
│       Assistant (data archives)      │
└─────────────────────────────────────┘
```

Position Description

As the name suggests, Tape Librarian is a position traditionally associated with mainframe computer installations that store data on large spools or cartridges of magnetic tape. Duties of the Tape Librarian or Archivist may include:

- classifying, filing, and retrieving tapes or disks containing backup or other data
- maintaining a library of documentation such as operations procedure manuals
- maintaining an inventory of software and supplies (such as tapes, disks, paper, etc.)

While some of these duties are also needed in PC-based networks, the person who carries them out there is more likely to be called an assistant systems administrator or technical assistant.

The "librarian" part of the job description suggests an overlap with library work; the position is somewhat similar to work done by library clerks or assistants. Some sort of classification system must be used to store tapes according to such criteria as intended user (or department), program or data set, and date run.

While this position is essentially clerical, it does involve some knowledge of how the data processing department is

structured and how programs are typically run. Depending on the employer's needs, the Tape Librarian may have the opportunity to help operate the computer system. Other related tasks can include keeping an inventory of software (version and number of users for each package) and supplies such as tapes, floppy disks, printer cartridges, and paper.

Salaries

This tends to be a low-paid entry-level position. Salaries depend on the general level of clerical wages in the community as well as the size of the employer and whether the workplace is unionized.

Employment Prospects

Because of the continuing decline of the mainframe computer system, demand for Tape Librarians/Archivists is expected be stagnant or even decline. Rather than counting on getting this particular position, the candidate should train for a variety of entry-level jobs such as computer operator, system administrator (trainee), or library assistant.

Advancement Prospects

There is some advancement potential within the position. Most individuals will use the job to gain some computer operations experience while preparing to move on to operations management, programming, or other positions.

Education and Training

This is a good "springboard" job for a high school graduate with some basic experience who needs to find a technical job without (or before) attending college. Having some college-level computer courses may help in getting an entry-level job.

Experience, Skills, and Personality Traits

Some experience working in a library or data processing facility is a plus. Basic skills needed include classification, filing, operating equipment (such as tape drives), using simple database or inventory programs, and communicating with coworkers.

Cross-Training for Tape Librarians/Archivists

Interests	Related Job Descriptions
working in a library	Library Assistant
operating or managing computer systems	Computer Operator or Systems Administrator
managing graphics archives	Computer Graphics Librarian/Archivist
organizing and managing multimedia materials	Media Specialist (School Libraries)

Unions and Associations

A Tape Librarian/Archivist may be considered to be a clerical employee, and thus belong to a local clerical union.

Tips for Entry

1. While in high school, look for volunteer work in the computer lab or school library where you can become familiar with data storage, retrieval, and filing.
2. Since the skills involved are similar, keep an eye out for library clerk or library assistant jobs in addition to jobs in data processing.
3. Once you get an entry-level position, decide whether you are more interested in programming, systems operation and administration, or library work, and try to gain experience and education that points in your chosen direction.

SYSTEMS ADMINISTRATOR

CAREER PROFILE

Duties: Responsible for managing the operation of a multi-user computer system or network so that it runs reliably and meets users' needs; updates and configures software and hardware; provides assistance to users and managers

Alternate Title(s): Computer Systems Manager

Salary Range: $40,000 to $75,000

Employment Prospects: Good

Advancement Prospects: Good

Prerequisites:

Education or Training—Generally four-year college with computer-related degree or course work, but appropriate experience can sometimes be substituted for academic qualifications

Experience—Familiarity with operating system (such as Unix or Microsoft Windows), utility software, backup and security procedures, basic programming or scripting

Special Skills and Personality Traits—Attention to detail; problem solving and good communications skills; reliable

CAREER LADDER

```
┌─────────────────────────────────┐
│  Manager, Information Systems    │
└─────────────────────────────────┘

┌─────────────────────────────────┐
│     Systems Administrator        │
└─────────────────────────────────┘

┌─────────────────────────────────┐
│  Assistant Systems Administrator │
└─────────────────────────────────┘
```

Position Description

Whether they are working in a business, government, scientific, or academic setting, people depend on their computer system and network being available and reliable. The Systems Administrator's most important responsibility is to monitor the operation of the system and fix any problems that arise, whether with data storage, network communications, or the running of software.

The Systems Administrator keeps track of user accounts, setting up accounts for new users and answering questions about system operations and procedures. If certain resources such as disk space or printers are limited, the Systems Administrator may have to allocate them to users according to various priorities.

The Systems Administrator must properly set up and maintain the various services on which users depend. This may include file servers, databases, access to the Internet and to the internal network (intranet), and software applications that run on users' individual PCs or on a central server.

Users must be educated about proper procedures for backing up and archiving data. (Data on a central server will probably be backed up automatically, but users may have data on their own PCs as well.) In today's security-conscious environment it is particularly important that users understand the need to use hard-to-guess passwords, to run antivirus software, and to avoid opening e-mail attachments from unknown sources. The Systems Administrator may also help create and enforce policies designed to prevent outside intruders from tricking users into revealing sensitive information. (Larger installations may have a separate computer security specialist with whom the Systems Administrator will coordinate security efforts.)

When users require new software, hardware, or capabilities, the Systems Administrator must install them and make sure they work smoothly with existing systems. It is common for bugs and even "security holes" to be found in software, so the Systems Administrator must keep up with information provided on software vendors' websites or through bulletins. By promptly installing updates or "patches" to software, the Systems Administrator can keep software up to date and as secure and reliable as possible.

Entry-level or assistant Systems Administrators in large installations will usually work under the supervision of senior staff. They will follow well-defined procedures and carry out routine monitoring, log problems, answer user questions, and install software. As they gain experience Systems Administrators can take on more complex responsibilities, including writing simple programs or scripts to automate procedures such as backups, or configuring and maintaining facilities such as file and Web servers. At the higher levels Systems Administrators gain managerial responsibilities such as supervising technicians, operators, or lower-level administrators. They can also help formulate policies and guidelines for computer use or help plan the purchase or upgrade of hardware or software.

Salaries

Salaries for Systems Administrators depend largely on the size and complexity of the installation for which they are responsible, as well as the duties and skills required. Other things being equal, Systems Administrators working in large corporate settings may be paid more than those in academic or government ones. While salaries are not bad, they tend to be toward the lower side for computer professionals because many people see the system administration field as a way to get experience before moving on to managerial or specialist positions.

Employment Prospects

Despite the recent downturn in some parts of the computer industry, the need for capable Systems Administrators remains strong. Candidates who have specific knowledge of particular operating systems (such as UNIX/Linux or Microsoft Windows XP) will be more competitive, as will those with experience in networking and Web applications (see the Network Administrator entry for a related position).

Advancement Prospects

Individuals who keep their skills up to date and demonstrate the ability to handle increasing responsibility have a good possibility of moving up the administrative ranks (in large institutions) or of qualifying for more advanced positions elsewhere. One route to advancement goes into management, with the goal of becoming a manager or director of information systems. Another possibility is to specialize in a particular area (such as networking or security) with a view to becoming a well-paid consultant.

Education and Training

Although most employers will expect a two- or four-year college degree in computer science or information systems, experience and demonstrated capabilities are often valued

more highly than academic credentials. Industry certifications relating to the operating system or networking software (such as the Microsoft Certified System Engineer, or MCSE) can be useful for demonstrating a base level of knowledge.

Experience, Skills, and Personality Traits

A person considering work as a Systems Administrator is likely to have used computer systems for a number of years and to have gained familiarity with the operating system and major software applications. Although details will be different depending on the operating and network system in use, the general skills needed for good systems administration are the same. These include technical skills (observation, analysis, problem solving) and communication skills, including the ability to write clear, accurate reports and to communicate with users who may be under considerable stress. Because much of the routine work involved in system administration can be repetitive and boring, the individual must be able to maintain motivation and discipline. At the same time it will be necessary to deal with stressful, challenging conditions if a crisis occurs, such as the system being attacked by a virus or the network going down.

Cross-Training for System Administrators

Interests	Related Job Descriptions
system configuration	Systems Analyst
programming	Programmer; Software Engineer
networking	Network Administrator
user support	Technical Support Representative; Technical Writer

Unions and Associations

Systems Administrators working in government (and a few private) installations may belong to clerical or office workers' unions. Most Systems Administrators do not belong to unions but may find it helpful to join general computer-related organizations such as the Association for Computing Machinery (ACM) or the Institute of Electrical and Electronics Engineers (IEEE).

Tips for Entry

1. Decide which of the two major computing environments (UNIX/Linux or Microsoft Windows) most interests you and delve into the details of the operating system and software on your home or school PC. However, try to learn something about the other operating systems as well.
2. In high school, see if you can help teachers or school administrators work with maintaining the computer systems. You might also volunteer to help local nonprofit groups set up or maintain their computer system, help

underserved groups (such as minorities or senior citizens) connect to the Internet, and so on. Document whatever experience you gain for future use in your résumé.

3. Consider getting an industry certification (such as MCSE), but be sure to check articles in the trade press to see which certifications are most in demand.

DATABASE ADMINISTRATOR

CAREER PROFILE

Duties: Takes responsibility for the overall operation and security of an organization's database systems; coordinates development and use of data resources; represents database operations in interdepartmental meetings

Alternate Title(s): Database Manager

Salary Range: $45,000 to $75,000 or more

Employment Prospects: Good

Advancement Prospects: Fair

Prerequisites:

Education or Training—Minimum four-year degree in computer-related field (usually MIS); business and management courses helpful

Experience—Experience designing and programming with major database software packages; management experience helpful

Special Skills and Personality Traits—Database design and programming; needs analysis; management and communications skills; needs to be a responsible person who is consistent but can adapt to changing needs

CAREER LADDER

Chief Information Officer

Manager, Information Systems

Database Administrator

Database Analyst/Programmer

Position Description

Databases are the heart of information processing in the business world. Detailed information about customers, orders, vendors, products, research, and other matters must be maintained accurately and without falling behind the flow of business.

The Database Administrator is in charge of all aspects of database operations. Typical tasks include:

- supervising Database Analysts or other programmers in the design or modification of the structure of the database, the input forms used to gather data, and the reports to be produced for managers and executives
- ensuring that all changes to the system are thoroughly tested so that accuracy can be certified
- configuring and maintaining the server computers that allow access to the database across the local area network (LAN)
- watching for potential security problems or vulnerability of data to natural disasters, and making contingency plans (such as for backup or recovery) to deal with these threats

- creating "Data Warehouses" that bring together data generated by many different departments into a form that can be used for evaluation of operations and for executive decision making
- creating Internet-accessible databases, such as product specifications, to be retrieved by potential customers

The Database Administrator must regularly run software that verifies the consistency of data formats and the relationships between databases. Often several different departments may use the same database and update different parts of the same records. Programs that access the database and add or change data must follow the same specifications, such as the format for dates. While good software design can help ensure that data is automatically screened before it enters the database, the Database Administrator must make sure that software developers follow good programming practices.

The Database Administrator will often assign programming tasks to Database Analysts to meet the need for changes in the database structure or changes in the way data is used. Supervision and training of junior database programmers or analysts is also important.

The installation must maintain adequate backups (including a backup kept offsite to guard against fire or other disaster). Since database often have confidential or proprietary information, the Database Administrator (possibly working with a computer security specialist) must make sure that persons accessing the database are using passwords that aren't too easy to guess, and aren't leaving written passwords lying around or leaving logged-in terminals running.

In interdepartmental meetings the Database Administrator may represent the data processing department, explaining operations to other managers and in turn listening to their information processing needs.

Salaries

Because of its importance and responsibilities, this is a well-paid position. Larger organizations with more complex data needs tend to pay higher salaries for Database Administrators. Small organizations may not have a separate person for this position, but rather include it in system administration.

Employment Prospects

The thirst for data in business and government shows no signs of slacking off. On the other hand, there are relatively few positions available at a given time, because this position is often the top of a career track. Individuals who have extensive experience and strong skills involving the most popular database systems will have the best chance—perhaps moving up from database analyst when the Database Administrator in an organization retires or moves on.

Advancement Prospects

Since Database Administrator is at the top of the database-related career path, further advancement is usually to either manager of the information systems department, or into general high-level management, possibly to the chief information officer level.

Education and Training

Minimum of four-year college degree with major in management information systems (MIS) or computer science; courses in business (management, marketing, operations, etc.) are a definite plus. Some software manufacturers offer certification that indicates an individual has mastered the use of their system; such certification can reassure potential employers that the candidate's skills are up to date.

Experience, Skills, and Personality Traits

The Database Administrator must have a solid background in the theory of database design and the detailed operation of commonly used database software packages such as Oracle and Windows-based systems such as Microsoft Access. Knowledge of SQL (Structured Query Language), a standard for database retrieval and processing, is also a must. With the increasing use of the Internet, the Database Administrator may be called upon to supervise the development of Internet-accessible database using the Java language, CGI (Common Gateway Interface) scripts, VBScript, Visual Basic, ActiveX, XML, and other tools.

An individual in this position needs a strong sense of responsibility, willingness to keep up with new challenges and changing needs, and good communication skills.

Cross-Training for Database Administrators

Interests	Related Job Descriptions
managing a computer system	Systems Administrator
designing database applications	Database Analyst
presenting data on the Internet	Internet Applications Programmer; Webmaster

Unions and Associations

Database Administrators often belong both to computer-science related organizations (such as the Association for Computing Machinery) and business and data management organizations.

Tips for Entry

1. While in school, combine computer science (with an emphasis on database theory and data modeling) with projects that help you master major database software packages currently in demand by business.
2. Look for entry-level programming jobs that will reinforce database skills. You may be able to "earn while you learn" by taking on small consulting jobs.
3. If you have a good track record and several years' experience you may be able to eventually move into the Database Administrator position at your current company.
4. Focus especially on the Internet and intranets, which are the main ways of accessing data today. Familiarize yourself with TCP/IP (Transmission Control Protocol/Internet Protocol), HTML (Hypertext Mark-up Language), and XML (Extensible Mark-up Language).

COMPUTER SECURITY SPECIALIST

Duties: Protects computer systems from illegal intrusions, viruses, data theft, fraud, or other forms of tampering

Alternate Title(s): Security Manager

Salary Range: $50,000 to $80,000

Employment Prospects: Fair

Advancement Prospects: Good

Prerequisites:

Education or Training—Four-year degree in MIS or computer science; courses in database, telecommunications, networking, and auditing/accounting helpful

Experience—Experience configuring and working with database, networking, and other software; Internet experience a plus

Special Skills and Personality Traits—Ability to recognize something that is wrong or out of place; attention to detail; investigation skills; personal integrity; polite but assertive when necessary

```
┌─────────────────────────────┐
│   Director of Security,      │
│   Information Systems        │
└─────────────────────────────┘

┌─────────────────────────────┐
│ Security Specialist or Consultant │
└─────────────────────────────┘

┌─────────────────────────────┐
│  Trainee or Assistant, Security │
└─────────────────────────────┘
```

Position Description

Recent movies and real-life stories in the media have shown how easy it can be for unscrupulous but clever people to break into computer systems. Once inside, they can introduce viruses (destructive programs), steal valuable data (such as credit card numbers), or simply wipe out important data. Add to that the possibility that terrorist groups might target vital computer systems, and you can see why computer security is one of today's fastest growing occupational areas.

The Computer Security Specialist is the security guard and detective of the high-tech world. His or her duties include:

- setting up automatic antivirus and security monitoring programs
- reviewing system logs for evidence of tampering
- educating users about good security practices (such as choosing hard-to-guess passwords and not leaving them lying around)
- keeping up with bulletins issued by software and operating system vendors and agencies such as CERT (Computer Emergency Response Team)
- cooperating with law enforcement officials in investigating computer crime

As a guard, the Computer Security Specialist must be constantly on the lookout for suspicious changes to programs and system files, or for accounts that may have been compromised. (For example, an account belonging to a high-level executive that is seldom used suddenly filling hundreds of megabytes of file storage.)

As an investigator, the Security Specialist must gather data such as logs of commands entered into the computer by a suspect. He or she must know the common behavior patterns of teenage computer "crackers" and experienced industrial spies, and respond appropriately in a variety of situations.

The Security Specialist must be an effective communicator within the organization. He or she must strike a balance between security that is so tight that it becomes a major inconvenience to legitimate users and systems that are so easy to access that they might as well display a "Steal Me!" sign.

The integration of the Internet into many corporate computer systems has added a new dimension of security concerns. The Security Specialist must now supply services such as:

- configuring and monitoring the "firewall"—a computer that allows users to access the Internet while insulating the system from direct outside contact
- guarding against new kinds of computer viruses found in Internet documents and their attached programs (called "macros" or "applets")
- configuring special secure connections that allow customers to safely send their credit card information over the Internet

Salaries

Large corporations with sensitive data (such as phone companies, utilities, and banks) generally pay the top rates. Government positions usually pay somewhat less, but may offer greater job security.

Employment Prospects

Recently publicized hacker attacks and growing public concern about identity theft and the need to protect sensitive information (such as credit card numbers) on the Internet are increasing the demand by businesses for Computer Security Specialists.

In addition, the new emphasis on homeland security following the recent terrorist attacks is likely to lead to increasing demand for Computer Security Specialists by federal, state, and local governments. Working with a company that provides computer security to business or government on a contract basis is also a possibility.

Advancement Prospects

An experienced Computer Security Specialist may find consulting to be attractive, both for the variety of situations encountered and the high hourly pay (up to $150 per hour or more). Very large organizations with critical systems (such as banks and telephone companies) will have a director of security and a large security staff that can provide a career path.

Education and Training

The basic requirement is a four-year college degree in computer science or information systems. The candidate must become familiar with a variety of topics, including network operation, telecommunications, behavior of computer viruses, security problems in common operating systems (such as UNIX), basic criminology, and human behavior.

Experience, Skills, and Personality Traits

Individuals preparing for careers in computer security need several years of hands-on experience in configuring and operating computer networks and relevant types of software, such as mail servers, transaction systems, firewalls, antivirus programs, and system monitoring software.

Essential skills include attention to detail, the ability to recognize patterns (what should be there or what shouldn't be there), the ability to interview and investigate as necessary, and willingness to confront wrongdoers (although direct physical confrontation is rare).

Cross-Training for Computer Security Specialists

Interests	Related Job Descriptions
testing accuracy of systems and data	EDP Auditor
educating users	Trainer; Technical Writer; Technical Support Representative
managing a computer system or network	Systems Administrator; Network Administrator
designing security devices	Embedded Systems Designer; Artificial Intelligence Programmer

Unions and Associations

Computer Security Specialists can join software engineering and management organizations. There are also specialized organizations in this field, such as the Computer Security Institute and the Information Systems Security Association. A related field is EDP auditing, so membership in the Electronic Data Processing (EDP) Auditing Association is a possibility. Security specialists often subscribe to newsgroups such as comp.risks and to bulletins from security agencies such as CERT (Computer Emergency Response Team).

Tips for Entry

1. Start with a good, well-rounded course of study in information systems or computer science and get a couple of years' experience as a programmer, computer operator, or assistant systems administrator. Security is a specialty, not a good entry point into the job market.
2. In the early days a few computer hackers became notorious, got caught, and were able to turn around and sell their services as highly paid consultants. While this still happens once in a while, breaking into computers is definitely not a recommended learning strategy.
3. On the other hand, reading books by hackers or publications like *2600* or *Phrack* will give you some insight into the mentality and techniques of computer intruders.
4. Read Internet news postings, webpages, and trade publications to keep up with the latest developments both in security threats and in protective software or techniques.

MANAGER, INFORMATION SYSTEMS

CAREER PROFILE

Duties: Oversees all operations in an information systems department, including technical support, training, network, and database operations

Alternate Title(s): Operations Manager (Data Processing)

Salary Range: $65,000 to $90,000

Employment Prospects: Fair

Advancement Prospects: Poor

Prerequisites:

Education or Training—Minimum of an undergraduate degree in information systems or computer science; course work in business operations and management is very helpful

Experience—Several years' experience working up the ladder as a computer operator, systems administrator assistant, or support technician

Special Skills and Personality Traits—Ability to schedule and prioritize tasks; ability to respond calmly to emergencies; good technical problem-solving skills (including programming and script writing); familiarity with the relevant operating system and commonly used software; good communication and management skills

CAREER LADDER

```
┌─────────────────────────────────┐
│   Chief Information Officer      │
│     (in large corporations)     │
└─────────────────────────────────┘

┌─────────────────────────────────┐
│  Director, Information Services  │
│   (medium-size organizations)   │
└─────────────────────────────────┘

┌─────────────────────────────────┐
│  Manager, Information Systems    │
└─────────────────────────────────┘

┌─────────────────────────────────┐
│     Systems Administrator        │
│       or Support Manager        │
└─────────────────────────────────┘
```

Position Description

The Information Systems (IS) Manager is in charge of all data processing activities for a small company, government office, or university department. (In larger organizations individual departments will have their own Information System Managers.)

The "bottom line" responsibility of the Information Systems Manager is making sure that everyone in the organization has timely, reliable access to the computer system and its databases and other resources. Typical duties of the IS Manager include:

- supervising computer operators and system administrators to make sure operations go smoothly
- preparing an operating budget, including new computer hardware, software, and training as needed
- planning for expansion or upgrading of equipment or software

- making sure computer users' questions, problems, or special needs are dealt with promptly
- seeing that computing resources are used efficiently
- working with other department managers to coordinate the use of computer resources and supporting the organization's overall goals

In smaller organizations the Information Systems Manager will perform most of the "hands-on" tasks of a system administrator in addition to the management duties above. In larger organizations the IS Manager will supervise and coordinate a staff of system administrators, operators, and technical support personnel.

Salaries

Salaries depend mainly on the size of the organization and its information processing operation and the number of people the IS Manager supervises.

Employment Prospects

There is a strong demand for candidates who have the right mix of technical and managerial skills. Many excellent programmers are not good management material, while a manager who doesn't understand technical requirements can bring operations to a grinding halt.

Persons already working in an organization who have compiled a good record as a system administrator or assistant IS Manager may be able to work their way into this position. Otherwise, it may require patience and good contacts to get a position.

Advancement Prospects

IS department managers in a larger organization who demonstrate outstanding ability are in a good position to move up the ladder to becoming director of information services, supervising all information systems throughout the organization. There are, however, relatively few such openings at any given time.

Education and Training

The most suitable four-year degree emphasizes information processing and business rather than computer science theory. While the IS Manager must be familiar with programming, system analysis, networking, auditing, security, and EDP accounting, the main focus of the job is management.

Experience, Skills, and Personality Traits

Hands-on experience with computer operations is essential. This should be supplemented with experience helping supervise operators or other personnel, in helping to plan budgets and expansion, or in technical support and user education activities.

The most suitable candidate combines a hands-on approach to problem solving, mastery of a variety of technical issues, and the leadership and communication skills needed to supervise subordinates and to interface with other managers. The individual must be energetic, self-motivated, and able to take responsibility.

Cross-Training for Information Systems Managers

Interests	Related Job Descriptions
designing efficient systems	Systems Analyst
managing details of computer operation	Computer Operator; Systems Administrator
freelance consulting for IS problems	Systems Consultant

Unions and Associations

Technical, management, and executive organizations are all appropriate for the IS Manager. Regular meetings and seminars on technical issues and management skills are part of ongoing career development.

Tips for Entry

1. If you are still in college, study the organization and operation of your school's computing center. See if you can get a work-study position or internship where you can learn about operations and technical support.
2. Be sure to supplement your information processing studies with courses in business administration and management, basic accounting, and other business-related subjects.
3. After a few years as a system administrator or manager of technical support you may be in a good position to move into the more general position of Information System Manager.

DIRECTOR, INFORMATION SYSTEMS

CAREER PROFILE

Duties: Takes ultimate responsibility for all information processing activities in a small- to medium-sized business, a government office, or a school district or university; develops budgets, expansion plans, contingency plans, and other strategic plans for an organization's information needs; reports to top executives

Alternate Title(s): Director of IS Operations

Salary Range: $80,000 to $125,000

Employment Prospects: Poor

Advancement Prospects: Poor

Prerequisites:

Education or Training—Usually requires graduate degree in information systems; MBA a strong plus; industry and management certifications

Experience—Extensive experience managing IS departments; planning, budgeting, and policy making

Special Skills and Personality Traits—Ability to think strategically, plan, and delegate authority; excellent verbal and written communication skills; ability to coordinate with professionals and managers; must have great personal energy, ability to focus, and ability to inspire people to work together

CAREER LADDER

```
┌─────────────────────────────────┐
│   Chief Information Officer       │
│     (large corporations)          │
└─────────────────────────────────┘

┌─────────────────────────────────┐
│   Director, Information Systems   │
└─────────────────────────────────┘

┌─────────────────────────────────┐
│   Manager (of a data processing   │
│          department)              │
└─────────────────────────────────┘

┌─────────────────────────────────┐
│     Systems Administrator         │
└─────────────────────────────────┘
```

Position Description

The Information Systems (IS) director is the person in charge of planning for and supervising all of an organization's information systems departments. For example, the Director of Information Systems for a university has responsibility for the school's computing center, which probably includes a campus-wide network, the school's presence on the Internet, and possibly supercomputers used by scientific researchers on campus.

The IS Director is an executive who is concerned mainly with the "big picture" rather than the day-to-day computer operations that are handled by various department or operations center managers. His or her main responsibilities include:

- working with top management to budget for all computer resources
- planning the expansion of computing facilities

- setting organization-wide standards for equipment, software, training, auditing, and other practices
- meeting with managers of departments that use computing services to find ways to provide better service

The IS Director is at the top of the ladder in IS management for small- or medium-sized corporations and for most universities, science labs, and other organizations. (Some larger organizations have a chief information officer or CIO as their top-level executive. See the following entry.)

As a top executive, the IS Director must be an excellent forecaster and planner. He or she must develop long-term plans that take expected trends into account (such as a university's growing student population and need for more extensive Internet connectivity). Policies in areas such as budgeting and purchasing, employment practices, and security and disaster recovery must be developed in coordination with the heads of appropriate departments. A consistent training and staff development program must be put in place so employees understand how to implement these policies.

Salaries

The high salaries for this position reflect the level of responsibility and the complexity of the duties of the IS Director. Corporations usually pay best, followed by university and government departments.

Employment Prospects

There are relatively few openings for this top management position at any given time. Individuals can be promoted from the ranks if they have solid experience as an IS manager, but there is often a nationwide job search and strong competition.

Advancement Prospects

There is little potential for advancement because this is the top IS position in many organizations. Individuals with strong business and management skills could move into the main executive track (such as vice president positions) or move to a larger organization that has a CIO (chief information officer) position available.

Education and Training

The IS Director normally has a very solid background, including a graduate degree in information systems and quite possibly an MBA (Master of Business Administration) degree as well (directors in academic institutions may have a computer science or science background instead).

Training may also include industry certification for the major networks and operating systems, and management courses or workshops.

Experience, Skills, and Personality Traits

A candidate for IS Director typically has five to 10 years of experience in computer operations, system administration, project management, and related activities. This experience has probably led to the individual becoming IS Manager for a department.

Cross-Training for Information Systems Directors

Interests	Related Job Descriptions
top-level executive position	Chief Information Officer
IS management for a department	Manager, Information Systems

Unions and Associations

At this level individuals are likely to belong to management and executive organizations as well as technical groups. There are numerous organizations devoted to management, both general and information systems-related.

Tips for Entry

1. It goes without saying that you will need extensive IS and management experience before you can apply for this position. As you plan your career moves, always try to find positions that have more extensive management responsibilities, while keeping up-to-date on technical issues.
2. You will need to be in the right place at the right time. Having good contacts with IS Directors and executives may give you the inside track for an upcoming opening.
3. Despite any advantages, you will probably be competing with top candidates from all over the country. Skills and areas of experience that closely match the employer's priorities may make the difference. Thoroughly researching the prospective employer will help you identify and highlight such matchups.

CHIEF INFORMATION OFFICER

CAREER PROFILE

Duties: Serves as the highest information services executive for a major corporation; responsible for long-term planning and setting organization-wide policy and standards relating to all computer-related activities

Alternate Title(s): Chief Technology Officer (CTO); Vice President, Information Systems

Salary Range: $125,000 to $200,000 or more (including nonsalary benefits)

Employment Prospects: Poor

Advancement Prospects: Poor

Prerequisites:

Education or Training—Graduate degrees in information systems and/or MBA

Experience—Ten to 15 or more years, including computer operations, analysis or research, and management with increasing responsibilities at IS manager or director level

Special Skills and Personality Traits—Visionary or strategic thinking; ability to delegate responsibilities; self-confidence and strong leadership skills

CAREER LADDER

```
┌─────────────────────────────────────┐
│     Chief Information Officer        │
└─────────────────────────────────────┘

┌─────────────────────────────────────┐
│    Director, Information Systems     │
└─────────────────────────────────────┘

┌─────────────────────────────────────┐
│    Manager, Information Systems      │
└─────────────────────────────────────┘
```

Position Description

The Chief Information Officer (CIO) is primarily a long-range strategic planner. For example, in a corporation that runs a nationwide chain of pizza stores, the CIO might be looking for ways to use information technology to gain an edge over competitors. He or she may direct assistants to research the possibility of using GPS (Global Positioning System) and wireless modems to link all stores with their delivery persons, providing real-time tracking and driving directions, while having another assistant study the possibility of having a nationwide Internet site automatically route pizza delivery requests to the nearest store, using a map database. Meanwhile, the CIO may decide to replace the chain's old DOS-based network and POS (Point of Sale, or "cash register" terminals) with a new Windows XP–based system.

As a high-level executive the CIO must know how to delegate responsibility, letting trusted assistants carry out research assignments or take charge of managing particular projects. The CIO must also be able to present proposals to the CEO (chief executive officer), the highest corporate executive, or to the corporation's board of directors.

The CIO must continually monitor how competitors are using information technology. If the corporation is looking toward expansion, he or she may also research possible mergers that would bring in new technology or resources.

In addition to planning, the CIO must set policies that ensure uniform standards for computer operations, including data integrity and security, plans for recovery from natural disasters, and standards for training new employees or the continuing training or education of professionals.

There is still some tendency to see the CIO as a sort of poor cousin to positions such as CFO (chief financial officer), but this is gradually changing.

Salaries

The Chief Information Officer is a relatively new position that represents the corporate world's recognition of the crucial role that information technology plays in business success. The CIO's actual job title, job description, and salary will generally reflect how much a given "corporate culture" actually believes this to be true. Some CIO positions at the lower end of the scale may be glorified departmental manager positions, while at other companies the CIO may be on the same level as the other traditional corporate roles such as senior vice president or chief financial officer (CFO).

Employment Prospects

Since CIO is a top-level executive position, there are few openings at any given time. An individual who has compiled an impressive track record as a manager may be in a good position to move up to CIO when that position is created for the first time in that organization, but there are no guarantees, since there may be a nationwide competition among top candidates.

Advancement Prospects

Since CIO is the top IS position, advancement possibilities consist mainly of moving into the CIO position in a larger corporation or (rarely) becoming CEO.

Education and Training

Reaching the CIO level reflects a solid background built up over many years. The foundation is a strong undergraduate and graduate background in both information systems (or computer science) and business management. A combination of a graduate degree in IS and an MBA would be strong.

Experience, Skills, and Personality Traits

A candidate for CIO will have begun by gaining hands-on experience supervising and managing IS operations such as networking, database management, training, and support. This experience will have led to becoming a department IS manager or director. This process generally takes a minimum of 10 years, with 15 being more common.

Management and leadership skills are the key to success in this position, although a broad understanding of technical issues is also important. Key skills are strategic thinking, planning, the ability to delegate authority while being alert for problems, excellent communication skills, and the ability to inspire people to share a common vision and goals.

Cross-Training for Chief Information Officers

Interests	Related Job Descriptions
top executive responsibilities	Chief Executive Officer
strategic planning	Vice President for Research (or Planning)

Unions and Associations

A CIO is an executive and will probably emphasize executive and management organizations. He or she may maintain membership in technical organizations in order to keep up with developments in areas of interest.

Tips for Entry

1. The suggestions given earlier for the IS director position apply here also, but to a greater degree. At this level there is no easy recipe for success.
2. Contacts and connections are always useful, particularly if you are working for (or learn of) an organization that is just now adding the CIO position.
3. Because you will be responsible for so many things, you will have to be careful to avoid spending too much time on "pet projects." If you really still want to have a hands-on interest in technical matters and problem solving, you might consider avoiding the IS Director or CIO positions and instead try to become a high-level IS management consultant who specializes in spending a year or two in a troubled company reorganizing and expanding their IS operations.

TRAINING AND SUPPORT

TECHNICAL SUPPORT REPRESENTATIVE

CAREER PROFILE

Duties: Answers questions from computer users and solves problems with the installation or operation of software; researches problems using manuals, help files, and online knowledge bases; walks users through procedures designed to fix the problem

Alternate Title(s): Help Desk Technician

Salary Range: $30,000 to $50,000

Employment Prospects: Good

Advancement Prospects: Fair

Prerequisites:

Education or Training—Four-year college with computer-related major preferred

Experience—Exposure to common software and operating systems through part-time or summer work, internship, etc.

Special Skills and Personality Traits—Problem solving; ability to search for information in printed or on-line sources; well-organized and able to manage time; good communication and listening skills

CAREER LADDER

```
┌─────────────────────────────────┐
│   Manager, Technical Support    │
└─────────────────────────────────┘

┌─────────────────────────────────┐
│ Senior Technical Representative │
└─────────────────────────────────┘

┌─────────────────────────────────┐
│  Technical Support Representative │
│    or Help Desk Technician      │
└─────────────────────────────────┘
```

Position Description

Modern computer software contains many sophisticated features. Software programs such as word processors, database programs, and communication packages must constantly interact with the operating system, the local network, and devices such as printers, scanners, modems, and CD-ROM drives. The complexity of these systems leaves room for problems ranging from minor "glitches" to complete system crashes.

Most users of office computers are familiar only with the basic features of their software. They know how to "boot up" the system, save files, print documents, and so on. When a problem occurs, however, it is usually accompanied by error messages that use highly technical language. At this point the user calls for help from his or her company's in-house help desk or the technical support line provided by the software manufacturer.

The person at the other end of the call is the Technical Support Representative. He or she must listen to the (often agitated) caller and ask questions like the following:

- What command did you give just before the system froze up?
- What is the exact error message you received?
- What version of the software are you running? Which operating system? (The user may well not know, and have to be instructed on how to find out.)
- How much memory does your computer have? How much free space on your hard drive?
- Were you running any other programs at the same time?

If the Support Representative doesn't know the answer to a problem right away, he or she usually consults a "knowledge base" of common problems and solutions provided by the software or hardware vendor. Hopefully the customer's problem will match one that has already been solved.

Sometimes, however, the Support Representative must ask the customer to experiment by changing program options or installing new versions of software downloaded from a Web site. It may take a series of attempts before the problem is solved. For some problems, the Support Representative must consult with engineers who may have to come up with a special program "patch" containing instructions that will fix the problem.

Most people using office computers are under pressure to get work done quickly. They are likely to be frustrated by the computer problem. The Technical Support Representative needs good listening and communication skills. He or she must sometimes let the customers vent their frustration and reply in as calm and helpful a way as possible.

Help desk work can often be stressful. The release of a new version of software is likely to bring a flood of calls from people who have just upgraded. Many questions will have nothing to do with program defects. Customers will simply want to know how to perform a particular task or use a new feature. While this material can usually be found in the manual or on-line help, many people will not read these documents.

Salaries

Salaries depend somewhat on the complexity of the support to be provided. An entry-level person who answers basic questions using information provided by the company may earn $30,000 or so. Questions that can't be answered by the "first line" representatives may go to an experienced representative who can do detailed troubleshooting and work with engineers if necessary. That person may make a salary in the $40,000 range.

Employment Prospects

The ever-growing use of software has led to a steady demand for Technical Support Representatives. Many companies, however, are starting to economize on technical support by putting detailed problem-solving information in the program's on-line help in the form of "Frequently Asked Questions" files or even adding interactive troubleshooting "wizards" to the software itself. This information is often supplemented on-line at the vendor's website. This trend may lead to reduced demand for "live" technical support people, although experienced people will still be needed for dealing with the tougher problems.

A growing number of companies are "farming out" their technical support to an agency or to consultants. Agency workers may have lower salaries and fewer benefits than in-house support personnel.

Another recent trend is that some companies are moving their entire technical support operation to other countries (such as India) where well-educated, English-speaking workers are available at considerably lower cost than their American counterparts. (Since technical support is provided over the phone or via the Internet, geography is no longer a barrier.) As a result, domestic demand for technical support personnel may decline further.

Advancement Prospects

An experienced Technical Support Representative with an interest in management can look for a position as a manager of a help desk or support department. Alternatively, experience gained in technical support can help a student who is working toward a career as a system administrator or systems analyst.

Education and Training

A four-year degree with a major in information systems or other computer-related courses is a standard requirement. Vendors often provide additional training in the support of their products. A certificate indicating expertise in particular software or networks can be helpful. The A+ certificate for basic technical knowledge is a popular choice.

Experience, Skills, and Personality Traits

Employers generally look for evidence that the candidate has had hands-on experience with software and systems similar to those to be supported. Work in a school computer lab, internship, or part-time job can provide sufficient experience for an entry-level job. Besides information retrieval and problem-solving skills, good "people skills" are essential. In the course of dealing with a problem a representative may need to speak appropriately to a busy engineer, a demanding manager, and a flustered data entry operator.

Cross-Training for Technical Support Representatives

Interests	Related Job Descriptions
managing technical support operations	Manager, Technical Support
writing user help material	Technical Writer; Technical Editor
combining software and hardware to solve problems	Systems Integrator; Systems Consultant

Unions and Associations

Technical Support Representatives may belong to technical organizations that deal with particular software or operating systems. If they have an interest in technical writing or information design, they may belong to organizations such as the Society of Technical Communications.

Tips for Entry

1. When you run into problems in your own use of computers, call the technical support number. Note how you are treated. Did the representative understand your problem or ask appropriate questions? Was he or she courteous and helpful?

2. In addition to your formal computer courses, try to gain a good overall knowledge of the most commonly used software (such as word processors, databases, e-mail programs, Web browsers, etc.) and operating systems (Windows, Macintosh, or UNIX). Visit vendors' websites and note the kinds of support materials posted there.

3. Try to help fellow students when they have computer problems. (After you've done this a few times, you are likely to become the local "computer guru.") Also, find out if your school (or a local nonprofit organization) has a volunteer or part-time opportunity where you can help people with computer problems. This will give you some experience to list on your résumé.

MANAGER, TECHNICAL SUPPORT

CAREER PROFILE

Duties: Supervises a technical support department or help desk operation for providing assistance to computer users; establishes standards and procedures for support; coordinates with software developers; trains and supervises support representatives

Alternate Title(s): Help Desk Manager

Salary Range: $50,000 to $65,000

Employment Prospects: Fair

Advancement Prospects: Fair

Prerequisites:

Education or Training—Four-year college degree with computer-related major; business courses helpful; certification from software or operating system vendors is a plus

Experience—Hands-on familiarity with common software and operating systems; experience working on a help desk; supervisory experience

Special Skills and Personality Traits—Mastery of technical detail and ability to organize and retrieve information; ability to supervise and evaluate employees; good communication and writing skills

CAREER LADDER

```
┌─────────────────────────────────┐
│   Director, Technical Support   │
│      (large organizations)      │
└─────────────────────────────────┘

┌─────────────────────────────────┐
│   Manager, Technical Support    │
└─────────────────────────────────┘

┌─────────────────────────────────┐
│    Shift Manager, Help Desk     │
└─────────────────────────────────┘

┌─────────────────────────────────┐
│   Senior Technical Support      │
│         Representative          │
└─────────────────────────────────┘
```

Position Description

There are two types of technical support operations. The first type is an in-house support department (or "help desk") that provides assistance to computer users within the organization. The second type of technical support is provided by the makers of computer software or hardware to anyone who buys their products.

In either setting, the Technical Support Manager typically has the following duties:

- hiring and training support technicians
- scheduling support people so that callers don't have to wait too long for help
- assembling and organizing the documentation (manuals or databases) that support representatives will check for answers to questions
- providing supplementary support such as material on the Web, bulletin boards, or recorded voice or "fax back" services
- working with engineers to provide timely program "fixes" for newly discovered problems

- surveying users or tabulating calls to determine what parts of the software are responsible for the most user problems
- working with program developers and technical writers to improve the usability of programs

The Technical Support Manager must supervise and evaluate help desk representatives to make sure they are knowledgeable and treat callers courteously, while at the same time promoting efficiency so that calls can be answered more quickly. He or she must keep in close touch with vendors to get the latest information on new versions of software or operating systems and must make sure that the support database is updated to reflect them.

Just as the support representatives have the job of solving problems so that computer systems run smoothly, the Technical Support Manager must solve any problems that keep the "machine" of the technical support department from working smoothly. If computer users in a company can't get their problems solved, work won't get done on time and the company won't get the benefit of its investment in computer equipment and software.

For software vendors, bad technical support can lose customers to the competition. Also, reviewers in the trade press often comment on the quality of technical support when evaluating products. People who feel victimized by bad support will often write critical letters to trade magazines or post their complaints in Internet newsgroups and discussion forums.

Although technical support can have an important influence on sales and profitability for software companies and the business users of computers, upper management tends to skimp on funding for support because it is not directly connected to the "bottom line." The Technical Support Manager may need to be a strong advocate for making good customer support a corporate priority.

Salaries

Salaries generally depend on the size of the help desk or support department to be managed, with bigger companies paying more. The complexity of the software to be supported is also a factor.

Employment Prospects

The demand for Support Managers in the software industry may be slowing down as more software companies merge or are consolidated and more support is provided via websites. The demand for help-desk Support Managers outside the computer industry grows with the expansion of business and with the complexity of office computer systems.

The trend toward moving major technical support operations offshore (such as to India) may also reduce the number of available domestic positions for Technical Support Managers.

Advancement Prospects

Large companies like Microsoft will have many separate support operations for their various products, and several rungs to be climbed on the management ladder. In smaller companies, Support Managers who want to advance their careers may have to cross-train for other managerial functions (such as in systems administration or as IS manager) or possibly become independent consultants.

Education and Training

The ideal candidate has a four-year technical degree with a solid background in computer systems and software and courses in management. A graduate degree may be required by larger companies.

Experience, Skills, and Personality Traits

A Support Manager needs extensive hands-on experience working at a support center or help desk. Important skills include the ability to prioritize and schedule, good writing skills (for creating policies or procedures), the ability to supervise and evaluate employees, and enough technical background to be able to communicate comfortably with engineers and software developers.

Cross-Training for Technical Support Managers

Interests	Related Job Descriptions
maintaining complex computer systems	Systems Administrator
managing computer operations	Manager, Information Systems
preparing technical documentation	Technical Editor; Technical Writer

Unions and Associations

Technical Support Managers will be interested in organizations devoted to information systems issues and groups involved with technical writing and communications, such as the Society for Technical Communications. Subscribing to on-line mailing lists devoted to technical support for particular products may also be helpful.

Tips for Entry

1. While in school, focus on classes or internships that will give you hands-on experience with the kinds of software and operating systems in use in the business world (unless you are primarily interested in academic, scientific, or engineering applications).
2. Take management courses and look for a position where you can get some management experience (perhaps managing work-study students or interns in the computing center).
3. When you start the job hunt, look for news stories or advertisements for new products from start-up companies. Such companies may be looking for people to help them set up their technical support. Technical support positions are also advertised by recruiters or contract agencies.
4. If you apply for a support position with a large company, ask about the likelihood of advancement into management after a couple of years as a support representative.

SERVICE TECHNICIAN

CAREER PROFILE

Duties: Installs, tests, repairs, or upgrades computers and related equipment such as circuit cards and memory boards

Alternate Title(s): Systems Support Staff

Salary Range: $30,000 to $40,000

Employment Prospects: Excellent

Advancement Prospects: Good

Prerequisites:

Education or Training—Two-year college or vocational program or undergraduate degree with computer or electronics-related major; industry certification

Experience—Hands-on familiarity with computer hardware, installation, and configuration

Special Skills and Personality Traits—Observation; problem solving; mastery of detail; some manual dexterity

CAREER LADDER

Manager, Service Department

Senior Service Technician

Service Technician

Position Description

When one considers how complex the circuitry inside a computer really is, it's remarkable that most computers run for months or even years without breaking down. Nevertheless, hard drives do crash, monitors blow out, or a loose chip starts causing intermittent memory problems. It's the Service Technician's job to diagnose and repair problems with computer hardware and its connections. Depending on the needs and organization of a particular work setting, the technician's job can include many other duties, such as:

- installing and testing new PCs
- installing network cards and wiring PCs into the local area network (LAN)
- running diagnostic software to find the source of reported problems
- installing upgrades such as more memory or a larger hard drive

Large companies often have a staff of in-house technicians who go to the various offices or laboratories where computers are used. However, most technicians work for computer manufacturers or computer stores, servicing the products they sell.

Salaries

Pay tends to go up with experience and seniority on the job. In-house departments in large corporations generally pay better than service departments in computer stores.

Employment Prospects

There always seems to be a shortage of experienced, skillful technicians. Once one gets that first job and compiles a good record, prospects for regular employment are good.

Advancement Prospects

An experienced Service Technician may be able to get senior status, working on the tough problems for higher pay. A technician with good management and general business skills can seek a position as service manager for a store or manager of in-house computer support.

Education and Training

Many two-year colleges offer an AS (associate in science) degree in computer or electronics technology, and vocational schools also offer programs in computer service and repair. Certification from industry groups or major hardware vendors can help prove one's preparation for a position. The military also offers applicable training.

Experience, Skills, and Personality Traits

The typical Service Technician has had a number of years of "hands-on" familiarity with PCs and other electronic equipment. He or she has probably built electronic kits and wired strange contraptions in the high school electronics shop or science lab. Skills needed include observation and problem solving, a methodical approach to performing procedures, and some manual dexterity for working inside crowded computer cases and doing delicate operations such as removing a CPU chip or soldering.

Cross-Training for Service Technicians

Interests	Related Job Descriptions
computer manufacturing	Computer Hardware Manufacturing Technician
putting together hardware and software into a working system	Systems Integrator
helping users solve computer problems	Technical Support Representative
working in a computer store	Sales Representative, Computer Products; Computer Store Owner/Manager

Unions and Associations

Some Service Technicians may belong to retail or industrial unions.

The National Association of Personal Computer Owners (NAPCO) provides technical certification, as does the Computing Technology Industry Association (CompTIA).

Other organizations for technicians include the Electronics Technicians Association and the International Society of Certified Electronics Technicians.

Tips for Entry

1. Take advantage of opportunities to get inside computers (with permission, of course) and study how they're put together. Help parents or friends who need to upgrade their system or install a new one.
2. Check local community colleges and trade schools for programs leading to an AS (associate in science) degree or certificate in computer technology or electronics technology with emphasis on computers. But always check to make sure the institution's curriculum is up-to-date and that any promises of job-placement help are accurate.
3. Check at local computer or electronics stores for part-time jobs that can give you more exposure to the technology. Also look for technical internships or work-study jobs (these are sometimes available at government agencies).

TRAINER, SOFTWARE APPLICATIONS

CAREER PROFILE

Duties: Teaches specific courses in computer software or operating systems; may work within a corporation or at a school such as a community college or adult continuing education program

Alternate Title(s): Instructor; Teacher

Salary Range: $35,000 to $50,000

Employment Prospects: Good

Advancement Prospects: Fair

Prerequisites:

Education or Training—Four-year college degree with emphasis on computer-related courses; graduate degree for some positions in academic settings

Experience—Extensive familiarity with the software to be taught

Special Skills and Personality Traits—Good organizational and communication skills; ability to work with people of differing backgrounds and experience levels

CAREER LADDER

```
┌─────────────────────────────────────┐
│   Manager, Training Organization     │
└─────────────────────────────────────┘

┌─────────────────────────────────────┐
│ Senior Trainer or Training Consultant│
└─────────────────────────────────────┘

┌─────────────────────────────────────┐
│     Trainer or Instructor, Basic     │
│           or Entry-Level             │
└─────────────────────────────────────┘
```

Position Description

The operation of business and government requires a steady stream of millions of workers who have basic computer skills such as word processing, data entry, and information retrieval. While computer literacy is increasingly a goal of public education, many people entering the workforce do not have the level of computer skills businesses need. Further, as newer, more complex versions of software come out, workers must be continually retrained on the job. Also, workers whose experience is in skills that are now obsolete (such as non-computerized typesetting) must be retrained for today's jobs.

Opportunities to teach computer skills include:

- in-house corporate training programs for new workers, or retraining of experienced workers
- vocational schools
- community colleges and extension or "continuing education"
- "computer camps" for children
- training programs funded by social services or employment agencies

Unlike academic courses that focus mainly on computer science or programming theory, most training courses are narrowly focused on teaching specific skills for using operating systems, software, and networks. For example, a training center might offer courses in Basic Windows XP skills, Beginning and Advanced Word XP, or Office XP, e-mail, PhotoShop and basic Internet skills. A company's Trainers may also offer courses on using their in-house database or document production systems.

Not all training fits this profile, however. A computer camp will probably offer computer theory and programming as well as use of applications software. Training in Internet browsing and on-line research is now being offered by some libraries and community colleges. Finally, there is high-level training that focuses on such things as problem solving and management skills. This kind of training is often done by well-paid consultants who travel to businesses and conduct workshops that usually last for several days.

Salaries

Salaries vary greatly with the work setting and the nature of the courses taught. At the low end they are comparable to salaries for beginning schoolteachers. Trainers who teach specialized skills or train managers can make considerably more.

Employment Prospects

The demand for skilled workers and the emphasis on computer-related courses in most schools should keep the demand for Trainers high. Still, competition for entry-level positions in desirable geographic areas may be high.

Advancement Prospects

An experienced Trainer has two typical advancement paths: He or she can become a manager in charge of supervising Trainers, or can become an independent consultant offering advanced or specialized training in the form of workshops.

Education and Training

The minimum requirement is usually a four-year college degree with a background in information systems or computer science. Courses in business operations are helpful for understanding employer needs and the context in which the skills taught will be used. Courses in technical writing and education can help the prospective Trainer learn how to organize and present information effectively. Persons teaching courses in elementary or high schools may need an education degree and state teaching credentials.

Experience, Skills, and Personality Traits

Experience is needed in two areas. The individual must have both general familiarity with the most common software and operating systems and detailed knowledge of the particular software to be taught. The skills involved in teaching must also be learned through experience. Work as a teaching assistant or computer lab aide or assistant can provide useful experience.

The skills and personality traits required are the same as for any teacher: good organization and time-management skills, the ability to speak effectively and prepare written materials, the ability to determine the abilities and needs of individual students, and a good bit of patience.

Cross-Training for Software Applications Trainers

Interests	Related Job Descriptions
advanced teaching	Training Consultant; Professor, Computer Science
preparing instructional materials	Curriculum Specialist; Technical Writer

Unions and Associations

Individuals teaching in a middle or high school classroom or computer lab may belong to teachers' unions such as the National Education Association (NEA) or American Federation of Teachers (AFT). Teachers or Trainers working in industry or as consultants may belong to technical organizations relating to their subject matter, as well as groups such as the American Vocational Association and American Society for Training and Development. There are also numerous organizations for consultants.

Tips for Entry

1. While in school, make notes of how the teaching is done in your computer classes or lab work. How do the teachers organize and present information? How do they relate to your individual needs as a student?
2. Look for work-study, teaching assistant, or intern positions where you can help teach software or other computer skills.
3. Look for opportunities to volunteer your services as an instructor, such as public libraries, adult education, or senior centers.
4. Keep track of the operating systems and software packages that have the largest share of the business computing market. Those are probably the ones you'll want to learn the most thoroughly.

TRAINING CENTER OWNER OR MANAGER

CAREER PROFILE

Duties: Owns or operates a training center or consultant agency that provides training in computer skills; markets training services or classes and develops uniform procedures for delivering them; hires and supervises training staff

Alternate Title(s): Manager, Training Services

Salary Range: $50,000 to $100,000 and up

Employment Prospects: Fair

Advancement Prospects: Fair

Prerequisites:

Education—Usually four-year college degree with reasonable familiarity with information technology; courses in business operation very helpful; financial investment also required for ownership

Experience—Experience as a trainer or manager in a training center

Special Skills and Personality Traits—Ability to track many kinds of details; ability to delegate responsibilities while keeping in touch with how staff is performing; willingness to take risks (as for all entrepreneurs); flexibility to adapt to changing circumstances

CAREER LADDER

```
┌─────────────────────────────────────┐
│   Owner/Operator, Training Center    │
└─────────────────────────────────────┘

┌─────────────────────────────────────┐
│     Manager, Training Center         │
└─────────────────────────────────────┘

┌─────────────────────────────────────┐
│  Assistant Manager, Training Center  │
└─────────────────────────────────────┘
```

Position Description

Because the public schools are lagging behind the demands of our information-centered society, an increasing number of parents are sending kids to private training or learning centers to give a boost to their computer literacy. Adults who find their lack of up-to-date skills is limiting their career advancement are also a good source of students for training centers.

A number of companies offer franchised learning centers. To be successful, the prospective Center Owner must usually:

- have an investment (often $100,000 or more) to buy the franchise
- find a good location where there is demand for training but not too much local competition
- find out what skills are in the most demand in the area
- effectively advertise the training services
- establish a curriculum that specifies the courses and what will be taught in each (this is often provided by the franchise company)

- hire teachers and support staff
- manage the teachers and staff to ensure training is of high quality

As a business owner, the Training Center Operator has numerous other duties, including complying with taxes, zoning regulations, state regulations for educational institutions, and the many regulations that affect employment. While the franchise company will probably provide some guidelines and help, running a business can be a daunting task. The employees may put in 40-hour weeks, but the owner-operator must put in as much time as it takes, even 60 hours or more.

An individual who does not want all the responsibilities of owning a business may be able to find a position managing a training center owned by someone else. In this case, the focus is on management skills: Depending on the job description the manager may be responsible for all of the tasks described above, or may be involved only with the supervision of trainers.

Salaries

The amount of income the owner will get from the business depends on many things, including the number of students served, the demand for training (and thus the amount that can be charged for it), and the efficient use of teachers and other staff, which can keep expenses reasonable. Annual income can thus range from nothing (if expenses outweigh revenues) to $100,000 or more.

A manager working for someone else will have a more certain, though lower, income, perhaps in the $40,000 to $50,000 range.

Employment Prospects

Anyone who has the money and the necessary skills and background can start a training center, but success depends greatly on finding the right balance between the number of people in a given area who want training and the number of competitors already offering it. Owners who can find an area (possibly outside of large cities) that has untapped demand and limited or no competition will have the best prospects.

Advancement Prospects

Successful Training Center Operators may make enough money to open new centers, or perhaps create their own franchise company to enlist other prospective owners.

Education and Training

While there are few formal qualifications for opening a training business, franchise companies will usually require at least a basic college degree that suggests the franchise owner has enough skills and preparation to succeed. While some knowledge of computer skills is useful, the Training Center Owner is primarily a manager, so business operation and management skills are more important. (Some training may be provided as part of the franchise package.)

Experience, Skills, and Personality Traits

Experience running or working in a small business will help individuals know what to expect as business owners. A fran-chise owner may have some experience working as a trainer, but that is not required.

The skills and qualities most needed are those common to many small businesses. First, the individual must be willing to take risks—there are no guarantees of success in any business. The owner must be able to master many business skills, including planning, management of details, marketing, and supervision of employees.

Cross-Training for Training Center Owner/Managers

Interests	Related Job Descriptions
training people in computer skills	Trainer, Software Applications
managing in-house user support	Manager, Technical Support
selecting or developing training materials	Curriculum Specialist (School Libraries)

Unions and Associations

As a business owner or manager, an individual in this field may join small business organizations, the local Chamber of Commerce, and training industry groups such as the American Society for Training and Management.

Tips for Entry

1. Take courses in business administration and management, as well as courses specifically focused on small businesses.
2. Use sources such as the Department of Labor and computer industry associations to determine what kinds of training are most in demand, and in what communities.
3. Before investing in any franchise opportunity, contact a local office of the Small Business Administration of the federal government or similar state agencies. They offer training for business owners as well as helping you to avoid questionable franchisers.
4. Be aware that you may make no income at all for the first year or two of operation. You may need to have savings to pay for your living expenses.

RECRUITER OR AGENT, TECHNICAL

CAREER PROFILE

Duties: Finds qualified employees for technical positions or helps employees or consultants find suitable positions

Alternate Title(s): Headhunter

Salary Range: $35,000 to $50,000

Employment Prospects: Fair

Advancement Prospects: Fair

Prerequisites:

Education or Training—Four years of college with computer-related and business-related courses or degrees

Experience—Knowledge of common software applications and of the computer industry; experience working in human resource departments or employment agencies

Special Skills and Personality Traits—Communication and other "people skills"; flexibility and adaptability; self-motivation

CAREER LADDER

```
┌─────────────────────────────────┐
│   Manager, Recruiting Agency    │
└─────────────────────────────────┘

┌─────────────────────────────────┐
│   Senior Technical Recruiter    │
└─────────────────────────────────┘

┌─────────────────────────────────┐
│      Technical Recruiter        │
└─────────────────────────────────┘
```

Position Description

The Technical Recruiter, or "headhunter," may work in one of several settings. In one typical scenario the headhunter, individually or as part of an agency, works from a list of positions that a company wants to fill. He or she then interviews people who are seeking technical positions. Using his or her knowledge of the industry and of employer needs, as well as various databases, the headhunter tries to match the candidate to a suitable position. If the candidate is hired, the headhunter receives a commission paid either by the employer or from a portion of the employee's initial earnings.

A Recruiter can also work for a company on salary, going to technical conferences or job fairs in order to meet professionals who might be interested in working for the employer.

Finally, a Recruiter can work the other side of the street, representing the job candidate rather than the employer. Just as athletes or writers might have agents who negotiate for them with employers, technical professionals (particularly advanced specialists) might also hire an Agent who takes on the task of "marketing" the professional's skills to employers and negotiating terms of employment. Such Agents are generally paid a commission based on the employee's earnings.

Regardless of whom the Recruiter or Agent works for, similar skills are required. The Recruiter must be familiar both with industry trends (including what skills and applications are currently "hot," for example, genetics, biotechnology, and security) and with the needs of particular prospective employers. It is also important to be able to read a résumé "between the lines" to determine whether a candidate is truly suitable for a particular position, and to ask questions if necessary to determine whether particular skills or experience are present. Although the Recruiter does not need to have a degree in computer science, he or she must understand the terminology used by programmers and other technical people and be able to identify the many acronyms used to refer to software applications, hardware, operating systems, and industry certifications. In some cases the Recruiter may be able to help an employer clarify what skills are really needed for a particular position.

Since much of the Recruiter's job involves talking with people (either candidates or employers), good verbal communications skills are essential to success in this profession. Because of the growing use of on-line job-matching services, many technical people are taking charge of their own career quest rather than going to recruiters. A good Recruiter still has much to offer—especially the kinds of personal contacts that usually can't be found on-line—but increasingly recruiters must sell themselves before they can sell anything else.

Recruiters must keep up with changes in technology that are affecting how jobs are advertised and sought. Today the Web is used extensively for posting positions and résumés, so Recruiters must know how to use various on-line services efficiently and integrate them with personal contacts, information from interviews, and other sources.

Recruiters must also be aware of ways in which technology is changing the nature of work and of the workplace. For example, the growth in telecommuting is bringing forward candidates who are looking for part-time or flexible work—for example, parents who want to be near their young children at home but are willing and able to work from a home office.

Increasingly, Recruiters must be aware of the desire (and legal necessity, in some cases) of employers having a more diverse staff drawn from a variety of backgrounds. The Recruiter must therefore be able to work with diverse candidates.

Salaries

Salaries tend to be fairly low for beginners but will be higher for large organizations or in specialized areas. The earnings of independent headhunters and agents will depend more closely on their success in placing clients in high-paying positions.

Employment Prospects

The growing use of on-line employment services may make it harder to find clients who are interested in the Recruiter's services. However, the current downturn in some sectors of the technology industry (particularly those related to the Internet) has increased the number of people chasing after a diminished pool of jobs, and this may motivate more job seekers to work with Recruiters or Agents. In general, Recruiters may want to specialize in areas that are in high demand, such as biotechnology (bioinformatics), data mining, or computer security.

Advancement Prospects

As the industry recovers from recent downturns, it is likely that there will be more positions for in-house Recruiters for major corporations, particularly for the more skilled positions. However, more routine positions such as technical support are increasingly being filled by immigrant workers or even "outsourced" to countries such as India, eliminating the need for Recruiters. Advancement for Recruiters and Agents will depend primarily on their ability to offer "added value" compared with the use of on-line job services, and upon the Recruiter's specialized knowledge and network of contacts.

Education and Training

Four years of college with a computer-related or business-related degree is useful, although individuals with a liberal arts degree and a reasonable amount of computer experience can also be successful. There is little formal training in technical recruitment, but courses in business administration (including human resources) are helpful, as is experience working in a human resources department or for an employment agency.

Although there is no certification for Recruiters as such, the Society for Human Resource Management (http://www.hrci.org) offers various certificates in human resource work.

Experience, Skills, and Personality Traits

The position of Technical Recruiter might best be described as a "people" job that also requires some technical knowledge and experience. Although a degree in computer science or information systems is not required, the Technical Recruiter needs to be able to use a variety of software (including Web browsers and search engines), as well as the skills and qualities needed for various technical positions.

To be successful in this kind of work a person should be comfortable interacting with people in a variety of settings. Frequent travel may be required. Adaptability to change in technology and the workplace is also important, as is self-motivation and the willingness to make the constant effort needed to gain and maintain an edge in this rather competitive field.

Cross-Training for Technical Recruiters or Agents

Interests	Related Job Descriptions
training	Trainer, Computer Applications; Training Center Owner
computer industry trends	Industry Analyst, Computer Products and Services
sales	Sales Representative

Unions and Associations

Recruiters generally do not belong to labor unions. They may join professional organizations, particularly if the Recruiter specializes in a particular application area, such as bioinformatics or robotics.

Tips for Entry

1. Consider whether you like working with people and bringing people together on the basis of their common interests. If you are more interested in technology than people, you are unlikely to be happy or successful as a Recruiter.
2. As you look for various jobs, note how the job-search process works today. What services are available to job seekers and employers? If possible, contact a Recruiter and ask him or her what this kind of work involves.

3. For your first job in this field, look for agencies that might need help with routine functions such as organizing résumés and employer data or obtaining information from job candidates.

4. If you have suitable technical skills, consider working for a while in the computer field yourself. Getting to know the field from the inside will help you become a better recruiter later.

5. If your background or experience gives you special insight into the needs of a particular community that is not well represented in the technical field (such as minorities, disabled persons, or women), look for ways to use this experience in seeking Recruiter positions or in working as a Recruiter.

TECHNICAL WRITER

CAREER PROFILE

Duties: Writes documents, books, or on-line help materials that explain how to use computer systems, software, operating systems, or programming tools

Alternate Title(s): Technical Communicator; Information Designer

Salary Range: $40,000 to $60,000 or $35 to $100 per hour; more for specialists

Employment Prospects: Good

Advancement Prospects: Fair

Prerequisites:

Education or Training—Four-year college degree; computer-related or technical-writing degree a plus but usually not required

Experience—One to two years writing or projects demonstrating writing ability; general familiarity with computer theory and software

Special Skills and Personality Traits—Writing; organizational ability; communication skills; self-discipline; ability to work under pressure

CAREER LADDER

```
┌─────────────────────────────────┐
│      Manager (publications       │
│  or documentation department)    │
└─────────────────────────────────┘

┌─────────────────────────────────┐
│     Senior Technical Writer      │
│        (or Consultant)           │
└─────────────────────────────────┘

┌─────────────────────────────────┐
│        Technical Writer          │
└─────────────────────────────────┘
```

Position Description

Technical Writers prepare the manuals, reference books, and on-line screens that computer users consult when they need to learn how to use computer software. Some of the possible projects for Technical Writers include:

- writing procedure manuals for employees
- writing documentation (manuals, reference cards, etc.) for commercial software
- designing on-line help screens for software
- creating interactive computer-based training (CBT) for software
- writing computer books for trade publishers

Many Technical Writers work in-house as staff members of software companies or in the information processing departments of other businesses. Much work is also available on a contract (freelance) basis, and computer book authors, like other authors, usually work as contractors.

A Technical Writer working in the publications department of a software company is usually assigned as part of a team

that creates documentation for a new program. Ideally, writers are part of the software development team, helping developers keep the users' needs in mind as they design the software. Writers and developers keep in close touch as the product evolves, and the writers have time to make all the necessary revisions when programmers add features or change the way the product's user interface works.

In the real world, however, Technical Writers tend to be somewhat "out of the loop." They're too busy with other work to write the new product's documentation until the product is within a few weeks of shipping. The programmers are too busy trying to stomp on the latest batch of "bugs" to keep the writers up-to-date on changes in the program. The writers pound furiously on the program, trying to discover and document how it works. Deadline pressure can become intense as the product's launch date nears.

Technical Writers who prepare documentation for in-house computer systems may be under somewhat less pressure, although the need to train workers in how to use a new version of a system can also be pressing.

While software users still expect a printed manual that explains how to use a program, many software companies now produce only a slim "Getting Started" type of manual. Detailed instructions on how to use the program are found in the on-line help or in the form of portable document files (PDFs) on disk. Technical Writers create the on-line help by writing and linking a series of topics and detailed how-to instructions. To do this, they use special hypertext tools such as those for standard Windows help screens or, increasingly, linked pages in HTML (Hypertext Mark-Up Language) that are read using a Web browser.

Technical Writers are also sometimes called on to write interactive training scripts, sometimes called CBT (Computer-Based Training). These screens demonstrate software features by having the user actually try out the commands and view the results.

Finally, because the manuals and on-line help can't cover the many complex possibilities for using software, there is a thriving market in computer books put out by well-known publishers. These full-length books cover popular applications software, operating systems, and programming languages. (There are literally dozens of different books on some popular programs—Adobe PhotoShop, for example.)

Writers with book ideas can send proposals to publishers. If the publisher likes the idea, the author may be asked to write an outline and sample chapter. Alternatively, many publishers develop long-term relationships with authors and regularly assign them books as new software enters the market. The publisher and author sign a contract that specifies what will be in the book, when it will be delivered, and how the author will be paid. Most typically the author is paid a royalty, or a percentage (usually about 10 percent) of the price of the books sold. Usually the author is given some money in advance based on the expected sales.

Salaries

In-house Technical Writers receive regular salaries, based on the size of the company, the writer's experience, and whether the writer has additional duties such as supervising other writers, which can bring salaries up past the $60,000 range. Contract writers are often paid hourly rates from $35 to $125, based on experience and the complexity of the work (special skills such as on-line help authoring and graphics design can bring higher rates). Computer-book authors are paid depending on how well the book sells. A book that takes four to six months to write might earn the author an advance of about $5,000 to $7,500 plus another $20,000 over a period of several years. However, many computer-book authors hold down regular jobs (such as teaching or software development) in addition to their writing.

Employment Prospects

The combination of writing and technical skills is not easy to come by, so Technical Writers are in strong demand. Most jobs are in software companies that are concentrated on the East and West coasts, but contract writers and book authors can live almost anywhere and do their work by modem.

Advancement Prospects

Experienced Technical Writers can become manager of a documentation department or can increase their rates as freelancers.

Education and Training

A four-year college degree is expected. Many companies are starting to ask for a technical degree (such as computer science or technical writing itself), but a person with a liberal arts degree and some solid computer-related courses can often break into the field.

Experience, Skills, and Personality Traits

A Technical Writer obviously needs good writing skills, which include the ability to organize ideas and make them accessible to readers who may not have much familiarity with them. Jobs such as writer for the college paper or teaching assistant can help build these skills.

Other skills needed include familiarity with word processing and desktop publishing software and basic graphic skills (working with screen images and creating diagrams). The move from print to on-line documentation means that many of the hypertext and multimedia skills used in creating webpages are also part of the technical writer's toolkit.

Technical Writers, particularly those working in-house, also need good communication skills and some assertiveness for dealing with software developers and managers. Self-discipline and the ability to work with little supervision and still meet deadlines are also important.

Cross-Training for Technical Writers

Interests	Related Job Descriptions
editing technical material	Technical Editor
creating hypertext material	Webpage Designer
creating documents	Desktop Publisher; Computer Graphics Technician

Unions and Associations

The Society for Technical Communications is the main professional group for technical writers. The National Writers Union also seeks to represent Technical Writers and secure them better contracts.

Tips for Entry

1. While in school, look for jobs that will help you build your writing skills. Good places to look include the

school newspaper, student organizations, and the computer center (which may need help creating instruction manuals for new users).

2. Get a good general background in computers, including courses in computer science, programming, user interface design, and, of course, technical writing.

3. Become familiar with the most widely used word processing and graphics programs.

4. Look at the manuals and on-line help that come with the software you use. Note the layout, use of illustrations, step-by-step-descriptions, and other features used to present information.

5. Browse books in the computer section of your favorite bookstore. Compare beginners' or "for Dummies" books and those for more advanced users.

6. If you can't find a job right away, leave your résumé and a writing sample with software companies and other businesses that you know hire writers. Offer to do a small project on a contract basis—if they like your work, you'll have a good chance of getting a permanent position.

7. Technical writing is also a good "sideline" for people whose main job is in programming, science, or engineering.

TECHNICAL EDITOR

CAREER PROFILE

Duties: Checks and revises technical writing; supervises technical writers; supervises artwork or production

Alternate Title(s): Technical Reviewer; Content Editor; Publications Editor

Salary Range: $40,000 to $60,000 or $35 to $75 per hour

Employment Prospects: Good

Advancement Prospects: Fair

Prerequisites:

Education or Training—Four-year college degree; computer-related or technical writing major preferred

Experience—Several years experience as technical writer or editorial assistant

Special Skills and Personality Traits—Ability to quickly absorb technical material and spot problems or inconsistencies; basic copyediting skills; familiarity with desktop publishing, layout, and graphics; must be well-organized; management skills helpful

CAREER LADDER

```
┌─────────────────────────────┐
│    Documentation Manager    │
└─────────────────────────────┘

┌─────────────────────────────┐
│    Senior Technical Editor   │
└─────────────────────────────┘

┌─────────────────────────────┐
│      Technical Editor        │
└─────────────────────────────┘

┌─────────────────────────────┐
│      Editorial Assistant     │
└─────────────────────────────┘
```

Position Description

Technical Editors work with Technical Writers, graphic artists, and other production staff to create software user manuals, in-house procedure manuals, on-line help systems and tutorials, or computer trade books.

A project usually begins with the Technical Editor briefing the writers on what is to be covered and the approach and style to be used. (Most trade publishers and many publications departments have style guides that specify such things as chapter organization, use of graphics, and layout of procedures, with examples.) Sometimes a separate individual called a developmental editor helps the writer create the outline and first chapter or two, and then hands off the project to a Technical Editor.

As chapters or parts of the project are completed, the Technical Editor reviews them. The most important concern is that material is well-organized, easy to understand, accurate, and complete. The Technical Editor may edit for grammar and phrasing, or this may be left for a copy editor.

Technical Editors generally check procedures to make sure no steps have been left out, and that the descriptions of programs match how the program actually behaves.

This technical review task is sometimes done by a separate person.

The Technical Editor often works with the graphics or production department to make sure that the screen images and diagrams are properly laid out and reproduced.

The computer industry has been moving away from printed publications toward on-line help screens and interactive tutorials. This work requires editors to be familiar with "authoring systems" such as Windows Help and CBT (Computer-Based Training), as well as HTML (Hypertext Mark-Up Language).

Most Technical Editors work in-house in a publications department, but many trade book publishers (and some software companies, particularly start-ups) may hire freelance editors.

Salaries

An editor who only reviews writing or does technical reviewing will probably be at the lower end of the salary scale. The higher end is occupied by Technical Editors who work with all parts of the publication process, including art and layout, and supervising writers. This can be a "manager-like" position.

Employment Prospects

As with technical writers, Technical Editors are in reasonably strong demand. There has been some consolidation in the computer book industry, through mergers, reducing the number of book titles. On the other hand, the demand for more elaborate on-line help and editors with a wide range of multimedia skills is increasing.

Advancement Prospects

Technical Editors already have some management functions, so a logical career move is into management of a publications department or becoming managing editor for a computer book publisher. The number of such positions available at any given time, however, is fairly small.

Education and Training

The general requirement is a four-year college degree that can be either technical or in liberal arts.

Technical Editors need not start out as "computer people," but they must become familiar with the world of software and operating systems, including the concepts and terminology. Introductory computer science or information processing courses are helpful. Editors must be good writers themselves so they can show others how to improve their writing. Courses in composition, technical writing, editing, and graphics or layout are all valuable.

Experience, Skills, and Personality Traits

Most Technical Editors start out either as computer experts who have an interest in writing, or as writers with a technical bent. They may work for several years as a Technical Writer before moving into editing, but it can go the other way around. Important skills include the ability to read and quickly master material, attention to detail, ability to evalu-

ate organization, composition, graphics, and layout; and increasingly, the ability to work with hypertext and multimedia. The Technical Editor must also be able to communicate well with writers and other staff members, and constructively criticize or supervise their work.

Cross-Training for Technical Editors

Interests	Related Job Descriptions
technical writing	Technical Writer
developing for multimedia and Internet	Multimedia Developer; Webpage Designer
selecting educational materials	Curriculum Specialist

Unions and Associations

Technical Editors can join the Society for Technical Communications as well as professional specialty groups (such as in graphics or book design). Individuals with an interest in computer science, operating systems, and programming languages may join groups such as the Association for Computing Machinery (ACM).

Tips for Entry

1. While in school, consider a major in technical writing if available. If this is not offered, take courses relating to: computer science theory, practical mastery of software (such as desktop publishing, graphics, layout, etc.), and writing and editing skills.
2. You can get writing and editing practice by volunteering for the school newspaper or literary publication, working as a teaching assistant in computer classes, or helping prepare documentation for student computer users.
3. Some areas have agencies or co-ops for editors. They may be a good way to find contract work. You may have to pass a test or complete a supervised project to qualify to be a full-fledged member.

GENERAL NETWORKING

NETWORK CONTROL OPERATOR

Duties: Performs routine monitoring and maintenance tasks for a computer network (local or wide area); installs and configures new network connections; maintains logs and produces regular reports

Alternate Title(s): Network Technician; Network Support Specialist

Salary Range: $30,000 to $40,000

Employment Prospects: Good

Advancement Prospects: Good

Prerequisites:

Education or Training—Two-year college degree or vocational certificate in information processing, computer science, or computer or communications technology; detailed knowledge of a major network operating system; industry certification helpful

Experience—Hands-on experience with networking utilities and other software

Special Skills and Personality Traits—Attention to detail; report-writing skills; trouble-shooting; reliable work attitude

```
┌─────────────────────────────┐
│   Network Administrator      │
└─────────────────────────────┘

┌─────────────────────────────┐
│   Network Engineer           │
└─────────────────────────────┘

┌─────────────────────────────┐
│   Network Control Operator   │
│       or Technician          │
└─────────────────────────────┘
```

Position Description

Most business, educational, and government organizations maintain one or more networks that connect the PCs or workstations of individual users to the organization's information resources (software, databases, document archives, etc.). These networks can be within a single office or department, where they are known as local area networks or LANs, usually with directly wired connections, or computers in many different offices can be linked using telephone lines over a wide area network, or WAN.

Each network has its own operating system software, control programs, and utilities. Two common network operating systems found in business are Microsoft Windows XP and Novell Netware, although Linux is increasingly seen as well. Many academic and scientific institutions have networks based on some version of the UNIX operating system. The TCP/IP protocol used on the Internet is often used as the basis for local networks, creating an "Intranet."

The Network Control Operator (or technician) is responsible for the tasks needed for daily operation of the network. Some typical duties include:

- setting up accounts for new users
- wiring new PCs or workstations into the network
- configuring peripheral devices such as printers to be shared by network users
- making sure there is enough storage space on file and database servers (larger computers that supply data to workstations)
- keeping detailed logs showing installation, repair work and use of licensed software
- watching for unauthorized network access or other security problems
- monitoring the performance of the network (such as how fast data is traveling and how long it takes programs to load)
- running regular backups of the file or database server
- monitoring connections between the local network and the Internet

Most Network Control Operators work in business information processing departments or in academic or government computing centers. Some, however, are hired as technical representatives for vendors who provide network hardware, software, and support. They can help new customers set up their networks or make service calls to respond to problems.

Salaries

Salaries generally increase with the size of the organization, the size and complexity of its network, and the individual's experience and skills.

Employment Prospects

The continuing growth in networking is creating a strong demand for network support services. Employment is most plentiful in large cities that have universities and major corporate headquarters.

Advancement Prospects

Experienced Network Control Operators who earn four-year college degrees and/or industry certification are in a good position to become Network Engineers or Network Administrators. It is very important for individuals to keep their skills and certification up to date as new versions of network operating systems enter the market.

Today most local networks are implemented as Intranets (using the same TCP/IP protocol found on the public Internet). The use of broadband (cable or DSL) and wireless network connections is increasingly common, and one will often be dealing with several different interconnected networks. Keeping up with this ever-changing infrastructure is important, as is attention to proper security procedures. (Becoming a network security specialist may be a good path to advancement.)

Education and Training

An undergraduate (two- or four-year) degree in a computer-related major is usually required by employers as evidence of background preparation, but the main focus will be on experience and demonstrated competence in particular networking systems, such as those from Microsoft and Novell or UNIX/Linux systems.

Experience, Skills, and Personality Traits

Skills in the various networking systems are demonstrated through work experience and certification such as the MCSE (Microsoft Certified Systems Engineer) and certification in Cisco networking systems. The individual needs to be able to work systematically, focusing on details but able to recognize anything that looks wrong or out of place. Other skills needed include some mechanical aptitude (for opening computers, installing circuit cards, and running wire cables), problem solving, clear writing (for logs and reports), and good verbal communications skills (for answering user questions and keeping managers well informed). Because the operation of the organization depends on keeping the network running, the Network Control Operator needs to be self-disciplined, reliable, and consistent.

Cross-Training for Network Control Operators

Interests	Related Job Descriptions
overall management of networks	Network Administrator
advanced network design and troubleshooting	Network Engineer
management of Internet or Intranet sites	Webmaster

Unions and Associations

Network Control Operators may be classified as clerical or paraprofessional employees and be members of labor unions, but this is rare. Those working toward network administration positions may wish to join organizations for network engineers and consultants.

Tips for Entry

1. Read the trade press and determine which networking systems and software are likely to be in the most demand in the next few years. Make sure you take courses that focus on these systems, but also become familiar with the other major systems to increase your job chances.
2. Consider taking certification courses in Microsoft, Cisco, Linux, and other networks. Employers tend to view the certificate as an assurance of basic competence and as a measure of discipline and hard work.
3. Look for nonprofit organizations or schools that might welcome volunteers to help run their networks. This is a good way to get some hands-on experience for your résumé.

NETWORK ANALYST

CAREER PROFILE

Duties: Plans for the installation or expansion of local or wide-area computer networks; performs complex configuration of servers, hubs, routers, and other network communications equipment; writes scripts or programs to automate network operations; trains network control operators

Alternate Title(s): Network Engineer

Salary Range: $45,000 to $70,000

Employment Prospects: Good

Advancement Prospects: Good

Prerequisites:

Education or Training—Four-year degree in computer science or information processing; industry certification or graduate degree helpful

Experience—Several years of increasing responsibility as a network assistant or technician

Special Skills and Personality Traits—Problem solving and analysis; mastery of details; ability to learn quickly and adapt to changes in the industry; good communication skills

CAREER LADDER

```
┌─────────────────────────────────┐
│     Network Administrator       │
└─────────────────────────────────┘

┌─────────────────────────────────┐
│   Network Analyst or Engineer   │
└─────────────────────────────────┘

┌─────────────────────────────────┐
│    Network Control Operator     │
└─────────────────────────────────┘
```

Position Description

As organizations grow and their information needs change, their computer networks must also change. For example, a small company used to own three restaurants and got by with just having a simple Windows-based network of three PCs in its modest central office, mostly handling payroll, billing, and other accounting tasks. Now, however, the company has acquired a dozen more restaurants. Not only will a larger network be needed to keep up with the increased record-keeping requirements, but management wants to set up a central inventory system so food and supplies can be bought in cheaper bulk quantities and distributed to the individual restaurants as needed.

For the inventory system to work, the restaurants will need to be linked over phone lines to the company's office network. Other devices, such as bar code wands, will need to be linked to the inventory system. Moreover, the company wants to start delivering food from the restaurants, and that may require mobile networking for scheduling and routing deliveries.

It's time for a new network and perhaps a new operating system. Should it be Windows or Linux? What kinds of servers and other software will be needed? Will ordinary phone lines work well enough, or is broadband access needed? What about the restaurant's website, with its postings of daily specials and discount coupons? Whatever choices are made will have implications for cost (including training and support costs), reliability, expandability, and security.

Network Analysts or engineers are the main planners or managers for small networks. (They assist the network administrator in larger organizations.) Their duties include:

- planning for expansion, including selection of operating system and hardware
- installing and configuring new network connections or new versions of operating software (sometimes assisted by network control operators or technicians)
- analyzing the performance of the network to find "bottlenecks" such as a file server that is too slow to keep up with database requests

- writing programs or scripts to customize standard network software to meet an organization's special needs
- improving data security through reliable automatic backups, backup power supplies or servers, and tight security to prevent unauthorized access
- analyzing log files and automatically generated reports to find possible problems
- documenting procedures to be used by control operators, managers, or users
- working with hardware or software vendor representatives to make sure equipment is properly installed and maintained

In a small organization (roughly 10 or fewer users or workstations) one person will probably have the combined role of network administrator, analyst, and control operator. As organizations get larger, the network support staff grows. Operators perform the routine day-to-day maintenance of the system. Analysts look at the larger picture, helping to plan for growth and for emergencies, and troubleshooting unusual problems. The network administrator has ultimate responsibility for the whole network and is primarily a manager, although not afraid to work with the technical details.

Organizations that are not large enough to require a full-time Network Analyst (or that are trying to reduce labor costs) often hire consultants who perform duties similar to those of the in-house Network Analyst. Some analysts may be hired only for specific projects, while others are "on call" for whatever problems may arise.

Vendors of networking software and hardware also hire analysts to install and maintain a customer's systems.

Salaries
Salaries tend to increase with the number of users in the network and the degree to which the analyst is expected to deal with complex problems or to perform managerial functions.

Employment Prospects
The growth in the number, size, and complexity of networks is showing little sign of slowing down. Small, simple networks may now have less need of Network Analysts because of the increasing use of automatic diagnostic and analytical software. But once networks get large enough to include several offices, require dial-up access, or need to provide rapid access to large databases there is a steep jump in the complexity of the network and the need for analysis and management.

Advancement Prospects
An experienced Network Analyst is well on the way to becoming a network administrator with managerial responsibilities and usually an increase in salary. An alternative path of advancement is to become a specialized consultant who can command a high hourly pay rate.

Education and Training
Network Analysts normally have a four-year degree in computer science or information systems with courses in programming, network design, telecommunications (including major network protocols like TCP/IP), and systems analysis. Senior positions may require a graduate degree. Industry certification in particular network systems is also recommended.

Experience, Skills, and Personality Traits
Network Analysts usually have several years of experience in performing tasks of increasing complexity, such as installing and configuring network workstations or file servers, performing backups and routine maintenance, and writing utility programs or scripts. Individuals must have good problem-solving skills, willingness to keep up with the many changes in the computer industry, and good writing and communications skills.

Cross-Training for Network Analysts

Interests	Related Job Descriptions
designing software for organization's production needs	Systems Analyst
designing network software	Systems Programmer; Applications Programmer
managing networks	Network Administrator

Unions and Associations
As professional employees Network Analysts, engineers, and consultants do not usually belong to labor unions. They can belong to professional organizations such as the Association for Computing Machinery (ACM) and join special interest groups devoted to networking issues.

Industry certifications include:

- Certified Local Area Network Professional, Certified Wide Area Network Professional, and Certified Internetworking Professional, from Learning Tree International
- Certified Novell Engineer (CNE) and Master Certified Novell Engineer, from Novell
- Microsoft Certified Systems Engineer, from Microsoft
- Several certifications from Cisco, a major networking hardware vendor

Tips for Entry
1. Get a solid background in computer science and information processing, including programming, systems analysis, and network design.
2. After you have a general background, look for opportunities to learn about and gain experience

with the major types of networks, such as Windows XP, Novell, and UNIX. (College computer centers are good for UNIX experience; local businesses or nonprofit organizations are likely to have Novell or Windows XP.)

3. If you can get an entry-level job as network assistant or technician, volunteer to help with planning or analysis. Document your achievements and get recommendations that can help you when you apply for higher-level jobs.

NETWORK ADMINISTRATOR

CAREER PROFILE

Duties: Takes overall responsibility for the operation and planning for a local or wide-area computer network; plans expansion; selects appropriate network operating system and software tools; configures major features; deals with connection between local network and Internet; establishes procedures for support staff and users; organizes technical support and training for network features; supervises technicians and programmers

Alternate Title(s): Network Manager; LAN Manager

Salary Range: $40,000 to $50,000 (small local networks); $60,000 to $80,000 and up (large or wide-area networks)

Employment Prospects: Fair

Advancement Prospects: Fair

Prerequisites:
    Education or Training—Four-year degree in computer science or information systems preferred; industry certification; business and communications courses recommended
    Experience—Several years' experience helping run computer networks with increasing responsibilities
    Special Skills and Personality Traits—Programming; systems analysis; problem solving and troubleshooting; management and communications; self-starter and able to assume responsibility

CAREER LADDER

```
┌─────────────────────────────────────┐
│    Manager, Information Systems      │
└─────────────────────────────────────┘

┌─────────────────────────────────────┐
│   Network Manager/Administrator      │
└─────────────────────────────────────┘

┌─────────────────────────────────────┐
│         Network Analyst              │
└─────────────────────────────────────┘
```

Position Description

Richard Hayman, president of a networking company, noted in *LAN Magazine* that "network managers are like airplane pilots—their days are 95 percent boredom and 5 percent sheer terror." Much of the job involves the consistent performance of routine procedures and the supervision of staff. But when the manager in a billing department or a college admissions department finds that the computer network is down or programs are running slow as molasses, the person who has to make sure the problem is fixed as soon as possible is the Network Administrator (or network manager). This position is part manager, part systems administrator, and part technical problem solver.

The basic duties of a Network Administrator include:

- making sure all routine tasks such as data backup, antivirus and security protection, and performance monitoring are done regularly. Larger networks will have network control operators or other assistants to do these jobs, but the Network Administrator must supervise them.
- working with department managers to meet their needs for additional capacity, such as more workstations or auxiliary file servers, more modem connections for telecommuters, and so on
- helping prepare budget requests and making reports to upper management
- selecting the major application packages to be run on the network and supported for users

- maintaining the local network's connection to the Internet, often through a "firewall" computer that prevents direct (and possibly unauthorized) access. This may be done in cooperation with a Webmaster.
- preparing training classes or materials for network users
- troubleshooting nonroutine problems with the network (this may be done with the help of network analysts)
- installing new versions of network software and troubleshooting any problems

Network Administrators must often solve problems under pressure from users or their managers. They must help upper management fit the network into the organization's overall business strategy, while trying to convince them to provide adequate funding and support for the network operation.

The ever-changing specifications for computer hardware and the rapid changes in networking technology (such as the transition from older networking methods to TCP/IP as used on the Internet) continually challenge the Network Administrator to keep on top of things.

Salaries

The lowest salaries are paid for administrators of small local area networks, such as those serving a single office or work group. Administrators of large LANs tend to get intermediate salaries (around $50,000–$60,000) with the highest salaries going to administrators of wide-area networks such as those run by corporations with nationwide or international offices.

Employment Prospects

Throughout the 1990s more businesses switched over from mainframes or minicomputers to networks of desktop PCs. Most desktop computers in business are now part of a local area network or Intranet. The growing use of the Internet, electronic mail, and networked databases has fueled a steady demand for experienced Network Administrators, especially for larger or more complex networks.

Advancement Prospects

The career path generally leads to management of larger or more complex networks. Of course competition for positions increases the further up the ladder one goes.

Education and Training

Some people who have perfectly respectable jobs find themselves becoming Network Administrators because they have computer skills and someone has to be the "computer guru." Generally, however, large corporations and other organizations are looking for candidates who have a solid technical education (four-year or graduate degrees in computer science or information systems, with coursework in network design and engineering). Management and business administration courses will be very helpful as well.

Experience, Skills, and Personality Traits

Network Administrators usually have several years of experience working as network technicians or assistants, although small organizations may let people learn on the job. Important skills include basic programming (or script writing), familiarity with network utilities and configuration menus, problem solving, writing skills (for reports to managers or executives), verbal communication skills, and the ability to adapt to a rapidly changing technical and business environment.

Cross-Training for Network Administrators

Interests	Related Job Descriptions
freelance network troubleshooting	Network Consultant (Analyst)
management of information processing	Systems Administrator; Manager, Information Systems

Unions and Associations

As professional employees Network Administrators can join organizations such as the Association for Computing Machinery (ACM) and join special interest groups devoted to networking issues such as security and user training. Membership in information systems management organizations can also be helpful.

Useful industry certifications include:

- Certified Local Area Network Professional, Certified Wide Area Network Professional, and Certified Internetworking Professional, from Learning Tree International
- Certified Novell Engineer (CNE) and Master Certified Novell Engineer, from Novell
- Microsoft Certified Systems Engineer, from Microsoft
- Various Cisco network certifications

Tips for Entry

1. Make sure your educational preparation includes the following "skills clusters": computer science and operations (programming, network architecture, systems analysis); management (business administration, budgeting); and communications (technical writing, employee relations). Note that some computer science departments now offer a concentration in networking.
2. When picking a college, look for one that not only has the appropriate courses but also provides internship opportunities where you can work with the school's networks.
3. Get the appropriate industry certification for the network operating systems you are likely to be working with.

TELECOMMUNICATIONS TECHNICIAN

CAREER PROFILE

Duties: Sets up, troubleshoots, or repairs data communication circuits such as standard telephone, fiber-optic, or wireless connections; installs and configures switches, routers, and other control hardware

Alternate Title(s): Video Technician; Satellite Technician; and other specialized terms

Salary Range: $25,000 to $35,000

Employment Prospects: Good

Advancement Prospects: Good

Prerequisites:

  Education or Training—High school diploma plus technician training such as at a community college or vocational school; Federal Communications Commission (FCC) certificate for working with wireless equipment

  Experience—Some hands-on experience working with electronic equipment; basic familiarity with telephony, computer operations, and networks

  Special Skills and Personality Traits—Ability to read wiring diagrams and follow complex procedures; problem solving or troubleshooting; some manual dexterity for making connections and using test equipment

CAREER LADDER

```
┌─────────────────────────────────────┐
│   Telecommunications Engineer        │
└─────────────────────────────────────┘

┌─────────────────────────────────────┐
│        Senior Technician             │
│     or Technical Supervisor          │
└─────────────────────────────────────┘

┌─────────────────────────────────────┐
│   Telecommunications Technician      │
└─────────────────────────────────────┘

┌─────────────────────────────────────┐
│   Trainee or Technical Assistant     │
└─────────────────────────────────────┘
```

Position Description

If computer processors are the brains of the Information Age, the wires, cables, or radio links that connect them are their nervous system. Managing these connections involves setting up special hardware such as hubs and routers that control the flow of data "packets" (analogous to letters in envelopes) between networked computers. Modems are used to allow PC users to dial into the large computers used by information services such as America Online, as well as Internet service providers. The medium of transmission is often traditional copper telephone lines, but the need to transmit large amounts of data quickly ("high bandwidth") is leading to the increasing use of fiber-optic cable that uses pulses of light to carry data. Radio transmitters can also be used to connect computers without the need for wires. Technology that enhances ordinary telephone lines is now competing with the use of television cable to provide higher-speed access to the Internet from home or business.

The work of the Telecommunications Technician can include such areas as the following:

- running cable and connecting it to hardware such as desktop computers with network cards, modem banks, routers, and hubs
- troubleshooting electrical problems with connections (for example, each chain of devices on an Ethernet network has to be properly "terminated" for the circuit to be complete)
- configuring the transmission or switching hardware to the correct protocol, or specifying how data is divided up into packets and how the packets are addressed for delivery on the network
- setting up wireless systems (such as infrared or short range radio, digital cellular, or satellite-based systems)
- configuring or troubleshooting specialized systems such as ATMs, credit card verification machines, automated toll collectors, and so on
- working with systems that use digital signals to send voice, video, or fax transmission

As the above list shows, there are many possible areas of specialization in this field, and most Technicians will be intensively trained in just a few areas such as fiber-optic, video cable, or wireless.

Technicians normally perform their work without close supervision, following detailed diagrams or procedure manuals provided by equipment vendors. The Technician can work for a variety of employers, including telephone or cable TV companies, information services and Internet service providers, or they can serve as in-house employees for organizations that maintain extensive networks.

Salaries

Although salaries for these positions tend to be on the low end for computer-related jobs, large companies generally offer higher salaries and a more generous benefits package.

Employment Prospects

The vigorous growth of the Internet, local computer networks, and digital telephone and video transmission should keep demand for Telecommunications Technicians high.

Advancement Prospects

Technicians can gain experience and become senior technicians or supervisors. Alternatively, they can get more advanced degrees or certification and become telecommunications engineers.

Education and Training

Technician is a good entry-level position for students with a high school diploma and one to two years of technical training at community college or vocational school (the military also offers technical training). Technicians working with wireless systems must have an FCC radio telephone license, which requires no special training.

Experience, Skills, and Personality Traits

A combination of mental and physical skills is needed for this position. The Technician must be able to read and understand complicated diagrams and procedures. He or she must work carefully and systematically—a wrong connection made now may take hours to find later.

Technician work is for people who don't mind "getting their hands dirty." Since people tend to put their wires and connections in out of the way places, a certain amount of crawling under desks or reaching through the ceiling may be necessary.

Cross-Training for Telecommunications Technicians

Interests	Related Job Descriptions
designing data communications systems	Telecommunications Engineer; Network Analyst
manufacturing hardware	Computer Hardware Manufacturing Technician
repairing PCs	Service Technician (PC)

Unions and Associations

Technicians working for government agencies, telephone companies, and some large corporations may belong to labor unions.

Tips for Entry

1. If you are approaching high school graduation, check local community colleges for certificate or degree programs in telecommunications or electronics technology.
2. If you are considering a vocational school, check with some possible employers to see whether they hire graduates of that school. If possible, ask a working technician which courses he or she found to be the best career preparation.
3. If a local cable or telephone company is expanding in your area, they may have part-time or temporary openings for installers and may be willing to train on the job.
4. Consider obtaining basic technical certification such as the A+ certificate for technicians.

TELECOMMUNICATIONS ENGINEER

CAREER PROFILE

Duties: Designs circuits that connect computer networks and other digital devices; selects and integrates hardware and software to meet the needs of network users

Alternate Title(s): Telecommunications Analyst; Telecommunications Consultant; various specialized titles

Salary Range: $45,000 to $65,000

Employment Prospects: Good

Advancement Prospects: Good

Prerequisites:

Education or Training—Four-year college degree, preferably with networking or telecommunications emphasis

Experience—Several years of experience as a technician or analyst; experience installing and configuring telecommunications equipment

Special Skills and Personality Traits—Ability to use reference manuals or databases; systematic thinking, analysis, and problem solving; some mechanical ability; good communication skills (for dealing with employers or clients)

CAREER LADDER

```
┌─────────────────────────────────────┐
│   Specialist Consultant or Engineer  │
└─────────────────────────────────────┘

┌─────────────────────────────────────┐
│    Telecommunications Engineer       │
└─────────────────────────────────────┘

┌─────────────────────────────────────┐
│    Telecommunications Technician     │
└─────────────────────────────────────┘
```

Position Description

A Telecommunications Engineer (or analyst or consultant) determines what combination of hardware and software is needed to perform the data communication tasks required by the employer or client. Some possible projects might include:

• setting up the connections between an Internet service provider's system and the Internet and configuring the racks of modems that users will dial into
• selecting and configuring equipment for a videoconferencing system that will allow executives in Tokyo, Los Angeles, New York, and London to see and hear one another
• designing the control and distribution system for a cable TV company
• replacing a bank's ATM and debit card system with faster and more secure connections

The Telecommunications Engineer must be familiar with many types of hardware such as routers, switches, modem banks, and workstations or terminals. He or she must know

what kinds of phone lines are offered by various companies and the advantages and disadvantages of each type for each kind of application. Since many telecommunications systems carry financial transactions or critical communications, reliability and security are very important issues. While the Telecommunications Engineer works mainly with hardware, he or she must also be familiar with the characteristics of the major network operating systems, such as how they package data and how sensitive they are to physical changes in the wiring.

The Telecommunications Engineer must be able to work with people as well as machines. He or she is often called upon to estimate both the start-up cost and the operating cost of whatever system is provided. Detailed technical information must be summarized and communicated to clients or managers who are more interested in the "bottom line" than in technical details.

Salaries

Salaries will depend on the type of employer and the complexity of the work to be performed. Consultants may be paid an hourly rate. Specialists or people who can work quickly in emergency situations may be able to earn more.

Employment Prospects

Philosophers of technology have noted that a "digital convergence" is under way. This means that many kinds of information such as voice, music, and video previously transmitted by analog (continuously varying) circuits are now carried by the ones and zeroes of digital data. There is a great demand for "bandwidth"—high-capacity circuits that can carry digitized movies to home TV viewers or live conferencing between offices. In turn, this creates a demand for Engineers who can design systems that "push the envelope" to get the best possible performance with available technology.

Advancement Prospects

Telecommunications Engineers can move up the career ladder to more senior positions or become managers or planners. Consultants can improve their earnings by gaining skills that are in high demand.

Education and Training

A four-year college degree is generally required, with emphasis in computer or telecommunications technology. The typical computer science major does not, by itself, provide the detailed understanding of telecommunications required. As training progresses, the future engineer may decide to specialize in particular areas such as video and cable networks, wireless networks, fiber-optics, or designing systems for Internet providers. Nevertheless, having a general familiarity with different computer platforms (types of hardware), network operating systems, and transmission technologies guards against being made obsolete by industry changes.

Some specialized training is available from hardware vendors. Keeping up with the latest developments is essential.

Experience, Skills, and Personality Traits

There is no simple, easy path into a field that is changing as rapidly as telecommunications. The job seeker must actively try to match his or her training to opportunities. For example, an individual who wants to specialize in configuring wireless data networks will want to read the trade press to find industry trends and possible contacts, check websites and newsgroups for job postings, and put a résumé on-line where people starting a new company will see it.

On the other hand, someone who wants to work for telephone or cable companies might choose to use more traditional job-hunting techniques such as classified ads (printed or on-line) and contacting companies directly.

Cross-Training for Telecommunications Engineers

Interests	Related Job Descriptions
designing computer networks	Network Engineer (or Analyst)
providing Internet access	Internet Service Provider

Unions and Associations

Telecommunications Engineers usually belong to the Institute of Electrical and Electronics Engineers (IEEE), the premier computer engineering organization. Contact with groups such as the Telecommunications Industry Association can provide job leads and promotion of one's résumé. Organizations like the Society of Telecommunications Consultants are useful for freelancers.

Tips for Entry

1. Read trade journals, newsgroups, and websites relating to the technologies that interest you.
2. Try to obtain information interviews with local telephone or cable companies or other heavy telecommunications users such as banks or broadcasters. This will help you learn what people are doing and their typical requirements. They may also remember you when they have an opening!
3. Some universities are major routing centers for Internet traffic. Find out how they meet their telecommunications needs and whether they might have internships available.

WEB AND INTERNET

INTERNET APPLICATIONS PROGRAMMER

CAREER PROFILE

Duties: Develops programs that add features such as animation and forms to websites or that provide tools to help users get the most out of the Internet

Alternate Title(s): Software Engineer (Internet); Internet Software Developer

Salary Range: $50,000 to $75,000

Employment Prospects: Good

Advancement Prospects: Good

Prerequisites:

Education or Training—Four-year degree in computer science preferred; courses in network architecture and multimedia; knowledge of HTML, XML, CGI and other scripting languages, and Java

Experience—Several years of experience implementing network software or webpage support

Special Skills and Personality Traits—Strong programming and problem-solving skills; knowledge of Internet educational and business applications; ability to deal with a rapidly changing technology and industry

CAREER LADDER

```
┌─────────────────────────────────────┐
│  Senior Analyst, Internet Applications │
└─────────────────────────────────────┘

┌─────────────────────────────────────┐
│        Programmer/Analyst,          │
│        Internet Applications        │
└─────────────────────────────────────┘

┌─────────────────────────────────────┐
│  Programmer, Internet Applications   │
└─────────────────────────────────────┘
```

Position Description

The business world increasingly uses the Internet (and tools based on the Internet) for both its internal networks ("intranets") and its public outreach. Home PC users are using the Internet as a reference source, for games and entertainment, and for shopping. There is thus an increasing demand for sophisticated software to support all of these features. Internet Applications Programmers write programs used for such applications as:

- browsing or surfing the net (Web browsers)
- finding information on the net (search engines)
- automatically saving the contents of an Internet site to disk
- providing regular updates of information to users ("Subscription" or "Push" technology)
- letting shoppers find and safely pay for products on-line (Internet commerce)
- adding features to e-mail, such as the ability to include video clips
- connecting users to multiplayer games

- providing live chat or conferencing on the net (including videoconferencing)
- creating interactive forms and customizing sites to each user's needs

Every week brings new features as Internet-based businesses compete for users to "hit" (click on) their sites.

Some Internet Applications Programmers work for companies such as Microsoft and Netscape, which have created powerful browser packages that combine Web browsing and searching, news, e-mail, and chat features. Others work for smaller companies that are creating useful tools that supplement the browser features. But most Internet Applications Programmers work with webmasters and webpage developers to write the programs or scripts that allow the site to interact with users. For example, a major Internet bookstore site includes these features:

- a powerful search engine that can find books from millions of possible titles
- a "shopping cart" that accumulates the user's purchases

- a secure credit card form for completing orders
- a way to remember information (such as credit card number and address and various user preferences) so that the user can return to the site without having to reenter the data
- software to track purchases and create customer profiles

The Internet Applications Programmer seldom uses traditional programming languages like C or C++ to provide these features. More commonly, he or she uses scripting languages such as JavaScript, VBScript, or the older CGI scripts; special plug-in Windows controls called ActiveX; or Java, a full-fledged programming language that is replacing C++ for most Internet applications. The Applications Programmer must also be fluent in HTML (Hypertext Mark-Up Language), the set of codes that tells Web browsers how to display text and images on the screen. Another increasingly important code is called XML (Extensible Markup Language). It allows information on a webpage to be structured in such a way that it can be searched and analyzed in a more database-like way.

Finally, the Internet Applications Programmer needs to understand how much data must be moved between website and user to make a given feature work. The more data that must be transferred, the slower the site will be in responding to the user. The programmer must decide whether the impact on speed is acceptable. A website that has gorgeous graphics, sound, and clever interactive dialogs but takes five minutes to load when a user with an ordinary modem connects will probably not attract many "hits."

The growing variety of tools and the ever-changing needs of website developers guarantee many new challenges for Internet Applications Programmers.

Salaries

Since Internet applications programming has really existed for only a few years, job descriptions and salaries tend to vary widely. In general, an Internet Applications Programmer is likely to be paid a salary similar to that of a traditional Software Engineer or Programmer/Analyst, especially if working for a large firm. A well-funded startup company may pay quite high salaries, while more marginal ones pay less but promise a share in any future profits.

Employment Prospects

The economic downturn and the failure of many dot-com businesses that began in 2000 have made it harder to find positions in e-commerce firms and Internet content providers. However, the Internet as a whole continues to grow and play a vital role in many businesses and other organizations. There are still positions for qualified Internet Application Programmers in business, particularly for traditional "brick and mortar" stores seeking to establish or upgrade their Internet presence. Outside the e-commerce world, the health-care,

biotech, security, and government areas have particularly strong demand for Internet professionals.

Advancement Prospects

The lack of a clear career ladder in this field makes it hard to assess advancement possibilities. One common path is to build a career as a consultant, gradually mastering tools and taking on increasingly ambitious contracts leading to higher pay.

As the Internet becomes more institutionalized as part of the business culture, more traditional career ladders will probably develop, similar to the programmer/analyst/project leader progression.

Education and Training

Because this field is relatively new, employers are generally more interested in what someone can do than in what degrees he or she has earned. A four-year degree in computer science or information processing is sometimes required, but evidence of experience and a good "demo disk" of sample projects can sometimes substitute for the degree.

More institutions now offer specific degrees in Internet-related programming, and industry certifications are starting to become important.

Experience, Skills, and Personality Traits

An Internet Applications Programmer must have some general programming experience and has probably built some websites and experimented with scripting tools. Besides programming and problem solving, the most important qualities are probably the willingness to take risks (since there is little job security) and the ability to constantly master new techniques.

Cross-Training for Internet Applications Programmers

Interests	Related Job Descriptions
building webpages	Webpage Designer
working with computer graphics and animation	Computer Graphics Artist/ Designer; Animation/ Special Effects Programmer
administering websites	Webmaster
developing multimedia products	Multimedia Developer; Multimedia Producer

Unions and Associations

Internet developers can belong to computer science or networking-related professional organizations. Some organizations specifically for Internet developers are starting to appear. Trade journals are also good sources for contacts.

Tips for Entry

1. You may find courses specifically about Internet applications programming; you can also take courses on Java, Visual Basic, HTML, XML, and scripting languages such as CGI or JavaScript, where available.

2. If you can't find the courses you need at school, you can obtain "learner's" versions of Visual Basic and Java at little cost and practice with them on your PC. You can also obtain free or low-cost website authoring programs.

3. As you master the tools, look for friends, local businesses, or nonprofit organizations that would like help in improving their websites. For smaller sites you may be able to create a job for yourself as combined Webmaster and applications developer.

INTERNET SERVICE PROVIDER

Duties: Operates a business that provides access to the Internet, hosting for websites, Internet commerce, and related services

Alternate Title(s): On-line Service Provider

Salary Range: From going broke in a year to $80,000 or more

Employment Prospects: Poor

Advancement Prospects: Fair

Prerequisites:

Education or Training—None specific, although some college background in business management, computing, or marketing would be helpful; for owners, requires an investment for start-up costs (anywhere from $10,000 to $100,000)

Experience—Experience running a small business and general familiarity with Internet services and features

Special Skills and Personality Traits—Must be a self-starter and a quick learner willing to work far beyond the usual 40-hour week; must have imagination and persistence to market services

Manager (at a large ISP)

Owner/Operator (of a small to medium-sized ISP)

Support Staff (at an ISP)

Position Description

Internet Service Provider (ISP) is a general term for a business that offers home or business customers an account through which they can connect to the Internet. This often includes space for the user's website. The most basic challenge of the ISP operator is, first, to attract enough paying customers, and second, to make sure service is reliable enough so the customers will stay. Typically, service must be provided 24 hours a day, 7 days a week. The tasks of the ISP operator or his or her assistants include:

- getting the right amount of phone line capacity from the local telephone company (ISPs connect to the Internet through special, expensive, high-capacity phone lines). Buying too much capacity can tie up needed cash, but not having enough capacity causes frustration and lost customers.
- arranging connections to nearby Internet "backbones" (usually larger ISPs that agree to pass your traffic through to the net)

- setting up and configuring the Internet server machine and the modems that pick up customers' calls
- setting up accounts for customers and providing them with instruction and technical support as needed
- constantly monitoring the local connections and creating alternate routes to the Internet if there are blockages.
- creating "added value" features (such as support for customers' webpages, consulting, Internet commerce services, and other resources)

As the business grows, the owner will be able to hire technical support staff applications programmers or consultants, and perhaps a systems administrator and marketing/advertising specialist. The owner will become more of a manager, but the management required will be of the "hands-on" variety.

Salaries

As a business owner, the ISP operator's "salary" will be the profits left over after expenses are paid and money is set aside for emergencies or possible expansion. There is no guarantee of success, of course.

A manager who runs an ISP as part of a larger company or on behalf of an owner must negotiate a salary, which will likely be tied to the overall success of the business.

Employment Prospects

Anyone who has the money can attempt to start a business, but the prospects of success for small ISPs are problematic. Although the Internet continues to grow rapidly, there has been a rush of people into the field. In the early days (which is to say before 1996 or so), it seemed that anyone who could set up an ISP and provide reasonably reliable service could make good profits. Today, however, large information service providers such as America Online as well as telephone companies are offering unlimited Internet access at about $20/month, and low rates for hosting webpages.

In order to compete with these big players, small, local ISPs must now offer "added value" services such as quality technical support, help in setting up websites, secure commerce facilities, conferencing systems, exclusive content, or other services oriented toward the local community.

Advancement Prospects

An ISP owner who builds a successful business can add service capacity and hire a larger staff, hopefully leading to larger profits. An individual might decide to use that experience to apply for a job such as director of on-line services for a corporation or nonprofit agency.

Education and Training

While there are no requirements, a good preparation for this field would include basic courses in information processing and telecommunications as well as courses in business administration, management, marketing, and advertising. The federal Small Business Administration is a good source for help with a variety of small business needs.

Experience, Skills, and Personality Traits

Any experience running a business is transferable to the business of running an ISP. A job in customer support or marketing for an established Internet business would also be helpful.

The skills and traits needed are those common to all entrepreneurs: self-motivation, willingness to work hard, ability to learn many different skills, and the ability to judge people and supervise employees.

Cross-Training for Internet Service Providers

Interests	Related Job Descriptions
running a website	Webmaster
creating Internet business applications	Internet Applications Programmer
Internet advertising or marketing	Internet Advertising Manager

Unions and Associations

The owner of a small ISP may belong to small business organizations. Managers working in larger ISPs might join professional and management organizations and emerging ISP trade organizations.

Tips and Entry

1. If you are in school, make sure your preparation includes both introductory technical courses and general business courses.
2. Make sure you have some savings or alternate income to live on while the business is becoming established.
3. Before deciding to start an ISP, do research to find out how much demand there is for Internet access in your community, and whether you will be able to compete with large, nationwide on-line service providers.
4. Look for a "niche" or area that is not being well served by existing services. For example, you might be able to create a service that is tailored for disabled or elderly people or that caters to concerns of a particular ethnic or language group.

INTERNET CONSULTANT

CAREER PROFILE

Duties: Helps with the design of Internet sites and configuration of Internet software and connections

Alternate Title(s): Web Consultant

Salary Range: $35,000 to $60,000 or $50 to $75 per hour; more for advanced programming or other specialized skills

Employment Prospects: Good

Advancement Prospects: Good

Prerequisites:

Education or Training—College programming, networking, graphic design, and multimedia courses can be helpful

Experience—Generally starts with designing small websites or making modifications to existing sites

Special Skills and Personality Traits—Java and scripting language programming; database access; graphics and multimedia design; understanding of Internet features for commerce; imagination, adaptability, and self-motivation are important

CAREER LADDER

```
┌─────────────────────────────┐
│   Senior or Specialized     │
│    Internet Consultant      │
└─────────────────────────────┘

┌─────────────────────────────┐
│    Internet Consultant      │
└─────────────────────────────┘

┌─────────────────────────────┐
│    Internet Assistant       │
└─────────────────────────────┘
```

Position Description

Internet Consultant is a "catch-all" job description that can include many ways in which one can help people access the Internet or help businesses on the Internet attract and serve their customers. Consultants generally use some combination of analysis, design, programming, and support skills. Some typical projects for Internet Consultants might include:

- creating a small website for a start-up software company
- helping a business add on-line ordering or product support to its website
- changing an office from a traditional Novell (IPX) protocol network to an intranet using TCP/IP networking
- creating an on-line survey that a hospital can use to find out about the health needs of a community
- providing Internet access to a library catalog or an employment development office's job listings

The Consultant must be able to communicate well, finding out what the client wants to do and discussing the advantages and disadvantages of alternative approaches.

The Consultant must be familiar with a wide variety of scripting, programming, database, and design tools, as well as the major Web server software packages, browsers, e-mail programs, and utilities.

After the Consultant and client come to an agreement, they normally draw up a contract. Payment may be either a flat fee (usually divided into portions corresponding to major phases of the project) or for an hourly rate.

A Consultant may also enter into a long-term agreement to provide technical support for an intranet or an Internet website.

Salaries

Most consulting is paid for by the hour, with rates of $50 or so for simple Web design or maintenance work, up to $75 to $150 for advanced programming or design of major corporate websites.

Employment Prospects

The growing desire of businesses and other organizations to "get on the net" led to strong demand for Internet Consultants. Larger companies, however, are more likely to hire-in-house webmasters or Internet applications programmers, and a number of software packages (such as Microsoft FrontPage) now make it possible for people to create simple websites without outside help. The downturn in e-commerce (dot-coms) has slowed demand in the business area, but other sectors such as health care and government are relatively strong. Prospects remain good for Consultants who have more advanced skills.

Advancement Prospects

Consultants generally advance by mastering skills that are in high demand and thus are able to charge higher rates. Alternatively, an Internet Consultant may be in a good position to get a job as a corporate webmaster with a good salary and benefits.

Education and Training

Most clients look at the Consultant's skills and recommendations from previous clients rather than formal education. Nevertheless, university computer science and information systems departments are offering more courses relating to Web programming and design. Eventually there may be accepted industry certificates that would be evidence of Web-related skills.

Experience, Skills, and Personality Traits

One usually doesn't become a Consultant overnight. The usual path is to take on small jobs (such as designing webpages for friends or small businesses) while learning more advanced skills. A portfolio of successful projects and recommendations from satisfied clients tends to attract more clients, and the individual eventually can get enough work to survive as a full-time Consultant.

Cross-Training for Internet Consultants

Interests	Related Job Descriptions
creating webpages	Webpage Designer
managing a website	Webmaster
creating advanced scripts and programs to support Internet sites	Internet Applications Programmer

Unions and Associations

There are many organizations for information systems consultants and a few for Internet Consultants. It is best to do a Web search to find groups of interest and then contact them by e-mail.

Tips for Entry

1. Regularly spend some time on the Web, looking at different examples of websites and how they use text, graphics, and interactive features.
2. Learn about the options available for individuals and businesses to access the Internet and to present webpages.
3. Master a webpage authoring program (such as FrontPage) as an introduction to Web design.
4. Learn some Java and scripting languages (JavaScript, VB Script, etc.).
5. Check to see if your school has some courses relating to Web design and programming. Try to master some advanced topics such as Web database access methods and forms programming.
6. Note that there is a lot of overlap between Web authoring and multimedia authoring. Learning both can increase your employment possibilities.
7. While in school or in your present job, look for small Web design projects that will challenge you without being too far beyond your skill level.
8. When you are ready to be a full-time Consultant, use a personal webpage and newsgroups to advertise yourself, but also check out businesses or nonprofit organizations in your own community. They may be looking for a way to get on the Internet.

WEBPAGE DESIGNER

CAREER PROFILE

Duties: Creates linked pages of text, graphics, and animation for display on the World Wide Web

Alternate Title(s): Web Author

Salary Range: $35,000 to $50,000

Employment Prospects: Fair

Advancement Prospects: Good

Prerequisites:

Education or Training—No formal requirements, but courses in programming, composition, typography, and graphic arts/multimedia helpful

Experience—Preparation of documents (desktop publishing) and use of graphics programs helpful

Special Skills and Personality Traits—Artistic approach; good composition skills; ability to work with a variety of tools and resources to create a unified whole; creative, artistic personality but with discipline and attention to detail

CAREER LADDER

```
┌─────────────────────────────────┐
│           Webmaster             │
└─────────────────────────────────┘

┌─────────────────────────────────┐
│      Internet Consultant/       │
│     Applications Programmer     │
└─────────────────────────────────┘

┌─────────────────────────────────┐
│        Webpage Designer         │
└─────────────────────────────────┘
```

Position Description

The Webpage Designer performs the "bread and butter" Internet job of creating attractive pages to be displayed on websites. Simple webpages consist of text, graphics, and links that the reader can click on to go to other pages (or other websites). More advanced pages can have frames (areas of the page that can be scrolled separately), animated graphics, sound, or even programs called "applets" that are downloaded to the viewer's computer to be run in the browser. Applets or an earlier technology (CGI scripts) can make pages more interactive by getting information from the user or creating customized information displays.

The World Wide Web actually started out as a system with only text and no graphics. It has evolved into a true multimedia experience that can include animation, video, and sound. Style manuals and guides for webpage design are also available.

How does one design a webpage? The designer begins by considering what kind of information is to be presented, the intended audience, and how readers will interact with the page. A simple page listing names and phone numbers of members of a college faculty will be quite different from a page that showcases some of the creations of a graphic arts studio.

Originally, designers had to code webpages "by hand" using HTML (Hypertext Mark-up Language). Today, however, the equivalent of word processors are now available for Webpage Designers. These programs include a variety of templates, or predesigned page layouts. There are facilities for inserting and arranging text and graphics, and even plugging in interactive features such as forms and tables. The Designer may be able to adapt one of the standard page layouts to the needs of a particular project.

More advanced designers can write scripts or programs and attach them to the page. These can provide such services as database searches, getting feedback from the user, placing orders for products, and even playing games. This kind of work marks the transition from Webpage Designer to applications programmer.

Salaries

Simple webpage composition or maintenance (or revision) of existing pages usually bring an entry-level salary. The ability to write original text and work with complex layouts and scripting or programming brings a higher salary.

Webpage Designers can work in-house, but many are consultants or work for a "design house." Small organizations may hire a single person who does page design but also acts as Webmaster for the whole site.

Employment Prospects

The tremendous growth in use of the Web for education, commerce, and entertainment created a strong demand during the 1990s for people who could create original material, adapt existing material, or set up Web-based links to existing databases. However, the availability of software that can put many kinds of information on the Web automatically has reduced the demand for routine webpage design. Furthermore, the shakeout in the e-commerce industry at the start of the new millennium has reduced the number of start-up Web-based businesses. Job seekers should widen their search to include government, education, science, health care, and other sectors.

Advancement Prospects

Advancement generally comes with mastery of more complex skills of composition or programming. A Webpage Designer who learns the technical details of maintaining a website can become a Webmaster. Alternatively, a Designer who becomes interested in programming (such as in Java or a scripting language) could become an Internet applications programmer. Either career is likely to mean a substantial increase in salary or consulting fees.

Education and Training

As with most Internet jobs, employers are more interested in what someone can show they know how to do than in what degree they hold. Web design is a good career for people who have a liberal arts degree, interest in writing or graphics, and basic technical knowledge. People with only a high school diploma can certainly pick up these skills, perhaps at a community college or art academy.

Experience, Skills, and Personality Traits

The best way to get experience is to start designing webpages, beginning with simple headings and text and gradually mastering graphics, link organization, and interactive features.

A good Webpage Designer combines the following skills:

- writing (to create text for pages)
- editing (or adapting existing text for Web display, such as by breaking it into logical screen-sized sections)
- manipulating graphics (obtaining, sizing, and placing graphics to be shown on the page)
- linking (creating logical links that allow the reader to explore and find related information on a topic)

- designing interfaces (buttons or tables of contents the reader can use to navigate through the connected pages)
- composition, or the art of placing different kinds of elements (text, graphics, headings, frames) so they fit well together into pages that are easy to read and work with

Personal characteristics that promote this kind of work include creativity, imagination, attention to detail, flexibility, and the ability to understand the needs of the people who want to present information and the readers who will be viewing it.

Cross-Training for Webpage Designers

Interests	Related Job Descriptions
designing complete websites	Webmaster
programming advanced Web features	Internet Applications Programmer or Internet Consultant
working with graphics	Computer Graphics Technician or Designer
working with stand-alone multimedia programs	Multimedia Developer; Multimedia Designer

Unions and Associations

Webpage Designers can join consultant groups or various groups for Internet content creators that are starting to appear. Individuals with an artistic bent can check out the Associated Web Artists Guild.

Tips for Entry

1. Try to obtain one of the word-processor-like webpage creation programs such as Microsoft FrontPage. Look at the sample pages and templates and tinker with them to explore page design ideas. (The latest versions of MS Word also include basic webpage creation facilities.)

2. Look at a variety of webpages belonging to different kinds of organizations or individuals. Ask yourself whether a given page is appropriate for the purpose and useful to you, the reader. How might you improve it?

3. If you are in school, you may be able to help create pages for your school's website. Also look for local non-profit groups or businesses that are willing to let you try out your Web skills. Start with simple projects that don't require programming or Webmaster-level skills.

4. Look for courses in graphic arts, writing (composition), and programming (basic HTML, then Java and scripting languages).

5. When you are ready to look for a full-time job, put together a portfolio that shows sample pages you have created. If you supply this on disk or via your website, employers can view the pages with their Web browser.

WEBMASTER

CAREER PROFILE

Duties: Creates or maintains a site on the World Wide Web; provides content and programming or supervises writers and programmers; monitors the performance and popularity of the site; provides secure forms and transactions for Internet-based businesses

Alternate Title(s): Website Administrator

Salary Range: $45,000 to $70,000

Employment Prospects: Fair

Advancement Prospects: Fair

Prerequisites:

Education or Training—Undergraduate degree with computer-related major preferred but not always required

Experience—A few years designing webpages or helping to maintain a website

Special Skills and Personality Traits—Writing; graphic arts; design; programming; administration; must be flexible and a quick learner

CAREER LADDER

```
┌─────────────────────────────┐
│         Webmaster           │
└─────────────────────────────┘

┌─────────────────────────────┐
│     Internet Consultant/     │
│   Applications Programmer    │
└─────────────────────────────┘

┌─────────────────────────────┐
│      Webpage Designer        │
└─────────────────────────────┘
```

Position Description

The Internet, which started as a network linking university researchers and government labs, has now become a mainstream way for individuals and organizations of all types to advertise their presence, offer services, or provide useful information. The heart of today's Internet is the World Wide Web, a way to link documents (including text, pictures, sound, and even videos) so that people can browse them using widely available software.

A website usually consists of a "home page"—a document that serves as a kind of table of contents and index—which in turn is linked to many pages of text and graphics. The contents of these pages depends of course on the purpose of the website: A business can offer a catalog of goods or services; a school will describe its courses and faculty members; an individual may describe his or her job skills, interests, or hobbies.

Creating and maintaining a website involves the following tasks:

- designing the overall structure of the site—the topics to be covered, the kinds of information to be provided, and any added features

- creating the documents (webpages) that contain the text, graphics, and other features, using an attractive, readable layout

- creating the links that take readers from one page to another. Links can use highlighted text or consist of "buttons" or graphic images. The links can go to other pages on the same site, or can refer to other sites that might be of interest to readers

- writing the programs or scripts that provide additional features, such as forms readers can fill out to request additional information, or use to order goods. Some features can be obtained and "plugged in," while others require custom programming

- testing the site to make sure all links work properly. This must be done periodically because outside sites linked from the page may change or disappear

- monitoring the number of people who visit or "hit" the site (important for evaluating the effectiveness of advertising)

- dealing with issues such as network congestion or security problems

- responding to feedback from readers and adding or revising material as appropriate

In most small businesses or other organizations one individual, the Webmaster, performs all these functions. Larger organizations usually have a Webmaster who takes overall responsibility and coordinates the efforts of programmers, writers, and graphics specialists.

Salaries

In some small organizations a person may fulfill the duties of a Webmaster as a kind of sideline to another job, such as being system administrator or a public relations specialist. As organizations (or their websites) become larger and more complex, it is more likely that an individual will be hired solely to be Webmaster. Organizations that use the Web as an essential part of their business strategy (such as on-line stores) require the most experienced, reliable Webmasters, and are likely to pay them the highest salaries. Software companies (which use the Web to publicize products and to provide technical support) may also hire full-time Webmasters.

Employment Prospects

Demand is strong for people who have the variety of skills needed to manage a large website. The ability to create simple websites using word-processor-like software is likely to reduce the demand for people with limited skills. The dot-com shakeout also means that there is more competition for e-commerce Webmaster positions.

Advancement Prospects

As the Internet becomes a more important part of an organization's strategy, the status (and pay) of the Webmaster position will continue to grow. This means some Webmasters may be able to "advance" without changing their job title. Others may want to look for positions in larger organizations as their skills grow, or work for companies that do all or most of their business on-line.

Education and Training

Smaller organizations are less fussy about formal education and training. Larger organizations or organizations requiring advanced design or programming skills may require a four-year college degree with major in computer science or information processing. In part, the requirements depend on whether employers think of the Webmaster as a programmer who can do some writing or as a writer/artist who can do some programming.

Standards and certification for Webmasters and Web designers are starting to emerge.

Experience, Skills, and Personality Traits

Webmasters will normally have at least a year or two worth of experience designing webpages or doing programming or maintenance for a website.

Necessary skills include writing, basic layout and graphics manipulation, familiarity with HTML and XML knowledge of languages such as JavaScript, CGI, or Visual Basic, and mastery of various utilities used to maintain webpages. More advanced skills in high demand include data access languages like Perl (for UNIX systems) or use of ActiveX controls (for Windows-based systems), XML, ability to write Java "applets," as well as knowledge of Internet commerce applications (for processing orders, etc.).

Cross-Training for Webmasters

Interests	Related Job Descriptions
advanced Internet programming	Internet Applications Programmer
managing a complete computer system or network	Systems Administrator; Network Administrator
producing multimedia products	Multimedia Producer

Unions and Associations

Webmasters must keep in touch with many aspects of the evolving Internet. The Internet Society is one of the oldest and most prestigious groups for people concerned about the future of the Net. Trade groups for Webmasters and Web-based entrepreneurs are also emerging.

Tips for Entry

1. Look for courses in the Web programming languages listed above, but also look for introductory courses in writing, layout, and graphic arts.
2. Look for opportunities to help with the expansion or maintenance of a website at school or at a local non-profit organization.
3. When you have mastered the basic skills, look for a small business or other organization that might want a part-time Webmaster.
4. Document your achievements to build a résumé suitable for full-time employment as a Webmaster with a larger organization.

INTERNET ADVERTISING DESIGNER

CAREER PROFILE

Duties: Creates effective advertising features for websites, including animation, sound, and text

Alternate Title(s): Interactive Advertising Designer

Salary Range: $40,000 to $60,000

Employment Prospects: Fair

Advancement Prospects: Fair

Prerequisites:

Education or Training—Four-year college helpful; liberal arts degree with some programming, writing, and graphic design courses makes a good combination

Experience—Generally starts with webpage design and working with graphics and animation; Java programming helpful

Special Skills and Personality Traits—Design; graphics; programming; writing; marketing and psychology; should be imaginative, a self-starter, and persistent in seeking opportunities

CAREER LADDER

```
┌─────────────────────────────────────┐
│   Director, Internet Advertising     │
└─────────────────────────────────────┘

┌─────────────────────────────────────┐
│    Internet Advertising Designer     │
└─────────────────────────────────────┘

┌─────────────────────────────────────┐
│      Graphic Artist (Internet)       │
└─────────────────────────────────────┘
```

Position Description

Advertising is one of the most widespread and important uses of the Internet and World Wide Web. Because the Web is now crowded with sites in almost every category, a business must do all it can to attract the attention of the casual browser (or "Web surfer") and motivate him or her to read the detailed text.

While an organization's Webmaster may consider designing simple logos and animations to be part of his or her job, a company that advertises extensively on the Web is increasingly likely to want the help of a designer who specializes in interactive advertising. Advertising agencies are starting to hire such specialists to work with their clients.

While the position of Internet Advertising Designer is new and not yet well defined, there are a number of features that are believed to increase the impact and effectiveness of online ads. These include:

- striking graphic symbols or logos
- eye-catching animations
- promotions (such as a contest where readers who fill out a survey get a chance to win a prize)
- combining ads with free services (such as search facilities, interactive Web guides, financial or vacation planners, and so on)
- customized information and recommendation systems (for example, an on-line bookstore that recommends new books based on the kinds of books the customer has previously purchased)

The Internet Advertising Designer must combine traditional advertising techniques (such as identifying target audiences and finding out what appeals to them) with the demands of the new interactive medium. For example, the World Wide Web offers the ability to present extensive textual information and get instant feedback from viewers, but the Web surfer, like the TV channel surfer, has a limited attention span. Techniques from print media and television may be applicable to the Internet, but the Advertising Designer must be a creative experimenter who cannot rely on tried and true rules.

An important part of the Advertising Designer's job is to continually monitor the effectiveness of the advertising. There are simple methods that make it easy to determine the number of "hits" or times that someone has clicked to go to a webpage. But this measure is very crude. It can't easily distinguish one-time-only visitors from repeat visitors. The Advertising Designer, perhaps working with the Webmaster, must try to get readers to respond to surveys about what they liked, didn't like, or want to know more about. Such responses not only provide useful information that can lead to revising the advertising, but also give the company a chance to create a relationship that can lead to repeat business.

More sophisticated programming can note what parts of a site a particular visitor uses the most frequently as well as what types of goods he or she tends to buy. The ability to customize what someone sees at a site is very powerful, but it can also lead to privacy concerns. It is also a fact of life that most Web users find flashy banner ads, garish animations, and especially pop-up ads to be a real annoyance. Indeed, software to suppress such displays is now a popular shareware offering. This means that Internet Advertising Designers are being challenged to use subtler techniques to convey their messages, such as integrating targeted advertising more seamlessly with the main text being read.

The mix of duties for this position can vary widely. Some Advertising Designers may have all the programming skills they need to implement their ideas, while others may create specifications for Internet applications programmers to use.

There are two main workplaces for Internet Advertising Designers. The first is advertising agencies; the second is Internet-based businesses with their own advertising staffs.

Salaries

Salaries for designers at advertising agencies will generally depend on the size of the agency and its commitment to the new interactive media. At present there are few Internet-based businesses large and successful enough to have a full-time Internet Advertising Designer.

Employment Prospects

The failure of many e-commerce businesses in the downturn of the early 2000s shouldn't obscure the fact that the Web is here to stay as a place to do business. However, Internet Advertising Designers are more likely to be working during the next few years for companies that have an Internet presence rather than for purely Web-based businesses. Skills used in creating on-line advertising might also be applied to educational, nonprofit, or government sectors. The underlying demand for advertising professionals with Internet skills is likely to remain strong. Because there is little track record of what works and what doesn't, employers often aren't sure who they want. The greatest challenge for the Internet Advertising Designer is likely to be selling him- or herself to prospective employers.

Advancement Prospects

The high growth in new Internet-based businesses has proved to be accompanied by a high failure rate. Individuals who work for advertising agencies may have a little more stability and a more defined career path, but the field is fiercely competitive. Individuals who work in-house for Internet-based businesses may find themselves working for a succession of start-ups, patiently building up skills. Becoming a consultant may be an attractive option for individuals who thrive on change.

Education and Training

This is a field where a liberal arts (or even graphic arts) degree with some basic computer and Internet knowledge may actually be better than a computer science degree. Training is nearly always gained on the job working with actual websites.

Experience, Skills, and Personality Traits

Several years of Web design or Webmastering experience is helpful. While some positions may combine advertising design and programming, larger organizations are likely to separate the two functions. A wide variety of skills are useful, including writing, layout, graphic arts, animation techniques, marketing, psychology, and familiarity with the general capabilities of Web servers, browsers, and plug-in controls.

Individuals who work as Internet Advertising Designers need to be creative and imaginative but also self-motivated and disciplined. This is not a good position for people who want security and the comfort of routine.

Cross-Training for Internet Advertising Designers

Interests	Related Job Descriptions
creating webpages	Webpage Designer
managing a website	Webmaster
programming special webpage features	Internet Applications Programmer
advertising for a computer-related business	Advertising Manager (Computer Products and Services)

Unions and Associations

Internet Advertising Designers may want to check general advertising organizations to see if they have an interest in people who are working on the Internet, Organizations for Internet graphic artists, page creators, and Webmasters may also be of interest.

Tips for Entry

1. As you browse the Web, note what catches your eye. What makes you want to read more? What distracts or annoys you? How does the site try to get feedback from you? What features and special effects are used?

2. Take courses in advertising and study the advertising industry. What traditional techniques are used? How might they be applied to the interactive world? Look for interviews or articles about people who are achieving success in Internet advertising.

3. You may not be able to find a position as an Advertising Designer, particularly if you have limited experi-ence. It may be easier to start as a page designer who does some advertising, or as a Webmaster for a small site. So it's important to gain basic familiarity with the skills listed in the entries for Webpage Designer and Webmaster.

INTERNET STORE MANAGER/ENTREPRENEUR

CAREER PROFILE

Duties: Identifies an opportunity and runs a business that offers goods or services on the Internet; designs the website or manages the Webmaster or programmers; markets products through Internet-based advertising

Alternate Title(s): Electronic Storefront Manager

Salary Range: Nothing to $50,000 or more

Employment Prospects: Poor

Advancement Prospects: Fair

Prerequisites:

Education or Training—No formal requirements; introductory computer courses helpful; business-related courses very important

Experience—Web-related or small business experience helpful

Special Skills and Personality Traits—Basic Internet skills; attention to detail; management and sales ability; good business judgment; confidence; energy

CAREER LADDER

```
┌─────────────────────────────┐
│   Internet Store Owner      │
└─────────────────────────────┘

┌─────────────────────────────┐
│   Internet Store Manager    │
└─────────────────────────────┘

┌─────────────────────────────┐
│   Internet Store Assistant  │
└─────────────────────────────┘
```

Position Description

According to a survey from Pew Internet and American Life about 29 million Americans had bought something on the Internet during the 2002 holiday season. Many traditional businesses have put their catalogs on-line and accept orders directly through their websites.

But what about stores that sell *only* on the Net? There have been a few notable successes such as Amazon.com and the auction service eBay. Certainly the idea has its attractions: Businesses can reach out to their customers electronically and avoid the expense of a walk-in store with counters to be stocked and clerks at cash registers. Besides a website, all an on-line business needs is a place to store the goods and someone to box and ship them.

Of course the reality is rather more daunting. Many on-line business plans (such as the grocery delivery service Webvan) have failed, either because there wasn't enough demand for the product or service, or it could not be delivered economically enough. In the excitement of the "Web rush" of the late 1990s, it was easy to forget such underlying considerations.

Further, the very growth of the Web threatens to overwhelm users with information and choices. A business can't just create a website and wait for people to stumble upon it. The site needs to be advertised in print or other media so people will learn that it's there. The site must be attractive and well-organized so that it will be recommended by reviewers and linked to popular Internet guide sites.

If the business is starting out small, one person may be owner, general manager, Webmaster, and advertising manager all rolled into one. If the prospective owner doesn't have all the necessary skills, finding individuals who know what they are doing can be a challenge in itself. (There's no guarantee that a person who calls him- or herself an "Internet consultant" can actually do the job.)

Someone starting an Internet business needs some money up front, of course. Because this kind of business is new and risky, it may be hard to get financing. A Web server and dedicated phone line represent a large start-up cost, while hosting one's site on a commercial Internet service provider's facilities may put one at the mercy of unreliable service. On the other hand, some ISPs specialize in on-line commerce and can provide help with site design and maintenance. Customers must be able to use their credit cards to order and pay for goods or services. This requires special "secure server" software that prevents unauthorized reading of card numbers.

Even more so than with small business in general, someone opening an electronic storefront must weigh risks against the potential profit. And while it's hard to guess what that potential may be, some factors to consider include:

- Is the product to be offered something that can be shipped easily? Nonperishable items like books or clothing can be shipped any where, but groceries probably could be delivered only locally.
- Are people likely to be comfortable shopping for this product on-line? Most people want to pick out their own fresh produce. People also like to browse books, so on-line bookstores try to offer cover "blurbs" or reviews.
- How much competition, traditional or on-line, is there likely to be? Is there a way to offer special services or added value that will distinguish one's business from the competition?

Remember that when people like Sears and Woolworth first built chains of stores, they had to experiment until they found techniques that worked. Today's on-line store owners are in the same position.

Salaries
For a store owner, income depends on the profitability of the business. It makes little sense to list a range of salaries, since many businesses fail and make no profit, while a few are spectacularly successful.

If more on-line businesses prove to be successful, there will start to be openings for salaried Store Managers. Salaries will depend on the size and complexity of the business.

Employment Prospects
Anyone who has the money, time, and willingness to take a chance can start an on-line business. Employment prospects as a paid manager for someone else are hard to predict, since the field is so new.

Advancement Prospects
Successful on-line business owners can expand or go into other types of goods or services. They could also set up shop as consultants to help other small businesses, or enter the management ranks in an Internet service provider, on-line information service, or other large Internet-based business.

Education and Training
There are no specific educational requirements for running an on-line business, although introductory computer courses and courses in finance, management, and marketing are certainly helpful. The federal Small Business Administration is a good source for information and help for new business owners.

Experience, Skills, and Personality Traits
Some experience designing webpages or as Webmaster can be helpful for understanding the technical end of Web-based business. Experience in running a small business or in sales or marketing is probably more important.

An on-line business owner needs all the traditional business skills of organization and attention to details, sales, and management. In addition he or she must be comfortable with rapidly changing technological possibilities and a marketplace that is often hard to pin down. A confident, adventurous, creative personality must be tempered by good judgment and disciplined effort.

Cross-Training for Internet Store Managers/Entrepreneurs

Interests	Related Job Descriptions
creating Internet advertising	Interactive Advertising Designer
marketing computer-related products	Sales Manager, Computer Products and Services

Unions and Associations
Many small businesses belong to local chambers of commerce, although on-line businesses usually don't have much connection to the surrounding community. "Virtual" chambers of commerce may emerge, bringing together Internet businesses with similar needs or interests. Not surprisingly, the Web is the best place to look for organizations, mailing lists, and newsgroups relating to Internet commerce.

Tips for Entry
1. If you're not familiar with the Web or with basic business procedures, take some courses, either at your present school or at community college.
2. Put yourself in the role of a customer looking for several different kinds of product on the Web. Start browsing. Note how hard it is to find each kind of product and what techniques on-line merchants use to attract visitors. Note how products are listed or displayed, and the order and shipping procedures.
3. Do some brainstorming. Can you think of a popular product or service that is not being offered on the Web? What problems might there be with selling it on-line?
4. Check with local merchants or craftspeople who might want to try marketing on-line. You may be able

to design and run a small site in exchange for a percentage of the profits—and valuable experience!

5. Interview small business owners to find out more about all the tasks they must perform, including dealing with taxes, regulations, and employment.

6. Using services such as eBay, Amazon shops, and Yahoo! may be a good way for you to start a small business selling crafts, collectibles, or other merchandise.

ON-LINE WRITER/EDITOR

CAREER PROFILE

Duties: Writes for or edits on-line publications (or on-line versions of print publications) or creates other written materials for websites

Alternate Title(s): On-line Journalist; Reporter; Content Provider

Salary Range: $30,000 to $50,000 (more for featured or specialized writing)

Employment Prospects: Fair

Advancement Prospects: Fair

Prerequisites:

Education or Training—College degree (liberal arts or journalism), some technical training helpful

Experience—Experience working with a newspaper or magazine and/or creating Web material is useful, as is a portfolio of writing

Special Skills and Personality Traits—Writing and editing skills; research and analytical skills; communication skills; flexibility; motivation; perseverance

CAREER LADDER

```
┌─────────────────────────────────────────┐
│   Managing Editor (on-line publications) │
└─────────────────────────────────────────┘

┌─────────────────────────────────────────┐
│         Senior On-line Writer            │
└─────────────────────────────────────────┘

┌─────────────────────────────────────────┐
│            On-line Writer                │
└─────────────────────────────────────────┘
```

Position Description

Today virtually every news publication from the *New York Times* down to the local shopping newspaper has a website. Typically the on-line offerings include selected articles from the print publication, breaking news, and features that are available on-line only. There are also magazine-like publications that appear only in on-line form.

On-line publications need writers who can provide original reports or articles and editors who can adapt existing material for the on-line format. Readers of on-line material have different expectations and needs than readers of traditional printed material. On the one hand, the typical computer screen cannot hold as much text as a newspaper page, so material must be arranged so it can be presented one screen at a time or scrolled in a Web browser window.

On the other hand, the on-line format is not bound by the limited space available in a printed publication, and there is no need to "jump" from the front page to some inner page to continue a story. Related material in a story can be highlighted and linked to other stories or to relevant websites. Thus a reader of a report on humanitarian efforts in Afghanistan might follow a link to a related story about con-

flict among Afghani warlords or click on another link that brings up a summary of the current population of Afghanistan and its breakdown into ethnic groups.

On-line publications can combine a newspaper's depth of detail with the immediacy of a TV news broadcast. However, this means that On-line Writers for news sites do not have the luxury of a magazine deadline or even the daily production cycle for a newspaper. On-line reporters may have to gather material and write a story within an hour or two of a major news event (although some publications just use copy from the news services).

A writer who has special expertise or reputation can become an on-line columnist, submitting regular essays on controversial political or social issues, scientific developments, reviews of the latest books and movies, or other matters of interest. Some on-line publications such as Salon (http://www.salon.com) emphasize original content and diversity of opinion.

On-line Writers and Editors do not need to be computer experts, but they must master a number of relevant technologies. Besides regularly using word processing and e-mail programs, the On-line Writer must be able to search for information on the Web quickly and efficiently. This requires familiarity with the major Web search engines, with Web portals such as Yahoo! that organize information into a hierarchy of categories, and with specialized websites in areas such as technology, economics, or military affairs. Regularly checking for new sources and "bookmarking" them will help ensure that the On-line Writer can quickly gather material when under tight time pressure.

Although detailed knowledge of HTML (the language used for formatting webpages) is not essential, the On-line Writer should be familiar with the elements of webpage design. The ability to use page design software (such as Dreamweaver or Microsoft FrontPage) can be helpful, particularly if the writer is performing a number of tasks for a small website.

Salaries

Individuals who perform routine editing or write small items for news websites are likely to receive modest salaries similar to those for beginning reporters or editors at traditional publications. Writers who create feature-length material or who have special expertise in a particular subject area (such as business or technology) can earn more. Freelance work is also a possibility and can allow combining on-line writing with other forms of work.

Employment Prospects

Currently this is a difficult field in which to make a full-time living. The steadiest work is with the on-line operation for a successful print publication, but competition will be stiff for these positions. The on-line-only publications have been largely unable to find a reliable source of revenue. Those who relied on selling advertising found that the dot-com downturn has led to the collapse of many potential advertisers and less willingness of the remaining ones to invest in an unproven medium. Others have tried to create a "subscription model" where readers pay a monthly fee for access to quality on-line writing, but this has been only modestly successful. (Perhaps the best-known publication of this type, Salon.com, was barely hanging on as of late 2003.)

However, the on-line world is here to stay and talented and motivated writers can find opportunities.

Advancement Prospects

To receive a higher salary (or higher fees as a freelancer), writers should develop one or more areas of expertise, understand the relevant research sources, and cultivate personal contacts—both as potential sources of work and as "insider" contacts who might be able to provide key information for a news story.

Education and Training

On-line writing is a good profession for individuals who have a liberal arts degree, ideally supplemented with some computer and journalism courses. A journalism degree is helpful for persons seeking work with on-line sites for newspapers. Experience and writing samples showing appropriate skills are at least as important as educational credentials.

Experience, Skills, and Personality Traits

Journalistic experience (such as working as an intern with a newspaper or magazine) is helpful, as is experience with designing or providing content for websites. Writing, research, and communication skills are most important. In terms of personality, self-discipline and self-motivation are important in an area where employment is often uncertain and work when found can be hectic and stressful.

Cross-Training for On-line Writers/Editors

Interests	Related Job Descriptions
Web	Webpage designer; Webmaster
journalism	Reporter, Computer-Related Publications
on-line research	On-line Researcher, Reference or Special Librarian
writing and editing	Technical Writer, Technical Editor

Unions and Associations

On-line Writers working with print publications may belong to newspaper workers' unions such as the Communications Workers of America. Most On-line Writers are not unionized, however. Possible affiliations include journalistic organizations such as the Society of Professional Journalists or the Online News Association.

Tips for Entry

1. Read a variety of websites for newspapers and magazines, as well as on-line-only sites such as Salon.com. Note the kinds of material found, how stories are arranged and presented, and the skills that might be needed to create this material.
2. Many individuals today create their own Web-based journals, called weblogs or "blogs." If you have access to a website, consider starting your own blog. Besides helping you practice your on-line writing, linking with and commenting on other blogs can be an enjoyable social experience.
3. Consider volunteering to create news or features for websites for community organizations or nonprofits— or for a school newspaper. You can use this opportunity to master webpage creation software.
4. Look for internships at newspapers or magazines, particularly those with on-line departments. Such contacts might be made through journalism classes.

GRAPHICS AND MULTIMEDIA

COMPUTER GRAPHICS ARTIST/DESIGNER

CAREER PROFILE

Duties: Designs computer art or images for use in documents, websites, multimedia, or games

Alternate Title(s): Graphics Artist; Graphics Designer

Salary Range: $30,000 to $75,000

Employment Prospects: Good

Advancement Prospects: Fair

Prerequisites:

Education or Training—Two-year degree with computer and art-related courses; four-year degree for advanced or technical design

Experience—Hands-on familiarity with major image and art software packages; general familiarity with program and interface design

Special Skills and Personality Traits—Sense of artistic style and composition; familiarity with various genres or styles of art; manual dexterity for using on-screen art tools; creative personality but able to work to detailed specifications

CAREER LADDER

```
┌─────────────────────────────────┐
│   Art Director (documentation   │
│     or multimedia department)   │
└─────────────────────────────────┘

┌─────────────────────────────────┐
│  Computer Graphics Artist/Designer │
└─────────────────────────────────┘

┌─────────────────────────────────┐
│   Computer Graphics Technician   │
└─────────────────────────────────┘
```

Position Description

During the 1970s the computer world was an endless expanse of text. Very few software programs used graphics as part of the user interface or to illustrate the information they presented. As the 1980s progressed, this started to change. The Macintosh and Windows operating systems used a graphical user interface and had support for graphic icons and other images built into the system. In the 1990s, the arrival of the CD, multimedia software, and finally the Web for education and entertainment have created a voracious appetite for graphic images and the artists and designers to create them.

Computer Graphics Artists (or Designers) create the images used for program buttons and icons, help files, and user manuals as well as "splash screens" and other illustrative art. The artist/designer must choose images that are both attractive and intuitive for the user.

In computer games, original art is usually created using paint programs and sophisticated tools for creating background textures, lighting, and other elements. The art must often be combined with animation or live footage of actors.

While website designers can draw on libraries of clip art or scanned photos for much of their graphics needs, people who want their sites to stand out may contract for original art. Original art is also needed for the growing amount of advertising on the Web.

Major multimedia and game companies normally hire in-house artists. Smaller companies and many Web developers hire artists on contract, paid hourly or by the project.

Salaries

Salaries depend on the size of the company, the artist's experience, and his or her role. Artists who do simple graphics (such as icons or buttons) or who work primarily with clip art or existing images will likely make an entry-level salary in the $25,000 to $30,000 range. More experienced artists who create original art or who have responsibility for overall design can make considerably more.

Employment Prospects

While there has been some consolidation and leveling of growth in the computer game industry, this has been somewhat made up for by the need for art for websites and multimedia. There is strong demand for artists who can demonstrate skill and who already know the software tools used in a given department or project.

Advancement Prospects

An experienced Computer Graphics Artist or Designer can advance to the art director (or equivalent) position in a game or multimedia company. Consultants can advance by mastering specialized skills and increasing their rates.

Education and Training

A two-year degree in a computer-related field plus courses in the graphic arts is a good entry-level qualification. Alternatively, a student with an art major can prepare by adding courses in computer graphics techniques and software. Advanced work in user interface or educational program design may require a four-year degree with background in computer science as well as communications and graphic design.

Experience, Skills, and Personality Traits

A successful Computer Graphics Artist or Designer needs hands-on experience with major software packages such as PhotoShop, Quark, PageMaker, Illustrator, and others. (Computer game companies often use specialized or proprietary software utilities and may train qualifying artists in them.)

Cross-Training for Computer Graphics Artists/Designers

Interests	Related Job Descriptions
manipulating or processing images	Computer Graphics Technician
organizing images	Computer Graphics Librarian/Archivist
selling digital images	Sales Representative, Digital Photos or Images
games	Computer Game Designer/ Programmer

Unions and Associations

Computer Graphics Artists can explore groups relating to their particular areas of interest, such as the Associated Web Artists Guild for Internet artists and the Society for Technical Communications for individuals who create user documentation.

Tips for Entry

1. Look at a variety of business, educational, and entertainment software and study how images are used both to communicate with the user and to provide content.
2. If your school doesn't have many courses that relate directly to computer graphics, take a general graphics art course and look for vocational-type courses in some of the basic graphics software packages.
3. If you know you are going to be interested in a particular kind of software, contact the company and find out if it has a special "student" or "learning" version, which is usually much cheaper than the full commercial version.
4. Volunteer to create art for local organizations that are working on websites, electronic kiosks, or other multimedia projects.
5. Accumulate a portfolio of images that can demonstrate your skills in a variety of areas. Send it along with a résumé to multimedia or game companies.

COMPUTER GRAPHICS TECHNICIAN

CAREER PROFILE

Duties: Performs routine work scanning, manipulating, and storing digitized photos or graphics images

Alternate Title(s): Technical Assistant (Computer Graphics); Graphics Assistant

Salary Range: $20,000 to $30,000

Employment Prospects: Fair

Advancement Prospects: Good

Prerequisites:

Education or Training—High school diploma; community college courses in computer graphics and graphic arts or photography helpful

Experience—Using a scanner; creating documents containing scanned images; work in a copy shop

Special Skills and Personality Traits—Sharp eyes and good artistic sense; ability to follow procedures consistently; reasonable communication skills

CAREER LADDER

```
┌─────────────────────────────────────┐
│   Computer Graphics Artist/Designer  │
└─────────────────────────────────────┘

┌─────────────────────────────────────┐
│    Computer Graphics Technician      │
└─────────────────────────────────────┘

┌─────────────────────────────────────┐
│          Assistant (computer         │
│         graphics department)         │
└─────────────────────────────────────┘
```

Position Description

Multimedia software and many websites use digitized photos or other images. For example, a multimedia history of the Civil War may include digitized maps from army records and the photographs of Mathew Brady. The developers of the project may wish to include other materials such as newspaper front pages, line drawings from magazines, posters, and illustrated envelopes. All this material must be scanned into digital form and often modified to make it suitable for the developer's needs. Graphics technicians do this processing. Some common tasks for the Computer Graphics Technician include:

- adjusting resolution, size, and color settings for scanning images
- cropping, reducing, or rotating scanned images
- making a variety of color adjustments using a program such as PhotoShop
- converting images from one file format (such as TIFF) to another (such as Windows BMP)
- organizing and possibly compressing images for efficient storage on CD
- creating printed copy or transparencies from image files
- linking images into documents, help files, or interactive presentations

Many Computer Graphics Technicians work for book, newspaper, or magazine publishers or for corporate documentation departments. Copy shops (many of which have evolved into sophisticated publishing services) may also hire people experienced with computer image processing.

The basic tools used by the Computer Graphics Technician include scanning software (which is often supplied by the scanner manufacturer) and an image manipulation program (Adobe PhotoShop, a powerful but quite complex program, is a common standard). Newspaper and book publishers may use more specialized (or older) software packages.

Computer Graphics Technicians must maintain a high level of accuracy in scanning and processing images. They must be able to work under deadline pressure and occasionally deal with "rush" requests.

Salaries

Entry-level positions at desktop publishing services or copy shops are at the low end of the salary scale. Positions that require considerable experience with PhotoShop or specialized software pay more.

Employment Prospects

There has been some consolidation and loss of jobs in newspaper and book publishing. Most webpage authors learn enough image manipulation skills to prepare their own images. Demand for business graphics (either through services or in-house departments) remains strong. In general an individual with good skills and some persistence should be able to find an entry-level job. Prospects are best in major metropolitan corporate centers.

Advancement Prospects

An individual with an interest in creative art can work toward an art or design position. Someone with an interest in management can work toward becoming manager of a copy shop or documentation department.

Education and Training

For entry-level positions there are no formal education requirements beyond a high school diploma. A two-year college degree with courses related to computer operations and graphic arts would be helpful.

Experience, Skills, and Personality Traits

The individual should have some experience using graphics programs and scanning graphics and text, and basic familiarity with Macintosh or Windows operating systems (depending on which the employer uses). Knowledge of desktop publishing programs and PhotoShop and Corel Draw is a plus. Retail experience is helpful for working in a print shop.

The important skills include attention to detail, ability to learn new programs and techniques, and good work discipline.

Cross-Training for Computer Graphics Technicians

Interests	Related Job Descriptions
art and design	Computer Graphics Artist/Designer
multimedia	Webpage Designer
creating documents	Desktop Publisher

Unions and Associations

Most small print/copy shops are not unionized. Individuals working for publications departments may belong to clerical workers' unions.

Tips for Entry

1. Become familiar with the basic graphics file formats and how to work with graphics files in the most common operating systems (such as Macintosh or Windows).
2. Take introductory courses in programs such as PhotoShop and PageMaker.
3. Look for local print or copy shops that might need part-time employment.
4. Document courses you have taken and skills you have mastered and submit résumés to publishers or multimedia developers.

COMPUTER GRAPHICS LIBRARIAN/ARCHIVIST

CAREER PROFILE

Duties: Organizes collections of digitized images; supervises graphics technicians; deals with copyright relating to use of images

Alternate Title(s): Image Manager; Photo Archivist

Salary Range: $30,000 to $40,000

Employment Prospects: Fair

Advancement Prospects: Fair

Prerequisites:

Education or Training—Undergraduate degree, computer-related or related to employer's subject area; graduate degree in library science required for some library jobs

Experience—Familiarity with graphics software; library experience helpful

Special Skills and Personality Traits—Classification; organization; basic familiarity with graphics formats and use of database programs; systematic person able to focus on details

CAREER LADDER

```
┌─────────────────────────────────────┐
│     Head Librarian or Archivist      │
└─────────────────────────────────────┘

┌─────────────────────────────────────┐
│ Computer Graphics Librarian/Archivist│
└─────────────────────────────────────┘

┌─────────────────────────────────────┐
│      Assistant, Image Archives       │
└─────────────────────────────────────┘
```

Position Description

There are several kinds of organizations that build large collections of computer images (usually scanned or digital photographs):

- Libraries may scan collections of old books or other documents for preservation and convenience.
- Museums may scan objects or specimens and distribute the images to scholars.
- Photo archives (nonprofit or commercial) scan their photo collections, or receive original digital photographs.
- Medical facilities need to manage medical images such as MRI or CAT scans.

There are many other possible collectors of scanned images. Whatever their origin or purpose, these image scans (which exist as computer files) must be organized for easy retrieval. This may be done using a classification system similar to those libraries use for books, a database of keywords, or a more specialized system.

In addition to collecting and organizing images, the Computer Graphics Librarian often must keep track of such information as the photographer who made the image, the owner of the object shown, the publication in which the image first appeared, and other details of ownership. If an image is copyrighted, people who want to use it for some commercial project have to contact the owner and obtain permission. Commercial image archives charge for the use of images depending on the purpose for which they will be used.

A Computer Graphics Librarian who works for a museum or public library may also have duties similar to those traditionally associated with curators or archivists. This might include writing descriptive material or creating exhibits using images. (Given their digital nature, it is easy to display selected images on the organization's website.) One concern of an archivist is always the safe preservation of the materials in his or her care. There is currently considerable controversy about how long data on CD-ROM or disks will be safe from decay.

Salaries

This field is rather new, and it is hard to find reliable salary information. Based on the nature of the duties involved, the low end of the salary scale would probably go to people who simply organize and store images for an organization. Work that involves the general skills of the librarian or archivist should pay more.

Employment Prospects

While this area is not in high demand, there is modest but steady demand from the growing number of libraries, museums, and other institutions that need to manage image collections, as well as the stock image industry that provides graphics for multimedia developers, Web authors, and traditional publishers.

Advancement Prospects

This position is not in a direct career path. At a commercial agency, a Computer Graphics Librarian or Archivist might gradually upgrade his or her job description (and thus, salary) as the size and complexity of the collection grows. Specialists in libraries may be able to advance along the librarian or library management tracks.

Education and Training

An undergraduate degree is usually required, with coursework including basic computer and graphics skills. For a specialized library or museum, a major in a subject area related to the organization's subject area (such as history or the arts) may be better, although good computer skills must still be demonstrated. Work in libraries may require a graduate degree in library science.

Experience, Skills, and Personality Traits

Experience involving classification and organization of materials is helpful. Clerical or library assistant experience would cover this area. The main skills are classification, record keeping, keeping up with details, and following procedures. This is a good position for a person who is well-organized and a steady worker. Some settings (such as commercial photo archives) may require more contact with the public and thus communication skills.

Cross-Training for Computer Graphics Librarians/Archivists

Skills or Interests	Related Job Descriptions
classification of documents	Librarian, Technical Services
retrieving information	Librarian, Reference
selling images	Sales Representative, Digital Photos or Images

Unions and Associations

Graphics Archivists working in a library setting may belong to the American Library Association (ALA) and Special Libraries Association (SLA).

Tips for Entry

1. Look for volunteer opportunities in your school's media department or local public libraries. Learn about the main methods for classifying and storing graphics images.
2. Learn how to use basic software for organizing graphics files (some of these programs are low-cost "shareware").
3. For job opportunities, search the Web using phrases such as "stock photos," "stock images," and "archives."

ART DIRECTOR (COMPUTER GRAPHICS)

CAREER PROFILE

Duties: Responsible for all use of art in the creation of books, magazines, brochures, or other publications; supervises artists and desktop publishers

Alternate Title(s): Production Director; Book Designer

Salary Range: $40,000 to $80,000

Employment Prospects: Fair

Advancement Prospects: Poor

Prerequisites:

Education or Training—Four-year college degree, preferably majoring in art or design; computer-related courses helpful

Experience—Several years in desktop publishing and graphics or design

Special Skills and Personality Traits—Ability to integrate graphics and text into an overall design; awareness of a publication's needs and objectives; ability to coordinate and supervise

CAREER LADDER

```
┌─────────────────────────────────────┐
│   Director (production department)   │
└─────────────────────────────────────┘

┌─────────────────────────────────────┐
│            Art Director              │
└─────────────────────────────────────┘

┌─────────────────────────────────────┐
│   Computer Graphics Artist/Designer  │
└─────────────────────────────────────┘

┌─────────────────────────────────────┐
│       Assistant or Technician,       │
│        Computer Graphics             │
└─────────────────────────────────────┘
```

Position Description

The Art Director is responsible for the creation of computer art (graphics) and its integration into the final product. That product could be books or magazines, educational material, advertising, or just about anything traditional graphics artists have done with pencil or brush.

An Art Director must have a detailed understanding of the software packages and other tools available for the creation of images, whether original art or imported photos or graphics, as well as desktop publishing programs. He or she must also have a strong sense of composition or design—the ability to combine art with text to create documents that are both attractive and easy to understand. Since art and text must fit together to make a successful design, knowledge of typography and layout is also essential.

The Art Director position involves the management of creative people—one of the most difficult tasks in any business. It is important to allow artists to experiment and exercise creativity, but the Art Director must always keep the overall needs of the project in mind, including style guidelines and corporate objectives.

A company with a small art or production department will probably have a senior artist who carries out the management and supervision tasks of an Art Director. Larger departments will have a separate Art Director who acts mainly as manager and creative director rather than working directly on the art.

Art specifications can be changed by designers or editors at the last minute, disrupting page layout and requiring much rearrangement. Combined with an approaching deadline, this can put pressure on the Art Director to get things done quickly.

Salaries

Art Directors who serve as full-time managers with responsibilities for major projects will get the best salaries. Salaries also depend on how important art is for the organization's products. A publisher of elaborately illustrated children's books is more likely to have an Art Director than would a publisher of fiction.

Employment Prospects

Many smaller publishers simply have an "art person" who is part of the production department, with an overall manager but no Art Director. The Art Director position is thus fairly hard to obtain.

Traditional publishing tends to be concentrated in the New York area. Since Art Director is an in-house job, relocation may be necessary. There has been considerable consolidation in the publishing industry; larger publishers have more jobs but also more competition for them.

Advancement Prospects

Since Art Director is high on the career ladder, advancement prospects are limited. An Art Director may be able to advance further into management as a publisher, or acquire the skills to move into the rapidly growing multimedia field, where salaries are likely to be higher than for traditional publishers.

Education and Training

The best background is probably an undergraduate degree in graphic arts or design, with basic course work in computer skills.

Experience, Skills, and Personality Traits

The individual must combine training in art and design with mastery of desktop publishing and graphics software. Other important skills are communication, management, and the ability to keep track of all aspects of a complex project. This position calls for a personality that can balance creativity and real-world considerations.

Cross-Training for Art Directors

Interests	Related Job Descriptions
create computer graphics	Computer Graphics Artist/Designer
create documents	Desktop Publisher
manage multimedia projects	Multimedia Producer

Unions and Associations

Art Directors at some newspapers or magazines may belong to a union, but this is generally considered a professional or management position. Art Directors may join groups involved with particular areas of interest, such as the Society for Technical Communications for producers of technical publications.

Tips for Entry

1. Try to expose yourself to different philosophies of design and style—everything from *Reader's Digest* to *Wired* magazine. Ask yourself how each design addresses the needs or expectations of its intended audience.
2. In addition to courses in art and design, get practical training in software packages such as Quark, PageMaker and PhotoShop.
3. Volunteer to try out your design skills with school or community publications.
4. Read the trade press such as *Publishers Weekly* to keep in touch with general trends and possible opportunities.
5. You may need to start with an entry-level job as a desktop publisher or graphic assistant, and work your way toward assignments that let you use your design skills.

ANIMATION/SPECIAL EFFECTS PROGRAMMER

CAREER PROFILE

Duties: Creates moving sequences of computer images that portray lifelike scenes for games or multimedia

Alternate Title(s): Computer Game Animator

Salary Range: $30,000 to $75,000 or more ($40 to $150 or more per hour)

Employment Prospects: Good

Advancement Prospects: Fair

Prerequisites:

Education or Training—Undergraduate degree emphasizing graphic arts with courses in computer graphics techniques

Experience—Portfolio of art or animation projects, such as work done in school

Special Skills and Personality Traits—Ability to visualize overall flow of a scene and precise details; creativity; concentration; ability to work under deadline pressure

CAREER LADDER

```
┌─────────────────────────────────────┐
│   Director, Multimedia Production    │
└─────────────────────────────────────┘

┌─────────────────────────────────────┐
│    Senior Animation Programmer       │
└─────────────────────────────────────┘

┌─────────────────────────────────────┐
│      Animation Programmer            │
└─────────────────────────────────────┘

┌─────────────────────────────────────┐
│    Trainee, Computer Animation       │
└─────────────────────────────────────┘
```

Position Description

Animation Programmers add the dimension of movement to computer graphics. The most spectacular graphics are usually found in computer games, but animation and related effects are also found in multimedia, education, and business presentations.

Traditional animation (as in cartoons) was done by drawing thousands of pictures (cells) that showed poses and positions that shifted slightly from frame to frame. Projecting the frames in rapid succession created the illusion of movement.

Some computer-based animation still uses drawings, but they are scanned into the computer and colors, shading, and textures are added. For much of today's animation (particularly 3-D animation), the images are created entirely in the computer. The artist interactively instructs the computer about the image and what movements it should make and how characteristics such as shading should progress as the scene plays out. The software can automatically modify the image to create the set of images that will be cycled through to produce the animated motion.

Animation requires much more skill than this bare description suggests. First, the animation designer or programmer must create a storyboard—a series of sketches showing the progression of the action in a scene in a game or other program. This becomes the "blueprint" for the animation work. In addition to creating the animation itself, the programmer must create lights, shading, and color changes to enhance the effect. He or she may also add special effects such as wipes, dissolves, and even "morphing"—a technique that might be used to change a frog into a prince in a fairy tale adventure.

The work of the Animation Programmer is detailed and intense. There is often deadline pressure, particularly for games.

Salaries

Animation Programmers who have experience with 3-D animation and the software used at high-priced workstations will receive the highest salary. Programmers who do 2-D animation, such as for simple educational software, are likely to receive an entry-level salary in the $25,000 to $30,000 range.

Employment Prospects

Demand is high for skilled animators. The computer game industry is very volatile, however, and a company might be a shining star of the industry one year and out of business the next. It is not uncommon for Animation Programmers to change employers frequently, or to be hired as independent contractors.

Advancement Prospects

Advancement can come either through upgrading skills (such as from 2-D to 3-D) or through going into management (such as becoming a multimedia producer).

Education and Training

The starting point is a good dose of raw talent in drawing and design. The preferred educational background is an undergraduate degree in graphic arts or a related field, plus courses in computer technology and software, with an emphasis on graphics and animation.

Experience, Skills, and Personality Traits

Employers often depend heavily on what they see in a candidate's portfolio—a CD with sample graphics and animation sequences. This means that actually creating art and animation, such as for class projects, is the best way to get started. Some employers will give art tests and train promising entry-level applicants.

Working in this exciting but uncertain field is best for a personality that is creative yet steady and focused; ambitious, yet adaptable to changing circumstances.

Cross-Training for Computer Animation Programmers

Skills or Interests	Related Job Descriptions
graphic design for publications	Art Director
putting together complete multimedia projects	Multimedia Producer
applying art techniques to multimedia production	Multimedia Developer

Unions and Associations

Animation Programmers can join general programmers' organizations (such as the Association for Computing Machinery and its SIGGRAPH graphics special interest group), as well as groups devoted to multimedia and game development.

Tips for Entry

1. When you're playing computer games, take note of how animation and other special effects are used. Read gaming magazines for reviews and other examples of creative use of animation.
2. Make sure you've mastered basic drawing and composition skills as well as the technical side of computer graphics.
3. As you create still art or animations for class projects, save the best examples for your future portfolio.
4. Use game developer publications and Internet newsgroups as well as websites to find out who is hiring entry-level Animation Programmers.
5. Animation is also used in webpages, although it is usually more rudimentary and written in a language such as Visual Basic or Java. Still, some techniques can be transferred to the medium of the Internet and crossing over into Web animation may be a good choice if you can't find work in games or multimedia.

ELECTRONIC SOUND PRODUCER

CAREER PROFILE

Duties: Creates the music, voice, and sound effects for multimedia or computer games; integrates sound into the overall design of the product

Alternate Title(s): Sound Producer; Electronic Musician

Salary Range: $35,000 to $60,000 or more

Employment Prospects: Fair

Advancement Prospects: Fair

Prerequisites:

Education or Training—Courses in music or sound production as well as computer programming, graphics, and multimedia

Experience—Sound studio or multimedia/game development

Special Skills and Personality Traits—Musicianship; knowledge of sound production techniques; ability to integrate sound into multimedia projects; ability to work under deadline pressure

CAREER LADDER

```
┌─────────────────────────────┐
│     Director, Multimedia     │
└─────────────────────────────┘

┌─────────────────────────────┐
│    Senior Sound Producer     │
└─────────────────────────────┘

┌─────────────────────────────┐
│       Sound Producer         │
└─────────────────────────────┘

┌─────────────────────────────┐
│   Trainee, Sound Production   │
└─────────────────────────────┘
```

Position Description

Anyone who plays computer games knows that sound is an important part of the entertainment experience. There is usually background music that changes to reflect the mood or level of tension. Many game activities (especially combat sequences) use sound effects ranging from the clash of swords to the roar of a jet fighter's engines. Game characters usually "speak" with realistic voices (often recorded from performances by actors).

While multimedia education products are usually not as "cutting edge" technically as games, there, too, sounds of birds or a recorded speech by Martin Luther King Jr. can help bring encyclopedia articles to life.

The Sound Producer must work with sounds from a variety of sources: recorded archives, live recordings of actors or "voice talent," digitized sounds and effects, synthesized music, and so on. He or she often supervises recording engineers who do the actual sound processing, but the Sound Producer is responsible for the final sound and its integration into the game or multimedia product. This includes making sure that the finished product will sound good on the kind of hardware (sound cards and speakers) likely to be installed by the target audience.

The Sound Producer must have a good overall grasp of the structure and objectives of the game or multimedia project in order to choose the type and quality of sound to be used. He or she must also be familiar with the tools used for digitally recording, mixing, and modifying sound. There must be close coordination with the designers and animators who are creating the on-screen action.

This position often includes some management responsibilities—supervising (and sometimes hiring) engineers or technicians and making sure the sound part of the project keeps up with the overall schedule. In large projects the Sound Producer may work closely with the art director who has overall responsibility.

Salaries

Salary goes up with the size of the company and the complexity of its typical projects, as well as with experience and management responsibilities.

Employment Prospects

Games and other media become more ambitious each year as designers are challenged to take advantage of ever more powerful computer processors, sound cards, and audio systems. Demand is good for people with top-notch skills, but the consolidation taking place in the game industry since the late 1990s may make it harder to get entry-level positions.

Advancement Prospects

A Sound Producer with good skills and track record can become a well-paid consultant. Alternatively, one familiar with graphic arts and animation could look for higher management positions such as art director.

Education and Training

Formal education is of minimal importance for this kind of work. Employers are looking for demonstrated skills. A portfolio of selections on CD can help. A college degree in music (with emphasis on electronic music and sound production) can also be helpful.

Experience, Skills, and Personality Traits

Employers are looking for individuals with several years of experience as an electronic musician or in a sound studio, although an impressive portfolio might make up for limited experience. Needed skills include musicianship; ability to integrate sound with visual arts; sense of dramatic structure; familiarity with sound-related hardware and software; ability to supervise, manage, and communicate well with other management personnel.

Cross-Training for Sound Producers

Skills or Interests	Related Job Descriptions
multimedia design	Multimedia Developer
overall management of multimedia projects	Multimedia Producer
game design	Computer Game Designer

Unions and Associations

Depending on local custom, Sound Producers may be affiliated with musicians' unions.

Tips for Entry

1. Analyze the sounds you encounter in computer games—particularly how the sound involves you in the action or heightens suspense.
2. Look for courses in acoustics (physics of sound), electronic sound production, and studio techniques. A music school or university music department may be your best bet.
3. Develop a portfolio based on school projects. Another possibility is to work with a game designer to do sound for a small self-published (or "shareware") game. While this is unlikely to result in much money, it can be valuable experience.
4. Read gaming and multimedia-related publications, newsgroups, and websites to find employment leads.

MULTIMEDIA OR GAME WRITER/EDITOR

Duties: Writes or edits the informational articles, narratives, or scripts for multimedia products or games

Alternate Title(s): Instructional Writer; Game Writer/Editor

Salary Range: $35,000 to $50,000 or more

Employment Prospects: Fair

Advancement Prospects: Fair

Prerequisites:

Education or Training—Undergraduate degree in liberal arts plus media courses helpful

Experience—Writing experience with educational materials, drama, fiction, or games

Special Skills and Personality Traits—Understanding of the audience; imagination; adaptability; ability to write in many styles or formats; ability to work under pressure

```
┌─────────────────────────────────┐
│   Project Editor, Multimedia    │
└─────────────────────────────────┘

┌─────────────────────────────────┐
│   Writer or Editor, Multimedia  │
└─────────────────────────────────┘

┌─────────────────────────────────┐
│       Assistant Writer or       │
│  Editorial Assistant, Multimedia│
└─────────────────────────────────┘
```

Position Description

Even though the graphics and sound may be more dazzling, most games and multimedia software also include extensive written material. Some examples of the kinds of work needed are:

- original articles for multimedia encyclopedias or other reference works
- editing articles from a "paper" encyclopedia into hypertext format
- questions, exercises, and feedback for an educational program
- instructions for following a procedure
- description of the background or setting for a fantasy game
- a script that determines what a game character will say under various circumstances

All of these kinds of writing have some similarities to their traditional printed counterparts, but the nature of multimedia changes the task of the writer in important ways. For example, a traditional encyclopedia contains articles that can range in length from part of a column to 20–30 pages or more, with longer articles divided by headings and usually including references to other articles.

A multimedia encyclopedia, however, is designed so that articles can be comfortably read on a computer screen. Often HTML (Hypertext Mark-Up Language) is used so that the articles can be read using a regular Web browser, with hyperlinks to different topics and to other articles. Because of the capacity of a CD-ROM, limiting the overall length (as with a printed book) is less important. The "clickable" links make browsing much easier than with heavy printed volumes. On the other hand, breaking a long article into many linked screens can lead to fragmentation and loss of the main narrative unless the organizing and linking is done carefully.

Similarly, a traditional work of fiction has one major plot (although it may have subplots). The reader does not influence decisions made by characters. A computer role-playing game, however, must allow for many possible plot variations depending on the player's choices and the outcome of battles or quests. A Game Writer must try to anticipate these variations and provide "scripts" for them, or gamers will complain that the game is too rigid.

A Game or Multimedia Writer must have a thorough understanding of how words, pictures, and sounds can work together to teach about something or to tell an exciting story. The film footage of Martin Luther King Jr. and his recorded voice, for example, are not just add-ons to telling the story of the Civil Rights movement: They help the viewer experience history. The Writer's words, in turn, help explore the significance and fill in the details.

The Multimedia Writer will usually work as part of a team that includes graphics and animation programmers, sound producers, and subject matter experts, under the overall direction of the multimedia producer or art director.

Editors may also be hired on larger projects that involve more than one writer. Besides making sure the writing is clear, the Editor must help the Writers achieve a consistent style and approach and make sure that there are no contradictions (such as a character having different names in different scenes).

Salaries

A Writer working in-house may start at a salary around $30,000 or so. Many Writers are hired to create scripts for games, or sets of articles or lessons, and are paid "by the piece." A Writer could make $50,000 or more for all the setting and character scripting for a major computer adventure game. Editors may also work in-house or be paid by the project.

Employment Prospects

It is hard to break into any kind of writing without some kind of track record. The best approach may be to get an entry-level job—almost any kind of job—with a game or multimedia company. Offer to help with miscellaneous writing tasks, and if you show talent, you may be remembered when regular writing assignments come up. Editors who have experience with multimedia are also in demand.

Advancement Prospects

An in-house career path may lead from Writer to senior (or lead) Writer or from helping to write parts of a script to writing a whole script. Writers with top skills can freelance, moving from one project to the next.

Education and Training

Employers may look for a four-year liberal arts degree as an assurance that the candidate has a broad background. Courses in drama, fiction writing, or multimedia (if available) are also helpful.

Proof of writing skill is the main qualification. Like artists, Writers need to accumulate a portfolio with samples that are similar to the kind of writing the employer needs.

Experience, Skills, and Personality Traits

There are a variety of possible sources for experience, such as creating one's own game using one of the available game authoring kits, writing material for an educational media publisher, or creating class projects. Besides writing skills, the individual must be able to adapt to a variety of different formats and objectives and work under deadline pressure. Educational media require an understanding of the teaching and learning process and the ability to write material for different reading levels. Game Writers need an imagination that can project them into fantastic worlds and allow them to see the world as the characters would see it.

Cross-Training for Multimedia or Game Writers

Interests	Related Job Descriptions
writing about computers and software	Technical Writer; Journalist (computer publications)
integrating writing, graphic arts, and sound	Art Director; Multimedia Producer

Unions and Associations

Writers may belong to the National Writers Union as well as organizations for various writing specialties such as dramatic writing, science fiction, fantasy, mystery, and so on.

Tips for Entry

1. Take courses that introduce different kinds of writing, such as drama (script writing), fiction, technical writing, or educational writing.
2. Become familiar with a major word processing program and the general principles of formatting text, using templates, and so on.
3. Keep looking for opportunities to write. Create a simple game that portrays different characters (there are a number of game-authoring programs that are limited but useful). Look for educational development houses that may need contract writers to create text for multimedia projects. "Get your foot in the door," then look for ways to show what you can do.
4. Develop a portfolio disk with samples of your best writing in each genre (such as games or education). Check *Writer's Market* for publishers who produce multimedia material, and read game and multimedia-oriented magazines and newsgroups.

MULTIMEDIA DEVELOPER

CAREER PROFILE

Duties: Uses design and programming skills to create interactive multimedia products that combine sound, images (still or moving), and text

Alternate Title(s): Multimedia Programmer

Salary Range: $40,000 to $60,000 or more

Employment Prospects: Good

Advancement Prospects: Fair

Prerequisites:

Education or Training—Undergraduate degree with computer-related courses preferred but not usually required

Experience—Programming related to graphics, multimedia, or webpage design

Special Skills and Personality Traits—Ability to create or implement a design by integrating text, images, animation, and sound; programming and graphic arts skills; creative, energetic, but focused personality

CAREER LADDER

```
┌─────────────────────────────────┐
│      Multimedia Producer        │
└─────────────────────────────────┘

┌─────────────────────────────────┐
│      Multimedia Developer       │
└─────────────────────────────────┘

┌─────────────────────────────────┐
│ Assistant, Multimedia Development│
└─────────────────────────────────┘
```

Position Description

Multimedia is a group of technologies that are transforming the way people obtain and use information. A multimedia product (such as an encyclopedia, reference, education, or home productivity title) combines the following elements:

- sources of images (such as digitized photographs or video clips)
- text, whether original writing or scanned from printed sources
- music and other sounds
- a software program that ties all the above into a unified presentation that the viewer can interact with
- the CD-ROM disk on which everything is recorded

In a large multimedia project, specialists such as graphics or image technicians, writers, and sound producers provide the material, while Developers (programmers) create the software that will present the material. For some products such as encyclopedias, existing software can be adopted to create the user interface. For example, the text and images can be coded in HTML (Hypertext Mark-Up Language) that can be browsed with an ordinary Web browser, combined with a search engine and utility functions. Other products (such as educational titles) can have custom programs written in languages such as C++ or Visual Basic that present material interactively and obtain feedback from the user. Commercial authoring software is also available. It allows Developers to work at a higher level without having to worry about technical details.

The Multimedia Developer must be able to use programming tools with a keen understanding of the overall structure and objectives of the project. Generally, he or she follows guidelines from the art director or multimedia producer.

Since the ability to integrate images, text, and sound is also key to webpage design, it is relatively easy to cross back and forth between that field and multimedia development.

Salaries

Because the multimedia industry is still rather new, salaries vary greatly. Very roughly, salaries tend to be comparable to beginning software engineers (or programmer/analysts) with higher salaries at larger, well-established companies.

Employment Prospects

Demand is generally high for people with good skills and some related experience. Multimedia development has become somewhat concentrated geographically in areas such as San Francisco's "Multimedia Gulch." However, many traditional publishers of reference works are moving into multimedia. Much work is done on a freelance or per project basis.

Advancement Prospects

Individuals who begin with a start-up company are likely to "grow with the company" if it is successful. Freelancers earn more as their skills improve and they become associated with successful projects.

Education and Training

Some colleges are starting to offer majors (or sub-majors) in multimedia studies. Most people moving into the field, however, have learned it on their own, even if they have a computer-related college degree. As the industry matures certifications and standards will probably emerge.

Experience, Skills, and Personality Traits

Any programming or Web design experience that emphasizes presentation of graphics and use of hypertext links is helpful. The needed skills include design, programming, and understanding of user interfaces. Knowledge of principles of education is a plus. Multimedia Developers should be both creative and detail-oriented. Long hours and deadline pressure require self-discipline and adaptability.

Cross-Training for Multimedia Developers

Interests	Related Job Descriptions
webpage design	Webpage Designer; Webmaster
teaching	Trainer (Software Applications)
graphic arts	Art Director (Publishing)

Unions and Associations

There are a number of organizations devoted to multimedia. The National Multimedia Association of America is the largest organization for multimedia professionals. The Interactive Media Association (IMA) is focused more on the use of multimedia in business and training applications.

Tips for Entry

1. Look for courses in webpage design, hypertext/multimedia, and programming languages such as Visual Basic.
2. Seek opportunities to work with educational software, such as in a school computer lab. Make notes about how material is presented in different kinds of programs.
3. Identify publishers of the kind of software you'd like to create, and send them a résumé and disk with projects you've created in school.

MULTIMEDIA PRODUCER

CAREER PROFILE

Duties: Takes overall responsibility for the creation and production of multimedia projects; supervises the multimedia development team

Alternate Title(s): CD-ROM Producer; Director (Multimedia Production)

Salary Range: $45,000 to $75,000 or more

Employment Prospects: Fair

Advancement Prospects: Fair

Prerequisites:

Education or Training—Few formal requirements; college degrees in fields such as film, media, or graphic arts are all applicable

Experience—General familiarity with computer graphics and sound capabilities, programming and authoring systems (but heavy-duty programming skill not needed)

Special Skills and Personality Traits—Ability to translate concepts into detailed specifications; good writing and communication skills; management and leadership skills; adaptable personality at home both with technical processes and people

CAREER LADDER

```
┌─────────────────────────────┐
│  Director (multimedia       │
│  production department)      │
└─────────────────────────────┘

┌─────────────────────────────┐
│  Multimedia Producer (for a project) │
└─────────────────────────────┘

┌─────────────────────────────┐
│  Lead Developer             │
└─────────────────────────────┘

┌─────────────────────────────┐
│  Multimedia Developer       │
└─────────────────────────────┘
```

Position Description

In seeking an organizational model, the multimedia industry tends to adopt terminology from its earlier counterpart, the movie industry. Just as a movie producer takes ultimate responsibility for all aspects of making a movie, the Multimedia Producer brings together the ideas and people that are needed to create a multimedia project.

For a typical project, the Multimedia Producer begins with an overall concept such as "an interactive guide to Boston's historic buildings" or "101 Home Improvement Projects." He or she must create a script or a set of detailed specifications that will tell developers what information is to be presented and how it is to be organized. The guidelines must also establish a suitable style and approach—a CD that introduces preschool children to animals is likely to be approached differently from a simulated dissection for a high school biology class.

The Multimedia Producer must then assign and schedule all aspects of the work, and deal with a variety of problems that might arise, for example:

- Getting copyright permissions to use photos is turning out to be too expensive, and threatening to the budget. Can less expensive pictures be substituted?
- A programmer has run into trouble using a third-party utility for displaying video sequences. Should she start over from scratch with another product, or take time to find a way around the problem?
- The program needs an imaginative introductory sequence to stir a user's interest, but the artists seem to be stuck with boring clichés. Would a brainstorming session help?
- A competing product will be coming out just before ours is scheduled to be shipped. Do we try to rush ours out ahead of schedule, or try to convince upper management that it's more important to have a polished, bug-free product?

As this list suggests, the Multimedia Producer must be familiar with all the technologies developers can use, together with their advantages and drawbacks. He or she must be able to supervise but also to suggest solutions, provide encouragement, and inspire creativity.

Salaries

Multimedia Producers who work in-house in a moderate-sized company are likely to start around $45,000. Larger companies, bigger projects, and more management responsibility all contribute to higher pay. Many Producers freelance on a per-project basis: with top skills and a hot reputation this can yield $100,000 per year or more.

Employment Prospects

There is strong demand for multimedia products, particularly in the education area. The large number of start-ups increases opportunities if one is willing to risk a company's first project falling apart and the company going bankrupt. A more conservative approach might be to find traditional publishers (such as textbook or reference book companies) that are just starting to go into multimedia and might be willing to hire a freelance Producer to direct their project.

Advancement Prospects

Advancement can take two paths: first, working in-house for larger companies that pay more, and second, becoming more skilled as a freelancer and being able to demand higher rates.

Education and Training

Multimedia production is still a new field, and students must largely put together their own curriculum. Since film shares many of multimedia's characteristics, film or video majors could add appropriate computer courses, as could graphic arts or communications majors. Some basic business and management courses could round out the preparation.

There is some formal training or certification available, but the individual needs to find projects where he or she can learn "on the job."

Experience, Skills, and Personality Traits

Any experience developing graphics or multimedia programs (or webpages) is useful for familiarizing the future Producer with the technological state of the art. While understanding the technology is important, the key skills are the ability to see "the big picture," translate it into practical terms, and provide the leadership the development team needs to succeed.

Cross-Training for Multimedia Producers

Interests	Related Job Descriptions
develop multimedia content	Multimedia Developer
lead a software development team	Project Leader

Unions and Associations

There are a number of organizations devoted to multimedia. The National Multimedia Association of America is the largest organization for multimedia professionals. The Interactive Media Association (IMA) is focused more on the use of multimedia in business and training applications.

Tips for Entry

1. Don't be bound by a school's departmental structure. Courses you want might be in different departments such as film, media, communications, or computer science.
2. There's no substitute for hands-on experience. In addition to doing class projects, consider volunteering at a local school to work with educational software. You might be able to help students use Visual Basic or authoring tools (such as Hypercard) to develop simple multimedia presentations.
3. Since Web development and multimedia development are similar in many ways, learn about Web design and don't be afraid to "steal" ideas from the Web for your multimedia projects. The same is true of computer games.
4. When looking for an entry-level job, check out areas such as "Multimedia Gulch" but also contact traditional educational and reference publishers. Look for a variety of job titles.

COMPUTER GAME DESIGNER/PROGRAMMER

CAREER PROFILE

Duties: Designs and/or programs computer games

Alternate Title(s): Game Developer

Salary Range: $40,000 to $80,000

Employment Prospects: Fair

Advancement Prospects: Fair

Prerequisites:

Education or Training—Undergraduate degree in computer science may be helpful, but not required

Experience—Should be able to demonstrate programming skill with a "demo disk" or shareware game

Special Skills and Personality Traits—Design and programming skills; ability to work long hours under pressure; willingness to live without much job security

CAREER LADDER

```
┌─────────────────────────────┐
│      Lead Developer or       │
│   Project Manager (games)    │
└─────────────────────────────┘


┌─────────────────────────────┐
│    Game Designer/Developer   │
└─────────────────────────────┘


┌─────────────────────────────┐
│ Assistant Programmer/Coder (games) │
└─────────────────────────────┘
```

Position Description

Developing today's computer games brings together programmers, artists, sound specialists, and writers, usually managed by a producer or project manager. While designing games and programming them are really separate skills, most real-world jobs require elements of both, so the two activities will be discussed together.

Computer games can be divided into the following genres or styles:

- simulation, where the player controls a realistic vehicle (such as a plane or submarine) or takes on a real-world role such as business tycoon or baseball manager
- strategy, where the player tries to conquer opponents through superior strategy and tactics
- role-playing, where the player controls one or more characters in a fantasy or science fiction world
- action or arcade, where quick decisions and hand-eye coordination are the keys to victory

All games, regardless of type, require that Programmers master such functions as graphics display, creating a user interface, and providing feedback to the player. Some form of artificial intelligence technique must be used to operate the computer opponent or players. Many games must keep track of the character's position on a map as well as tracking data about the game character or vehicle's level of skill, weapons, or other capabilities.

Recently there has been a strong demand for games that can be played by many players together on the Internet or another network. Such multiplayer games are more complex to program than games where players take turns and only one plays at a time.

The type of game does influence the programming specialty that is most in demand. A business simulation will place more emphasis on accurate mathematical models, while a "shoot-em up" 3-D dungeon game would emphasize fast, smooth, detailed graphics.

As with multimedia projects, the development process usually begins with an overall concept created or fleshed out by a Designer. The Designer or project leader creates a detailed outline (sometimes called a "pseudo code") that describes the modules or routines needed to implement all the game's features. Programmers must then translate these specifications into actual code in languages such as C++ (most frequently used) or Visual Basic.

In smaller projects one person may do the design and a large portion of the programming, assisted by artists, writers, and other specialists. For large projects (including most best-selling games) the management, design, and programming tasks are done by separate people.

Salaries

An entry-level Programmer who performs simple coding tasks in a small company or start-up may begin at about $30,000. Programmers with specialty skills (such as 3-D graphics) or who also do design work will be paid considerably more.

Employment Prospects

Despite some consolidation in the computer game industry that has seen some once famous companies fall by the wayside, demand for talented Game Programmers remains rather strong. As with other software development, employment is concentrated in geographical areas such as Silicon Valley south of San Francisco and the East Coast. It should be noted, however, that the skills involved in game design and programming are very similar to those used in multimedia and Web development, so individuals willing to pursue all three areas have a better chance of finding employment.

Advancement Prospects

Moving to an in-house position at a larger company that includes design duties usually results in a substantial salary increase. Freelancing is also quite possible, especially for "hot shot" designers or graphics programmers.

Education and Training

A four-year degree in computer science provides a good general background for software development, but the skills most in demand by game companies are seldom taught in school. A high school student who can show some dazzling 3-D texture-mapped graphics may be of more interest than a college graduate who has extensive theoretical knowledge. There are no certification standards in this field, although membership in professional game design organizations may help show professionalism.

Experience, Skills, and Personality Traits

Many Game Designers/Programmers started out by writing one or more "shareware" games and making them available on the Internet. A shareware game can be downloaded and played by anyone for free, although the user is expected to pay the developer a small fee if he or she likes the game and plays it regularly. While a few Game Designers can actually make a pretty good living creating shareware games full time, the objective is usually to gain experience and get feedback about one's programming skills rather than make money.

A Game Designer/Programmer must be a "systems thinker" who can visualize how the many parts of a game fit together, and can balance games so they can be played by people with different levels of skill. Ever-sharpened programming skills must be used to get that last bit of detail or graphics performance that will give a product an edge over the competition and attract reviewers' attention. The work is intense and approaching deadlines bring added pressure.

Cross-Training for Game Designers/Programmers

Interests	Related Job Descriptions
developing multimedia applications	Multimedia Developer
managing game or multimedia development	Multimedia Producer
testing games	Playtester

Unions and Associations

There are few well-established organizations for Game Designers, but there are a number of possibilities to check out on the Web, including the International Game Developer's Association.

Tips for Entry

1. Look for program code for games written in easy to learn languages such as Visual Basic, and study and tinker with it. Even though you'll probably be switching to C++ or Java later, the principles will remain the same.

2. Create a simple game or two, then possibly work on a larger shareware effort that will become the centerpiece of your portfolio.

3. Take some courses in computer science, especially those dealing with principles and algorithms ("recipes") for decision making, data structures, and graphics. Combine this with courses in specific programming languages (especially C++ and Java, the latter being popular for Internet-based games).

4. Read magazines and newsgroups on game development and look for companies with entry-level programming positions. If your portfolio isn't very good yet, try to "get in the door" as an in-house playtester, documentation writer, or assistant and then volunteer to take on simple programming tasks.

PLAYTESTER, COMPUTER GAMES

CAREER PROFILE

Duties: Thoroughly and systematically tests computer games and gives feedback to developers

Alternate Title(s): None

Salary Range: $18,000 to $25,000

Employment Prospects: Poor

Advancement Prospects: Fair

Prerequisites:
    Education or Training—No formal requirements
    Experience—Familiarity with a variety of computer games
    Special Skills and Personality Traits—Ability to follow detailed procedures and to be systematic; good written and spoken communication skills; patience and persistence

CAREER LADDER

```
┌─────────────────────────────────┐
│    Games Designer/Programmer     │
└─────────────────────────────────┘

┌─────────────────────────────────┐
│      Technical Assistant         │
│      (game development)          │
└─────────────────────────────────┘

┌─────────────────────────────────┐
│      Playtester (in-house)       │
└─────────────────────────────────┘

┌─────────────────────────────────┐
│      Beta Tester (volunteer)     │
└─────────────────────────────────┘
```

Position Description

To be interesting, a game must allow for many possible approaches and playing styles. Player demand and competition have led to most games having many features. For example, it is no longer enough to have a World War II strategy game with just a few types of tanks, infantry, and other units. Players want every model of German, Russian, or American tank (including the experimental ones), and they want game results to reflect the different performances of the tanks' engines, turret, armor, and guns. Similarly, players in on-line fantasy games don't just want to kill monsters. They also want to be able to join a guild, buy or sell goods, perhaps even marry another character and build a home. A baseball simulation will annoy purists if fly balls travel as far on a drizzly day as they do when it is dry and breezy.

The result of such complexity and "featuritis" is that it becomes very hard to make sure there aren't combinations of data and player actions that will cause "bugs" or errors. Many things can cause problems. A programmer may have mistyped (or left out) a key piece of data. The programmer may have tested a particular routine under every reasonable condition—but many game players are notoriously *unreasonable*.

Game companies face two competing pressures. On the one hand, the marketers want the product to ship on time. If it doesn't, they will lose sales, and a precious spot on store shelves may be lost to a competitor. On the other hand, programmers and developers want to create a product that is as bug-free as possible. This is partly a reflection of professional pride, and partly based on the fact that bugs lead to the need to release and distribute revised versions of the program ("patches") and to answer technical support questions.

Many gamers are perfectly willing to help test a game that is still in development in exchange for being able to play it before anyone else. These "beta testers" are usually paid only with a copy of the final version of the game. Many companies use both in-house paid Playtesters and volunteer beta testers. (Some companies try to save money by using only beta testers, but this less systematic testing can let more bugs get through. Other companies do *only* in-house testing because they are afraid that beta testers may freely "pirate" or illegally distribute the game.)

Salaries

Because spending one's time playing computer games is so attractive to many gamers, companies don't have to pay very much for entry-level Playtesters. Once in the door, however, a tester may be able to gain increased responsibilities, such as coordinating and writing up test reports or helping develop a better user interface. This can lead to an increase in salary and perhaps the opportunity to move into design or development work.

Employment Prospects

The attractive nature of this work, particularly for young people, means that there is considerable competition even for low-paid entry-level work. It helps to be able to show special experience or expertise—such as game reviews one has written and published.

Advancement Prospects

The Playtester position is usually either something one does for a while before moving into one's "real" field, or a stepping-stone to design or development work. Advancement depends on demonstrating one's skills and good work habits so that one will be considered when a position opens.

Education and Training

There is no formal educational experience required, other than perhaps a high school diploma (on general principles).

Experience, Skills, and Personality Traits

Besides loving computer games and having played them for hours on end, a Playtester must be able to follow detailed instructions and have good written and verbal communication skills. A mildly obsessed personality can be helpful as long as the individual doesn't lose touch with the requirements of the job.

Cross-Training for Playtesters

Skills or Interests	Related Job Descriptions
designing or developing games	Game Designer/Programmer
test software (general)	Quality Assurance Specialist
write about games or other software	Technical Writer; Reporter (computer-related)

Unions and Associations

Playtesters might consider joining organizations related to game development as a way to pursue career leads.

Tips for Entry

1. Check newsgroups and websites for game companies that are looking for beta testers. If you are accepted, make sure you follow the procedures and give as much useful feedback as possible. This may give you an inside track if the company also seeks paid Playtesters.

2. Read magazines such as *Computer Gaming World* and *Game Developer* to keep up with trends in game design and to identify the companies that make the kinds of games that interest you the most.

3. Playtesting can be fun and can lead to other opportunities, but don't neglect the courses and skills needed for long-term career advancement, whether in computer science, graphic arts, multimedia, or other fields.

VIRTUAL REALITY DESIGNER/PROGRAMMER

CAREER PROFILE

Duties: Develops software that immerses people into virtual worlds where they see, hear, feel, and interact with a computer-created environment

Alternate Title(s): Virtual Reality Developer

Salary Range: $40,000 to $60,000

Employment Prospects: Poor

Advancement Prospects: Fair

Prerequisites:
　　Education or Training—Undergraduate degree in computer science with strong graphics and design background
　　Experience—Graphics, game, and user interface design experience are helpful
　　Special Skills and Personality Traits—Technical skill; imagination and visualization; inventiveness; and persistence

CAREER LADDER

```
┌─────────────────────────────┐
│      Project Leader         │
│ (virtual reality development)│
└─────────────────────────────┘

┌─────────────────────────────┐
│ Senior Developer (virtual reality) │
└─────────────────────────────┘

┌─────────────────────────────┐
│ Virtual Reality Designer/Programmer │
└─────────────────────────────┘
```

Position Description

Most computer users sit in front of a screen and interact with software via the keyboard or mouse. But a new technology called virtual reality (or VR) in effect puts the user inside the computer screen. A pair of special goggles shows computer graphics that change as the viewer moves his or her head. More advanced systems include position trackers that move the user in the virtual world as he or she walks around the floor. Special gloves can use pressure and tactile sensations to make it feel like someone is grasping real objects. Some examples of virtual reality (VR) applications might include:

- games where the player can wield a sword in combat or swing a golf club with realistic results
- "tours" of museums or historical sites where the user can walk around and look at objects as if he or she were physically present
- training systems for airline pilots or operators of Martian robot rovers
- systems that can let a customer design and then walk through a dream home by arranging furniture and other elements, with the system calculating prices

- a system that can either help train surgeons or actually use imagery of the patient's body to allow operations to be performed by remote control

Like artificial intelligence, virtual reality has been a "hot" and exciting field, but there is a considerable gap between ideas and proposals and doable products. Most commercial applications involve games, while cutting-edge research is done in university or government labs. Nevertheless, the equipment is within the reach of start-ups who have the potential to create successful products.

Salaries

In commercial VR, salaries are generally similar to that of software engineers, starting at about $40,000 and going up with experience. Researchers in academic or government labs are paid similarly to other scientists and engineers, starting higher but with less potential for income growth.

Employment Prospects

The speculative nature of the field makes employment uncertain, and it is difficult for beginners without proven skills to break in. Someone who can start as a technical assistant and help maintain and configure equipment might be able to work up to a full-fledged programming job.

Advancement Prospects

There really isn't much of a corporate ladder in this field. An individual could move up to the equivalent of lead programmer/project leader status and make a salary similar to a senior systems analyst. A VR researcher in the academic world would advance along the traditional track (associate professor, professor, etc.).

Education and Training

A four-year degree in computer science is good for general preparation, but VR as such is unlikely to be part of the curriculum. A strong background in computer graphics, modeling, and interface design and user psychology would be a well-rounded preparation.

There is little formal training or certification available.

Experience, Skills, and Personality Traits

The Virtual Reality Developer must be familiar with interfacing and troubleshooting computer hardware, since most VR outfits have to be created using parts from different vendors. Experience in computer graphics and game design/development would be helpful. Since the object of VR is to create a compelling, believable world, imagination and the ability to understand how people interact with their environment is also essential. The personality of the classic inventor—drive, curiosity, and persistence—fits well here.

Cross-Training for Virtual Reality Developers

Interests	Related Job Descriptions
designing computer games	Computer Game Designer/ Programmer
creating computer graphics	Computer Graphics Artist

Unions and Associations

Individuals interested in the computer science aspects of the field could join the Association for Computing Machinery (ACM) and special interest groups relating to virtual reality. Game and multimedia developer organizations are also a possibility.

Tips for Entry

1. It probably isn't a good idea to plan one's whole career around the goal of doing virtual reality. Consider making it one of several related interests, such as computer graphics, game design, user interface design, and multimedia.
2. You can learn something about VR without the goggles and gloves. Many computer games use VR ideas, and there is a language called VRML that can create scenes you can "walk through" via the Internet.
3. Relatively inexpensive goggles and control gloves are available for use with some computer games. If you buy them, get the technical manual as well and experiment with creating simple walkthroughs.
4. Look for VR labs or game development companies that use VR ideas, and try to get a job as a technician or assistant to "get your feet wet."

MANUFACTURING

COMPUTER HARDWARE DESIGNER/ENGINEER

CAREER PROFILE

Duties: Designs chips or other computer components or systems

Alternate Title(s): Computer Chip Designer; Electrical Engineer

Salary Range: $55,000 to $75,000 or more

Employment Prospects: Excellent

Advancement Prospects: Good

Prerequisites:

Education or Training—Undergraduate degree in computer science or electrical engineering; graduate degree helpful

Experience—Some computer engineering experience helpful but not always necessary

Special Skills and Personality Traits—Design skills; ability to visualize physical systems; problem solving; analysis; troubleshooting; ability to perform exacting work under deadline pressure

CAREER LADDER

```
┌─────────────────────────────────────┐
│    Lead Engineer/Product Manager     │
└─────────────────────────────────────┘

┌─────────────────────────────────────┐
│       Senior Designer/Engineer       │
└─────────────────────────────────────┘

┌─────────────────────────────────────┐
│      Computer Designer/Engineer      │
└─────────────────────────────────────┘

┌─────────────────────────────────────┐
│     Designer/Engineer (entry-level)  │
└─────────────────────────────────────┘
```

Position Description

Designing the central processing chip (CPU), memory chips, and supporting chips and hardware for modern computers is an exacting task. For a CPU, a team of designers must create detailed specifications for the chip's built-in arithmetical, logical, and storage operations. The many layers of microscopic circuits that make up a thumbnail-sized chip must be laid out with the assistance of special software and methods for manufacturing them selected.

According to an industry maxim called Moore's Law, computer processors double in power about every 18 months or so, a rate of progress unheard of in any other manufacturing industry. Nothing stands still: It is like a basketball game in which the hoop is raised higher every week.

Hardware Engineers must understand the performance characteristics of materials and the electrical laws that govern a circuit's behavior. For example, the closer together the individual parts of a CPU can be placed, the faster the chip, because of the shorter distance electrical signals have to travel. But as the gap gets shorter, it becomes harder to prevent components from interfering with each other and there is also more heat that has to be gotten rid of before it damages the chip.

In addition to the CPU, Hardware Designers and Engineers create the chips and circuits that control the computer's devices, such as hard, floppy, and CD drives, video and sound cards, modems, and many others. Performance and reliability are the twin goals, and competition can be fierce. The demand for new features and better performance must always be juggled against the pressure of deadlines and the need to preserve market share as original equipment manufacturers (OEMs) decide whose components to buy.

While Hardware Engineers must also understand the principles of programming, the programs they are concerned with are not the words and symbols of languages such as Basic or even C++, but machine code, a set of instructions that specify how parts of numbers or single characters can be manipulated. One might say that Computer Engineers are the architects who build the houses that other programmers live and work in.

In addition to designing components, Engineers can specialize in testing them. A single undiscovered logical flaw in a chip can cost its manufacturer millions of dollars in replacement costs. Tests and analysis by Engineers can also make manufacturing more efficient, increasing the percentage of chips that can be certified as reliable and sold.

Salaries

This is one of the highest-paid entry-level positions for recent graduates. The high starting salaries reflect the amount of education required and the limited number of people who have engineering degrees. The growing number of foreign-born engineers coming into the American market may be causing some downward pressure on salaries.

Employment Prospects

Employment prospects are excellent for qualified graduates, especially those with graduate degrees. Major computer and semiconductor manufacturers send recruiters to campuses in an aggressive attempt to secure the services of recent graduates.

Advancement Prospects

Computer Hardware Designer/Engineers can advance to senior status for higher pay, or can become project or department managers, combining technical and leadership roles.

Education and Training

Generally the minimum requirement is a four-year degree in electrical engineering or computer science (plus engineering-related courses). Individuals with advanced (master's) degree are in higher demand and have a better chance of getting an entry-level position even without work experience.

Individuals need to keep their skills and certifications up to date through continuing education.

Experience, Skills, and Personality Traits

Because the education requirements are stiff and reflect hard work, this is one of the few computer-related areas where education often substitutes for experience. Nevertheless, it is important for engineering students to take on tough class projects that allow them to exercise design and implementation skills.

Computer hardware engineering requires the ability to visualize the complex interaction between components—not only the intended operation but also the limits imposed by the laws of physics. These limits often become problems that must be worked around to create a design that meets specifications. Analyzing performance and diagnosing problems requires good analytical skills and mastery of detail.

Contrary to stereotype, an Engineer need not be antisocial or unable to get along with people. Indeed, designing complex systems is necessarily a team effort and requires good communication skills. The Engineer must also be able to concentrate and maintain focus, often for many more than the standard 40 hours a week.

Cross-Training for Computer Hardware Designers/Engineers

Interests	Related Job Descriptions
designing special-purpose computers	Embedded Systems Designer
designing computers that interact with the environment	Robotics Engineer

Unions and Associations

The Institute of Electrical and Electronics Engineers (IEEE) is the premier professional organization in this field. Individuals can also belong to special interest groups devoted to specialties such as chip design or graphics products.

Tips for Entry

1. Since education is so important in this field, take the time to choose an undergraduate or graduate program that has a good reputation (which will help you in the hiring process) as well as challenging courses in areas that interest you (such as robotics).

2. Because you will be working with hardware and the physical world, not just ideas, make sure you have a solid background in mathematics, physics, electronics, and material science.

3. If you are about to graduate from a well-regarded school, the jobs may come to you—in the form of campus recruiters. But make sure you are well prepared for interviews, such as by studying technical problems typically faced by the kinds of companies likely to be recruiting. This will make it easier for you to answer the "What would you do if . . . " type of question.

COMPUTER SYSTEMS DESIGNER

CAREER PROFILE

Duties: Creates complete computer systems for vendors by integrating components from various manufacturers

Alternate Title(s): None

Salary Range: $50,000 to $75,000

Employment Prospects: Fair

Advancement Prospects: Fair

Prerequisites:

Education or Training—Four-year or graduate degree in engineering-related field

Experience—Experience in support for computer hardware company helpful

Special Skills and Personality Traits—Visualization of complete system; understanding of industry trends and marketing issues; ability to balance competing considerations; attention to detail; good communication skills

CAREER LADDER

```
┌─────────────────────────────────┐
│     Chief Designer or Manager   │
│        (design department)      │
└─────────────────────────────────┘

┌─────────────────────────────────┐
│  Senior Computer Systems Designer │
└─────────────────────────────────┘

┌─────────────────────────────────┐
│    Computer Systems Designer     │
└─────────────────────────────────┘

┌─────────────────────────────────┐
│       Entry-Level Computer       │
│        Systems Designer          │
└─────────────────────────────────┘
```

Position Description

The "name brand" computer systems sold through stores or by direct phone order must be created by carefully selecting each component, such as motherboard, processing unit, disk drives, and video systems, out of the many available from various manufacturers. The Computer Systems Designer is responsible for creating a complete system by specifying the components for each model of system sold by a vendor and ensuring that everything works together.

The designer begins with information provided by the vendor's marketing department. Every system has an intended market that determines what features will be emphasized. For example, a computer designed as an entry-level machine for home users will have only a moderately powerful processor, but it will have good graphics and sound capabilities and probably include a built-in modem. These features match the typical needs of the home user, which include running games and multimedia software and logging on to the Internet.

On the other hand, a machine designed to be the file server for an office network will probably have a more powerful processor and a large disk drive. That's because the machine needs space for large programs and data files used by businesses and must be able to keep up with the needs of the network users. This machine will not emphasize video and sound, however, since it is unlikely people will be playing games on it.

Laptop computers have their own design problems. Users want lightweight machines that they can easily carry though airports. They also want batteries that will last several hours. On the other hand, users also want their laptops to be able to run the same powerful programs they use in the office. Designers generally create several models to meet different priorities, ranging from a heavy but powerful laptop that is almost as powerful as a desktop machine, to a lightweight "notebook" or even handheld computer that is used mainly to keep track of addresses and e-mail or for making brief notes.

Once the designer has considered the needs of the machine's "target market," he or she must deal with other issues. One is that of price versus reliability. A cheaper component may make it possible to sell the system at a more competitive price, but if it results in a high rate of failures what is gained in sales may be lost in support costs and the loss of customers to other vendors. Another issue is expandability (or flexibility). Generally a computer that is designed to be easy to upgrade will cost more than one that is more limited. Whether to design for upgradability will depend on whether the vendor thinks that would be enough of a "selling point" with the intended market.

When the design is completed, the engineering begins. The components have to be put together into a prototype or "breadboard" where they can be tested to make sure they work well together. The extensive testing tries to catch incompatibilities or subtle problems such as overheating that may occur only after hours of use. The final design is then turned into detailed instructions for the assembly plant that will actually manufacture the system. This can include diagrams and procedures for manufacturing technicians, as well as instructions for CAM (Computer-Aided Manufacturing) machines that can automate much of the assembly process.

Salaries

The combination of design and engineering skills needed for Computer Systems Designers is hard to come by, so qualified graduates can earn high entry-level salaries of $50,000 or more. A graduate degree can push this higher, and experience can bring top designers up near the $100,000 mark.

Employment Prospects

The growth in home and business PC sales has slowed because of the recent economic downturn. Business users seem more willing to wait an extra year or two before upgrading their existing PCs, and the home market is becoming saturated. Furthermore, a few large companies, such as Dell, Gateway, IBM, and Compaq, now dominate the PC market. All of these factors have reduced the demand for Computer Systems Designers. There are still positions to be had with the major companies, but openings are limited and entry-level designers working there are likely to be involved only with small parts of the total system. To be more competitive, seekers for design positions might want to look beyond the desktop PC to other areas, such as laptop and notebook computers, handheld computers, mobile systems, and even the new generation of multifunction cell phones. Gaining engineering expertise may be another alternative.

Advancement Prospects

As a Computer Systems Designer gains experience, he or she can advance either by moving to a larger manufacturer or by moving up to a senior (or management) position. A more viable alternative might be specialization and consulting.

Education and Training

Employers are looking for solid preparation in an undergraduate course of study that includes electrical engineering, computer architecture and design, and related fields. An advanced degree can be helpful.

Experience, Skills, and Personality Traits

While education is considered more important than experience for this position, experience working with or integrating computer systems or doing technical support is useful because it helps familiarize the future designer with the "real-world" needs of different kinds of computer users.

The important skills include the ability to visualize how parts of a system fit together, good analysis and problem-solving skills, and the ability to communicate with marketers or major customers. The individual must be able to plan a variety of tasks, juggle schedules and priorities, and work under pressure.

Cross-Training for Computer Systems Designers

Interests	Related Job Descriptions
adapt computer systems and software to users' needs	Systems Integrator
design chips or other hardware components	Computer Hardware Designer/Engineer
design new devices	Telecommunications Engineer; Embedded Systems Designer
provide technical help to computer users	Technical Support Representative

Unions and Associations

An individual in this field can join engineering organizations (such as the Institute of Electrical and Electronics Engineers, or IEEE) and industry groups such as the American Electronics Association. An interest in marketing might lead to joining organizations in the marketing and business fields such as the Computers and Electronics Marketing Association. Joining user groups can be a good way to keep in touch with the public's demand for system features.

Tips for Entry

1. Get a solid background in computer science (especially system architecture) as well as computer engineering. Business-related courses that would help you understand user needs can be helpful, too, as well as courses in technical communications/technical writing.
2. While working for your degree, try to get some hands-on experience in technical support or systems integration. You may find opportunities in helping your school plan its computer purchases, or consulting with a local nonprofit organization or small business that needs technical help. Another possibility is working for a local store that assembles its own "no name" systems from generic components.
3. Get in the habit of reading the computer trade press to keep up with trends in system design and the opinions of reviewers about new systems. Join professional organizations such as the IEEE to keep in touch with trends in design.

COMPUTER HARDWARE MANUFACTURING TECHNICIAN

CAREER PROFILE

Duties: Implements and tests designs for computer components, usually under the supervision of engineers

Alternate Title(s): Electronics Technician

Salary Range: $25,000 to $45,000

Employment Prospects: Fair

Advancement Prospects: Good

Prerequisites:

Education or Training—Minimum of a two-year (associate) degree in electronics; good background in physics, mathematics (including statistics and failure analysis) is helpful

Experience—Employer will train qualified individuals, but hands-on familiarity with computer or laboratory equipment is very helpful

Special Skills and Personality Traits—Attention to detail; analysis; problem solving; manual dexterity; technical communications skill; should have steady work habits but be able to show initiative

CAREER LADDER

Senior Manufacturing Technician
or Supervisor

Manufacturing Technician
(computer products)

Technical Associate (or Assistant)

Position Description

After a computer system or component has been designed by engineers, the design must be turned into a working model or prototype. Computer Hardware Manufacturing Technicians build and test these prototypes, using their knowledge of electronics theory. They must be skilled in building circuits and in using instruments such as oscilloscopes and signal generators. Mathematical and analytical skills are needed for interpreting readings and results. The Technician must keep extensive logs and reports that document the research and development process, and must be able to work closely with engineers and assistants.

Technicians are also needed for configuring and maintaining the automatic machines that do much of the assembly work in some factories. Technicians may also supervise technical assistants or assemblers who perform more routine tasks. The Technician's problem-solving and troubleshooting skills come into play for fixing specific problems and as part of the attempts to continually improve the manufacturing process so that more reliable components are built.

More advanced Technicians sometimes write special diagnostic programs that put a computer system or component through its paces thousands of times, automatically recording how well it performs.

Technicians must keep up with the rapid changes in technology, including changes in component specifications, test equipment, and software.

Salaries

Entry-level salaries tend to be fairly low (mid-$20,000 range) but salaries for experienced or specialized Technicians can be considerably higher.

Employment Prospects

Prospects are generally good for individuals with electronics degrees who can demonstrate good basic skills, even if they lack specific experience. Employers are often willing to put such employees in trainee positions and build their skills.

The growing use of automation in chip and component manufacturing, and the moving of operations to countries with lower labor costs, has reduced the demand for routine assemblers, but not for skilled technicians, who are needed to maintain factory equipment.

Advancement Prospects

Entry-level Technicians may start out performing routine tests and other simple procedures. As they gain experience and take advantage of the opportunity to demonstrate more advanced skills, Technicians can move up the ladder to senior or supervisory status. Another option is to work toward an engineering degree at night and then move into an engineering position.

Education and Training

The basic two-year program in electronics technology offered by many community colleges can provide good preparation for an entry-level position. The military offers equivalent training. Solid coursework in physics and mathematics is helpful, as well as general familiarity with computer architecture and programming. An FCC license is required for working with equipment that generates radio frequency waves, but this license does not require any special training.

Experience, Skills, and Personality Traits

Many people who aim for Technician careers started at an early age building electronics kits or putting together computer systems from various components. Other ways to gain experience include class projects or work-study or internship positions in electronics labs, or working as a repair assistant for a computer or electronics store.

Technicians need good analytical and problem-solving skills, good written and oral communication skills, and some manual dexterity for soldering and working with small, delicate components. Individuals should enjoy working with details, performing somewhat repetitive tasks, and working alone or under minimal supervision.

Cross-Training for Computer Hardware Manufacturing Technicians

Interests	Related Job Descriptions
repairing computer equipment	Service Technician
designing equipment	Computer Hardware Manufacturing Designer/ Engineer; Computer Systems Designer
selecting and customizing equipments	Systems Integrator

Unions and Associations

Technicians working for the government or some large corporations may belong to labor unions. Technicians who are working toward an engineering career may wish to join organizations such as the Institute of Electrical and Electronics Engineers (IEEE).

Tips for Entry

1. Look for kits, projects, old computers, or other equipment that you can take apart, rebuild, or tinker with. Learn how to read circuit diagrams and schematics and how to follow step-by-step procedures.
2. Before signing up for a college electronics program, ask about its job placement services and how many graduates find jobs shortly after graduation.
3. Read computer and electronics magazines to familiarize yourself with the latest kinds of equipment and techniques. Sometimes school curricula may be a few years out of date—and a few years can be a long time where computers are concerned!

EMBEDDED SYSTEMS DESIGNER

CAREER PROFILE

Duties: Designs computer control systems for devices such as manufacturing equipment, appliances, or entertainment products

Alternate Title(s): Firmware Engineer

Salary Range: $40,000 to $60,000 or more

Employment Prospects: Good

Advancement Prospects: Fair

Prerequisites:

Education or Training—Undergraduate degree in electrical engineering or related engineering discipline; graduate degree may be required for senior positions

Experience—Familiarity with specialized microchips and low-level programming

Special Skills and Personality Traits—Ability to visualize systems and interactions; electronic and mechanical engineering; programming; reasonable communication skills; creativity combined with self-discipline and a methodical approach

CAREER LADDER

```
┌─────────────────────────────────────┐
│   Manager, Embedded Systems Design   │
└─────────────────────────────────────┘

┌─────────────────────────────────────┐
│  Senior Designer, Embedded Systems   │
└─────────────────────────────────────┘

┌─────────────────────────────────────┐
│      Embedded Systems Designer       │
└─────────────────────────────────────┘
```

Position Description

Most people are aware of only a small fraction of the computers that surround them. Desktop or laptop computers are readily recognizable. A moment's thought is enough to make one realize that little brother's Nintendo computer game unit is really a special-purpose handheld computer. But what about the electronic gadget that the FedEx driver uses when someone signs for a package? Or the electronic controllers in cars, air conditioners, even appliances like toasters? These are all special-purpose computers, also called embedded systems.

Embedded systems have these general characteristics:

• They are built into a device such as an appliance rather than being separate objects.
• They control the device's operation, usually in response to feedback from the environment (such as by automatically selecting a camera's shutter speed in response to light conditions).
• They are controlled by a program in permanent ROM (read-only memory), not in the changeable memory most desktop programs run in.
• They are usually programmed using low-level programming languages such as C or assembly language.

The Embedded Systems Designer normally works with designers and engineers who are creating a product. He or she must have the ability to visualize not only computer-type operations but also the interaction of electrical and mechanical connections, switches, and sensors. Unlike most computer programs, which work with abstract data, embedded programs interact directly with the physical environment, measuring or timing things and responding to changes.

A related field is the design of "firmware" such as the "boot ROM" that contains the instructions a computer uses to set up its devices (such as clock, memory, and disk drives) when the power is turned on. Many peripheral devices such as disk controllers and video boards also contain extensive ROM programming.

Salaries

Salaries for Embedded Systems Designers are similar to those for other mid-level engineers. Positions that mainly involve maintaining (revising) code for existing devices are likely to pay less than positions that involve original design work or management of other engineers.

Employment Prospects

The use of computerized controllers in more and more devices, as well as the growing number of features and functions in consumer products such as portable phones, is likely to keep demand for Embedded Systems Designers strong.

Advancement Prospects

Experience will automatically bring some increase in pay in most large corporations, but significant advancement comes either from having a major design role in a project or having significant management duties.

Education and Training

The minimum requirement is generally a four-year degree in computer science, electronics, or a related field. An individual generally starts out with general engineering training and then decides to specialize in the embedded systems field.

Experience, Skills, and Personality Traits

Most people don't have the opportunity as students to build devices with embedded control systems "from scratch," since the equipment needed is specialized and rather expensive. However, class projects or kits can provide the opportunity to study how existing devices work and to write simulated control software and run it on a regular computer. An entry-level job will generally bring some training and experience that starts with testing and maintenance tasks or working as an assistant to a more senior engineer.

This position calls for a mixture of visualization, design, and practical implementation skills including computer architecture, electronics and electromechanical engineering, and programming. The ability to work well with other members of the product development team is also important. The individual needs to be creative yet self-disciplined and methodical.

Cross-Training for Embedded Systems Designers

Interests	Related Job Descriptions
designing machines that perform complex tasks	Robotics Engineer
designing computer chips and circuits	Computer Hardware Engineer/Designer
designing communications equipment	Telecommunications Engineer
controlling automated manufacturing systems	Computer-Aided Manufacturing (CAM) Technician

Unions and Associations

As an engineer, the Embedded Systems Designer is likely to belong to the Institute of Electrical and Electronics Engineers (IEEE) as well as specialized groups for Embedded Systems and Robotics Engineers.

Tips for Entry

1. There are many electronics and robotics kits that include sensors and motors that can be controlled through the serial port of an ordinary PC. Building such projects can help you learn the general principles of control systems as well as programming.
2. A work-study or internship as a technical assistant to a company that makes controllers or devices that use embedded systems can provide additional experience.
3. In addition to your general computer science program, look for courses in specialized programming or embedded systems. Introductory engineering courses can also be helpful.
4. Read specialized journals and newsgroups devoted to embedded systems design.

COMPUTER-AIDED DESIGN (CAD) TECHNICIAN

CAREER PROFILE

Duties: Uses computer-assisted programs to create detailed design drawings and to compile specifications and cost data

Alternate Title(s): Drafter; Design Assistant

Salary Range: $25,000 to $40,000

Employment Prospects: Fair

Advancement Prospects: Fair

Prerequisites:

Education or Training—Two-year college or vocational program in drafting and design; background in a particular area of manufacture is a plus

Experience—Work as assistant to designer

Special Skills and Personality Traits—Visualization; ability to read drawings and diagrams; manual dexterity; attention to detail; background in specific industries; steady work habits

CAREER LADDER

```
┌─────────────────────────────────────┐
│           CAD Manager                │
└─────────────────────────────────────┘

┌─────────────────────────────────────┐
│        Senior CAD Technician         │
└─────────────────────────────────────┘

┌─────────────────────────────────────┐
│           CAD Technician             │
└─────────────────────────────────────┘

┌─────────────────────────────────────┐
│  Assistant CAD Technician or Drafter │
└─────────────────────────────────────┘
```

Position Description

In the past, engineers and designers created detailed pen-and-ink drawings that showed how all the parts of a device fit together, as well as specifying dimensions, lists of part numbers, and other data. This was a tedious process and it was difficult to make corrections or change a design without starting over.

Today skilled Technicians use CAD (Computer-Aided Design) software and high-resolution graphics workstations to create such drawings. Not only are computer-created drawings easy to correct, they also can be shifted or rotated to any desired perspective, helping engineers and technicians better visualize structure and function. Parts are shown in three dimensions, and it is easy to attach notes to them that will pop up when the part is clicked on with a mouse.

CAD programs make the actual task of drawing much easier. For example, the Technician can start with predesigned shapes (templates) and resize them, then specify what texture and/or color will be used to fill in the shape. A company is also likely to have extensive "object libraries" containing commonly used parts that can be simply "plugged into" a new design.

The CAD software can also be used to help with the overall management of production. For example, it can automatically connect to a parts database to create lists of part numbers and estimate the total cost.

In addition to having these general skills, CAD Technicians usually specialize in a particular area of design, such as mechanical engineering, architecture, electronics, automotive, or even fashion design.

Salaries

Entry-level salaries are fairly low, with experience or appropriate specialized skills bringing higher pay.

Employment Prospects

Employment prospects tend to vary with the economic strength of the industries that hire CAD Technicians. Currently an overall decline in the economy is making it harder to find jobs in the design/drafting departments of automobile, electronics, or other companies.

Having good general skills plus specialization in more than one industry can help overcome the effects of possible layoffs.

Advancement Prospects

Most large companies have several grades of CAD Technicians, from entry-level or assistant to senior level. Another advancement possibility is movement into management of a CAD department.

Education and Training

The basic requirement is generally a two-year degree or certificate program in drafting/design technology from a community college or vocational school. Courses in mathematics (including geometry and trigonometry), introductory engineering courses, and general computer skills are also important.

Experience, Skills, and Personality Traits

In addition to experience gained during school training, experience working as design assistants or technicians in specific industries can also be helpful. The most important skills are visualization, the ability to understand spatial relationships, dexterity in using computerized drafting and drawing tools, and general knowledge of mathematics, technical terminology, and technical writing. Individuals with a personality oriented toward detail work are more likely to be successful.

Cross-Training for CAD Technicians

Interests	Related Job Descriptions
managing a design department	Computer-Aided Design (CAD) Manager
technical communications	Technical Writer; Technical Editor
designing computer equipment	Computer Hardware Designer/ Engineer; Computer Systems Designer

Unions and Associations

CAD Technicians working in the automotive or other large industries may belong to labor unions. They can also help develop their careers by joining groups such as the American Design Drafting Association.

Tips for Entry

1. You can obtain low-cost commercial or "shareware" CAD software that runs on an ordinary PC. Use it to introduce yourself to basic drafting and graphics skills.

2. When it's time to look for a community college or vocational program in drafting, compare the subjects and skills covered with job requirements specified by local employers. Ask for information about job placement for graduates.

3. To get a broad background, take courses in computer graphics, desktop publishing, design, drafting, mathematics, engineering, and related subjects.

COMPUTER-AIDED DESIGN (CAD) MANAGER

CAREER PROFILE

Duties: Manages the CAD (Computer-Aided Design) department for an architectural or engineering firm; trains employees; coordinates work and scheduling; works with architects or engineers to meet their drafting needs

Alternate Title(s): Manager, Drafting Department

Salary Range: $50,000 to $80,000

Employment Prospects: Fair

Advancement Prospects: Fair

Prerequisites:

Education or Training—Four-year or advanced degree combining background in computers and in architecture or engineering

Experience—Several years work with CAD software in a design department

Special Skills and Personality Traits—Understanding of CAD features and procedures; ability to train, supervise, and coordinate workers; good communication skills for dealing with workers and architects or engineers; energetic and assertive but flexible personality

CAREER LADDER

```
┌─────────────────────────────────┐
│         CAD Manager             │
└─────────────────────────────────┘

┌─────────────────────────────────┐
│  Senior CAD Technician/Designer │
└─────────────────────────────────┘

┌─────────────────────────────────┐
│        CAD Technician           │
└─────────────────────────────────┘

┌─────────────────────────────────┐
│        CAD Assistant            │
└─────────────────────────────────┘
```

Position Description

Architectural and other design firms use Computer-Aided Design (CAD) technology extensively. The CAD Manager is responsible for all aspects of this operation, including:

- specifying and configuring the computer workstations and software
- training new technicians or operators
- helping the department move from one technology to another (such as from traditional manual drafting to CAD, or from mainly 2-D to fully 3-D modeling)
- working with the architects (or engineers) to make sure the drawings and other data are as useful as possible to them

Managers in engineering firms will also work with a related technology called CAM (Computer-Aided Manufacturing), which involves programming the operation of machines that assemble, paint, or otherwise process components on an assembly line.

In smaller firms there will likely be only one manager in charge of all aspects of CAD or CAM. The manager may therefore also have many of the responsibilities of a system or network administrator. In larger firms there will be a separate management information systems director in charge of all computer facilities, and the CAD Manager will have to work closely with that individual, as well as competing for computing resources with other departments.

A busy firm is usually working on several projects at once. Each project has its own schedule and has a priority set by upper management based on its importance to the firm. This means that the CAD Manager will often have to juggle work assignments—for example, taking technicians off a project that is ahead of schedule to help with one that is nearing deadline. On the other hand, moving people around can have a long-term negative impact on efficiency since technicians will have to spend more time getting up to speed on different projects. On top of all that, the Manager must be responsive to worker complaints and suggestions, and be able to keep them motivated while keeping the architects or engineers happy with the work output.

Salaries

Salaries at entry-level are based on the individual's education and experience. An individual with a four-year degree in architecture and good knowledge of CAD may start at around $50,000. The size and complexity of the CAD/CAM operation is also a factor in salary. A Manager with an advanced degree and experience in systems and networking as well as CAD/CAM could earn $80,000 or more in a large department.

Employment Prospects

The demand for architecture and the volume of manufacturing is closely related to the overall health of the economy. As the economy gradually recovers from the 2001–2 downturn, it is likely that the number of CAD/CAM available positions will grow. Candidates should look for specialties and sectors that are likely to be strong as a result of recent events—for example, security, surveillance, or the development of architecture that is resistant to terrorist attack.

Advancement Prospects

If an individual is managing a department that is growing substantially both in number of employees and complexity of systems, he or she should be able to demand an increasingly high salary. Alternatively, the individual can look for an opening in a larger company. Of course, the better the position, the more likely it is that the individual will face competition from other highly qualified candidates.

Education and Training

CAD Managers generally have a four-year or graduate degree in architecture (for CAD) or engineering (for CAM). General courses in computer technology plus specific training in major CAD/CAM software packages are also important.

Experience, Skills, and Personality Traits

An individual moving into management needs at least a couple of years of experience working as a technician in a CAD/CAM department. Needed skills include detailed familiarity with the software and workstations, the ability to quickly master new technology, attention to detail, and the supervisory and communication skills that make up good management. The individual should be energetic and assertive when necessary, but also flexible and diplomatic in dealing with other department heads, architects, or engineers who may have conflicting needs.

Cross-Training for CAD Managers

Interests	Related Job Descriptions
operating CAD or CAM systems	CAD Technician; CAM Technician
managing information systems departments	Manager, Information Systems

Unions and Associations

As a manager, the CAD Manager may join groups involved with management, such as the American Management Association. Groups related to the drafting and CAD/CAM industry such as the American Design Drafting Association may also be helpful, as well as groups relating to the employment industry.

Tips for Entry

1. While in school, get a good general background in the area of architecture or engineering in which you plan to work. Since your courses may not be fully up to date technologically, supplement them by reading technical journals.
2. In addition to computer-related courses, look for courses in management and technical communications to help you develop the "people skills" that are as important as technical knowledge.
3. If you get an entry-level job as a CAD technician, look for opportunities to help with the overall management of the department, such as becoming an assistant manager (in effect if not in title).
4. Try to add some specialized skills (such as familiarity with particular kinds of software, or applications for particular kinds of architecture). If you can "fit" these special skills to a prospective employer, you will have an advantage over other job applicants.

COMPUTER-AIDED MANUFACTURING (CAM) TECHNICIAN

CAREER PROFILE

Duties: Sets up and maintains complex computer-controlled machines that automate the manufacturing process in many factories

Alternate Title(s): None

Salary Range: $22,000 to $45,000

Employment Prospects: Good

Advancement Prospects: Fair

Prerequisites:

Education or Training—Two-year degree with good background in mathematics, computer skills, general engineering, electronics, etc.

Experience—Work-study or apprenticeship program

Special Skills and Personality Traits—Good combination of visualization, computer use, mathematical, and manual skills; attention to detail; able to keep focused but also to communicate well with coworkers

CAREER LADDER

```
┌─────────────────────────────┐
│      CAD/CAM Manager         │
└─────────────────────────────┘

┌─────────────────────────────┐
│  Senior or Lead CAM Technician │
└─────────────────────────────┘

┌─────────────────────────────┐
│      CAM Technician          │
└─────────────────────────────┘

┌─────────────────────────────┐
│      CAM Trainee             │
└─────────────────────────────┘
```

Position Description

Many of the routine tasks formerly done by assembly line workers are now done automatically by computer-controlled machines. Examples might include screwing or bolting components together, inserting parts onto a chassis or electronics motherboard, or painting or treating components.

The CAM Technician has two major areas of responsibility. The first involves all the steps needed for setting up a factory to manufacture a new product or component. The technician must determine exactly what parts are needed for the assembly, where they are located, and how they can be fed into the workstation where the assembly will take place. This involves detailed understanding of size, shape, measurements, and other characteristics of all the pieces involved. The necessary information is typically obtained from computer databases (manufacturing inventory and specifications data) as well as drawings and diagrams.

Once the information has been gathered, the machines, which can range from relatively simple automated lathes to sophisticated robots, must be given the precise instructions needed to perform the assembly operations. The machines must be tested and the resulting products carefully analyzed

to make sure they are all "within spec"—with everything having a position or dimensions that are close enough to those specified in the engineering drawings.

The other part of the CAM Technician's job involves the continuing monitoring and adjustment of the machinery once regular production has begun. This can involve both programming and good old fashioned mechanical tinkering.

Salaries

Individuals can often start at an entry-level or apprentice salary scale around $20,000. Satisfactory work experience results in step increases in pay. Senior or supervisory status brings the highest pay.

Employment Prospects

While many older large-scale manufacturing industries have been on a long decline in the United States and have gone overseas, domestic manufacturing has been able to compete mainly by "working smarter" and using technology to make workers more and more productive. CAM is a key part of this technology for everything from automobiles to computer components. There is thus a strong demand for qualified CAM Technicians, tempered by a currently stagnant economy.

Advancement Prospects

There are several ways to advance. Experience and supervisory duties can lead to higher pay grades with the individual's current employer, with an eventual move to becoming a department manager. Gaining specialized skills in high demand can bring higher pay. Pursuing engineering courses can lead to moving from technician to full-fledged engineer status.

Education and Training

Individuals with a high school diploma who can get into an apprenticeship program can get entry-level jobs, but a two-year college degree is more common, with basic courses in the different fields of engineering (electrical, mechanical, hydraulic, etc.), mathematics (particularly geometry), computer operations, and drafting. Adding business and communication courses can help prepare for later managerial duties and for working with engineers and other technicians.

Experience, Skills, and Personality Traits

Apprenticeship programs sponsored by state governments and/or employers can provide structured, well-rounded experience. The skills needed by CAM Technicians can be broken down into several categories:

- computer operations (use of databases, forms, and reports; manipulating drawings; programming specialized instructions for machines)
- visual (interpreting drawings, visualizing components in an assembly from various angles)
- mathematical (geometry, calculating dimensions and tolerances, statistics, analyzing test products and comparing to specifications)
- subject-related or specialized (familiarity with the symbols and terminology used for particular kinds of manufacturing, such as electronics or engine components)

The successful CAM Technician is likely to be a person who is comfortable with managing many details and with the need for high accuracy and consistency. Adaptability to new kinds of products and everchanging technology is also important. Good communication and interpersonal skills are helpful both for getting along well with colleagues and for moving into supervisory or managerial positions.

Cross-Training for CAM Technicians

Interests	Related Job Descriptions
computer-aided design	CAD Technician
managing the design process	CAD/CAM Manager
designing computer components	Computer Hardware Designer/Engineer

Unions and Associations

CAM Technicians in some industries (such as automotive) may belong to labor unions. CAM Technicians may join professional groups such as Computer-Aided Manufacturing International, or groups involved with specific industries such as automotive, aerospace, or electronics.

Tips for Entry

1. While in high school look for solid courses in algebra, geometry, statistics, and other kinds of mathematics. Also take classes in drafting, computer graphics, technical illustration, etc.
2. Look for community colleges that offer two-year degrees in drafting or related areas, with a strong emphasis on CAD and CAM skills.
3. Alternatively, check with your local state employment development department for information on apprenticeship programs that could prepare you for an entry-level position.

ROBOTICS ENGINEER

CAREER PROFILE

Duties: Designs robots (or robotic systems) for use in manufacturing, service, or research

Alternate Title (s): None

Salary Range: $50,000 to $80,000 or more

Employment Prospects: Good

Advancement Prospects: Good

Prerequisites:

Education or Training—Graduate computer science or engineering degree; courses in artificial intelligence, electronics, and mechanical engineering helpful

Experience—Work as laboratory assistant on artificial intelligence or robotics projects, research on vision and locomotion, etc.

Special Skills and Personality Traits—Comprehensive knowledge of engineering subsystems that make up robots; imagination and ability to visualize actions and procedures; mechanical skill; willing to work hard on projects that may have uncertain results

CAREER LADDER

```
┌─────────────────────────────┐
│   Lead Engineer, Robotics   │
└─────────────────────────────┘

┌─────────────────────────────┐
│  Senior Robotics Engineer   │
└─────────────────────────────┘

┌─────────────────────────────┐
│      Robotics Engineer      │
└─────────────────────────────┘

┌─────────────────────────────┐
│ Trainee, Robotics Engineering│
└─────────────────────────────┘
```

Position Description

Most people's image of robots owes a lot to science fiction—the witty C3PO or the cute R2D2 of *Star Wars,* for example. Today's real-world robots generally don't look much like people, however. They are usually squat boxes with arms and other attachments that do things such as mount parts on a chassis, assemble electronic circuits, or paint or weld machine parts. They are the tireless automated workers that have replaced people for many routine assembly line jobs. Most Robotics Engineers design such industrial robots, trying to adapt them to new tasks, making them more adaptable, or improving their ability to deal with unexpected problems such as a container or screws that's a little farther away than it should be.

Some Robotics Engineers work with what are called "service robots." These robots are more like R2D2 and his friends because they are not fixed to a platform in a factory. Rather, they travel around, doing things like delivering supplies in a factory or hospital, or even helping fight fires or negotiate with dangerous criminals. This kind of robotics is perhaps more exciting and challenging because the engineer's creation must move around in a real world filled with obstacles and unexpected situations.

Finally, a small number of Robotics Engineers specialize in the experimental research projects in university, government, or industrial laboratories. They apply the principles of artificial intelligence to give a robot a better chance of being able to solve problems. They also use "pattern recognition" techniques to enable a robot to recognize signs or even human faces. This kind of research may eventually lead to more humanlike robots.

Regardless of specialty, Robotics Engineers must combine knowledge of computer science and artificial intelligence, electronics, mechanical engineering, sensors, motors and locomotion, and many other fields. Robotics is perhaps the most comprehensive kind of engineering.

In addition to designing robots, Robotics Engineers must often help train or supervise robotics technicians. They must also work with factory managers and other users to determine how a given robot will be used and what it is expected to be able to do.

Salaries

Salaries for Robotics Engineers are comparable to that of other experienced engineers in electronics or other fields.

Top engineers who act as consultants or partners in start-up companies might make much more.

Employment Prospects

There has been a steady increase in the number of robots used in industry, and some growth in the use of service robots. While there may not be as much need for Robotics Engineers as for the more common kinds of engineering, the specialized nature of the field means there are likely to be about as many openings as there are graduates entering the field.

Demand for Robotics Engineers may suffer in a declining economy, because companies tend to not make major investments (such as in new robots) when the future is uncertain. On the other hand, rising labor costs could lead to more companies seeking to replace workers with robots.

Advancement Prospects

Besides the usual in-house advancement based on experience, Robotics Engineers can become consultants or partners in a start-up company that is planning a new kind of robot. Those willing to take the risk of failure have an opportunity to be very successful.

Education and Training

This field normally requires a graduate degree in engineering. Since there are few academic programs specifically in robotics, the student must try to choose courses wisely so as to gain a broad familiarity with computer-related subjects (such as artificial intelligence and programming), electronics and mechanical engineering, and specialties like vision, manipulation, and locomotion systems.

Experience, Skills, and Personality Traits

A student who seems well prepared may be offered a trainee position that will provide the needed hands-on experience. Student projects can help. The variety of skills that a Robotics Engineer is likely to call upon include problem solving, programming and system design, visualization of engineering possibilities, and mechanical aptitude. The successful individual is likely to have a personality that is adaptable yet focused, with a good measure of imagination.

Cross-Training for Robotics Engineers

Interests	Related Job Descriptions
creating programs that act intelligently	Artificial Intelligence Programmer
setting up manufacturing processes	CAM Technician

Unions and Associations

Robotics Engineers can belong to computer science and engineering groups such as the Institute of Electrical and Electronics Engineers (IEEE), the American Association for Artificial Intelligence, various AI and robotics special interest groups, and robotics industry groups such as the International Service Robot Association.

Tips for Entry

1. There are actually some neat, fairly inexpensive kits that you can use to build and program simple robots that can do things like travel around a room without getting stuck. That plus a couple of books can give a high school student a chance to see if he or she is interested in robotics. Going to one of the "robot rodeo" contests held at some universities would also combine fun and education.

2. Another way to learn or practice robot programming is to try some of the games or educational programs (some freely available on the Internet) that create "simulated robots" that move around a world depicted on the computer screen.

3. In undergraduate college, the best preparation for robotics is probably to become the best possible all-around engineer, learning about computers, electronics, and mechanical systems.

4. For graduate work, it's important to look into several of the schools that have advanced robotics research, such as Stanford, Caltech, or MIT. This is especially true if you want to go into research rather than industrial applications.

ROBOTICS TECHNICIAN

CAREER PROFILE

Duties: Sets up, "trains," maintains, and repairs industrial robots and automated machinery

Alternate Title(s): None

Salary Range: $30,000 to $45,000

Employment Prospects: Fair

Advancement Prospects: Fair

Prerequisites:

Education or Training—Two-year certificate in electronics technology or related fields

Experience—Factory automation experience; apprenticeship may be available

Special Skills and Personality Traits—Analytical and problem-solving skills; ability to read and interpret specifications and diagrams; understanding of a variety of mechanical systems; physical dexterity; willingness to "get one's hands dirty"

CAREER LADDER

```
┌─────────────────────────────────────┐
│  Supervisor or Team Leader, Robotics │
└─────────────────────────────────────┘

┌─────────────────────────────────────┐
│      Senior Robotics Technician      │
└─────────────────────────────────────┘

┌─────────────────────────────────────┐
│         Robotics Technician          │
└─────────────────────────────────────┘

┌─────────────────────────────────────┐
│   Entry-Level or Trainee Technician  │
└─────────────────────────────────────┘
```

Position Description

Many people have an image of factory workers standing next to an assembly line repetitively turning bolts or sticking parts into a car as it goes by. While there are still routine assembly jobs like this in many developing countries, factories in industrialized countries like the United States use a high degree of automation. Instead of the workers building the car or other product directly, the workers tend machines, often robots, that do the actual assembly. The person who is responsible for setting up a robot properly and keeping it running is the Robotics Technician.

Industrial robots are much more flexible than the automated or "numerically controlled" machinery serviced by CAM technicians, although there is some overlap. The key difference is that robots can be programmed to perform a much greater variety of actions, and can use their arms and grasping "hands" to handle objects rather than having the objects inserted directly into the machine.

The Robotics Technician can work in several different settings:

- helping robotics engineers in a research laboratory design or test new robots
- programming robots in a factory to perform new tasks

- periodically servicing the various systems (electronic, electromechanical, hydraulic, etc.) that make up the robot
- diagnosing and fixing the problem when a robot has broken down on the job

Unlike a person who does only one kind of work (such as an electrician or pipe fitter), a Robotics Technician must understand and know how to work with every kind of system in a robot. He or she is the "general practitioner" doctor for these machines.

The working conditions for a Robotics Technician can range from a sterile "clean room" in a computer assembly plant to a noisy, hot, potentially dangerous factory. While robots share much of their basic "anatomy," their different sizes, tasks, and work settings will affect the kinds of problems a technician must deal with. He or she must therefore be adaptable.

Salaries

Entry-level or trainee Technicians start a bit over $25,000. Experience, specialized skills, and managerial skills bring higher salaries.

Employment Prospects

While not growing as fast as areas such as programming and systems analysis, there is a steady demand for Robotics Technicians as factories continue to transition from human and semi-automated assembly techniques to the use of robots.

Advancement Prospects

Robotics Technicians working in factories can gain seniority and supervisory (or team leader) status. Robotics Technicians can also gain higher pay as manufacturer representatives or trainers for companies that make robotic equipment.

Education and Training

The basic requirement is a two-year college or vocational school certificate in electronics technology or a related field. The individual should be sure to take courses that give a solid grasp of mathematics, drafting, basic engineering principles (electronic, electromechanical, hydraulic, sensors, etc.). A few college programs offer a specialization or introductory course in robotics.

Experience, Skills, and Personality Traits

In addition to the school workshop, internship or apprenticeship programs can offer experience with robotics technology.

The individual needs a mix of intellectual (mathematics, analysis, problem-solving), communication (interpreting terminology and diagrams), and mechanical skills (understanding mechanical systems, good hand-eye coordination and dexterity).

An individual whose personality is focused yet adaptable will do best in this position. Individuals who want to move toward management should like to work with people and have good personal communication skills.

Cross-Training for Robotics Technicians

Interests	Related Job Descriptions
designing robots	Robotics Engineer; Artificial Intelligence Programmer
controlling automated machinery	CAM Technician
drafting	CAD Technician

Unions and Associations

Robotics Technicians (especially those who are working toward an engineering career) can join engineering groups such as the Institute of Electrical and Electronics Engineers (IEEE), the American Association for Artificial Intelligence, various AI and robotics special interest groups, and robotics industry groups such as the International Service Robot Association.

Tips for Entry

1. In high school, look for opportunities to work with robot-type machinery such as building kits or entering a science fair. Make sure you take courses in math, physics, and drafting if available.
2. In college, tell your adviser that you are specifically interested in becoming a Robotics Technician, and get his or her help to plan a curriculum that covers all the necessary skills, not just what is required for the electronics technology certificate. You may be able to obtain helpful material from one of the organizations listed above.
3. Meet with recruiters on campus if possible. Read trade journals to find more job leads.

COMPUTER INDUSTRY SPECIALISTS

RETAIL CLERK, COMPUTER PRODUCTS

CAREER PROFILE

Duties: Demonstrates computer systems in a store and helps customers make purchases

Alternate Title(s): Salesperson; Sales Clerk

Salary Range: $18,000 to $25,000

Employment Prospects: Fair

Advancement Prospects: Good

Prerequisites:
   Education or Training—High school diploma
   Experience—Retail sales experience
   Special Skills and Personality Traits—Basic computer skills; familiarity with computer terminology; attention to details; good communication skills; pleasant personality

CAREER LADDER

```
┌─────────────────────────────────────┐
│   Computer Store Owner or Manager    │
└─────────────────────────────────────┘

┌─────────────────────────────────────┐
│   Assistant Manager, Computer Store  │
└─────────────────────────────────────┘

┌─────────────────────────────────────┐
│  Retail Clerk, Computer Products     │
└─────────────────────────────────────┘

┌─────────────────────────────────────┐
│   Trainee or Stock Assistant,        │
│       Computer Products              │
└─────────────────────────────────────┘
```

Position Description

Computer stores (either chain or independent) sell desktop and laptop computer systems, software, and various accessories such as printers, modems, and removable storage drives. The Retail Clerk is the person who deals directly with customers in the store. Some typical duties include:

- recommending appropriate computer systems, accessories, or software to fit a customer's needs
- demonstrating computer systems and software
- answering questions about products
- filling out the paperwork and completing transactions
- providing basic after-sale support to customers
- setting up demonstration computers and stocking the shelves with software or other products

The Retail Clerk must be able to keep track of the features of the systems and products the store sells, as well as store policies, prices, and payment terms. He or she must have the basic skills needed to hook up computers, monitors, printers, and other equipment. The Clerk must have enough familiarity with the operating system and major software packages to demonstrates the system to customers and to answer questions such as:

- I have a computer with 128 MB of RAM (Random Access Memory). Is that enough to run this software?
- About how many sheets of text can I print with one of these printer cartridges?
- What is the difference between these two kinds of laptop screen displays?
- Does that system have everything I need to get on the Internet?

In addition to mastering technical details, the Retail Clerk must be polite and helpful, with good communication skills. A customer who feels that he or she is being treated well is more likely to buy products at that store and to recommend it to others.

Salaries

Retail Clerk is an entry-level job that generally starts at a low salary. Large companies tend to offer some additional benefits. Individuals may start as trainees at the lowest pay level and then move up after a few months.

Employment Prospects

Recent years have seen intense price competition where "entry-level" computer systems are being sold for $500 or less. In addition to chain stores, many computer manufacturers are now selling systems directly to customers by phone or over the Internet. Software is also being sold at discount prices by large chains and on-line. The result has been a steep decline in "mom and pop," or small, local, independent computer stores. These trends are limiting employment prospects for retail computer store clerks. Clerks in large chains (such as Circuit City) generally do routine work without much opportunity for initiative.

Advancement Prospects

A knowledgeable and hardworking clerk may become the store's informal "computer guru," and a possible candidate for assistant manager or eventually, store manager. Retail Clerk experience can also be a stepping-stone to a better paid job as a sales or technical support representative who works more extensively with customers.

Education and Training

There are few formal requirements, although employers generally want a high school diploma as evidence of basic literacy. Computer-related courses are helpful, of course, as well as introductory business or economics courses.

Experience, Skills, and Personality Traits

Most employers prefer to hire people who have some retail sales experience, although not necessarily in a computer store. Basic computer skills and understanding of computer terminology are also desirable, although stores are often willing to train individuals who seem to be intelligent and quick learners.

Because the Retail Clerk works with people more than with machines, an outgoing personality, the ability to listen and speak clearly, and reasonable grooming are all important.

Cross-Training for Retail Clerks

Interests	Related Job Descriptions
helping customers solve computer problems	Technical Support Representative
working extensively with customers	Sales Representative, Computer Products
managing a computer store	Computer Store Owner/ Manager
teaching people how to use computers	Trainer, Computer Software

Unions and Associations

Retail Clerks in larger stores or chains may belong to clerical or retail clerks' unions.

Tips for Entry

1. Look for part-time or summer jobs where you can work in a store and learn how to deal with customers. (It doesn't have to be a computer store.)
2. Visit some computer stores and observe how merchandise is displayed. Ask clerks some questions. Do they seem to be well organized and knowledgeable?
3. If you don't know much about computers, take introductory courses in computers programming, software, or hardware technology.
4. If you have experience working as a Retail Clerk and want to move forward with your career, look for community college programs in either computer technology (if you want to go into technical support) or business and management (if you want to become a store manager).

SYSTEMS INTEGRATOR

CAREER PROFILE

Duties: Combines computer hardware and software from a variety of manufacturers to create the best possible system for a client's needs

Alternate Title(s): Computer Systems Engineer; Manufacturer's Representative

Salary Range: $28,000 to $50,000

Employment Prospects: Fair

Advancement Prospects: Fair to Good

Prerequisites:

Education or Training—Undergraduate degree with emphasis in computer-related and business courses; graduate degree in computer science preferred for specialized areas such as scientific computing

Experience—Experience in installing and configuring computer hardware and software, perhaps in a computer store or as an office's informal "computer expert"

Special Skills and Personality Traits—Problem solving; attention to detail; good communication skills

CAREER LADDER

```
┌─────────────────────────────┐
│      Systems Engineer       │
└─────────────────────────────┘

┌─────────────────────────────┐
│     Systems Integrator      │
└─────────────────────────────┘

┌─────────────────────────────┐
│     Technical Assistant     │
└─────────────────────────────┘
```

Position Description

Many Systems Integrators work for manufacturers of computer equipment or for agencies that do consulting. Others work for a large corporation's information systems department, providing consulting to other departments on their information processing needs.

When an organization or department needs more computer resources, it will often call for consultation. The Systems Integrator typically takes these steps:

- visits the client's site and determines what computer resources (PCs, peripherals, networking, software, etc.) are needed, both for now and to accommodate planned growth
- determines what brands, models, or versions are needed to create a system whose parts will all work together
- recommends specific purchases; may include preparing a bid (if the consultant's agency is competing for a contract)
- oversees the installation of the new system, fixing the inevitable problems and often helping to train workers in its operation
- monitors the performance of the system and provides optimization or customization as needed

A Systems Integrator who works for a systems vendor will normally be provided with an extensive database of technical specifications and problem fixes for all the products involved. Such a consultant will normally be limited to recommending only products sold by the vendor. An independent Systems Integrator will have to create his or her own database but will have greater flexibility in recommending products.

Salaries

Salaries for Systems Integrators depend on who they work for and the scope of their duties. A Systems Integrator who is basically a sales representative with knowledge of a few basic configurations is at the low end of the scale. At the other end of the scale is a Systems Integrator who has extensive knowledge of many products and who functions more as a systems consultant or systems analyst.

Employment Prospects

Demand for simple system configuration is being reduced by the fact that many computer vendors now sell systems that have a complete, well-matched set of components previously sold separately (such as sound and video cards, modems, etc.). Several large mail-order firms allow users to specify exactly what equipment they want and order it directly. Of course some systems integration work is still done by personnel in computer stores and by manufacturers, especially in putting together a package for a whole business or department.

Demand for Systems Integrators with advanced skills for work in-house in corporate information systems departments is stronger. While it is somewhat harder to establish oneself as an independent consultant, they are also in demand, particularly if they have specialized knowledge (such as networking).

Advancement Prospects

Advancement for the Systems Integrator is best achieved by working toward becoming a full-fledged systems analyst (if working in-house) or systems consultant (if working as a contractor).

Education and Training

An undergraduate degree with a major in computer science or information processing and a minor in business is the basic foundation for entry into this field, although trade school or community college may be sufficient.

Experience, Skills, and Personality Traits

A couple of years of experience installing or customizing computer hardware and software is preferred. Some vendors will train candidates who look like they have a solid background.

The most important skills are analysis, problem solving, mastery of detail, and ability to communicate with vendors and clients. While the position is technically focused and demands a disciplined, organized personality, good social skills are also important. Since computer technology and software features are constantly changing, the Systems Integrator must be adaptable and comfortable with the idea of continual learning.

Cross-Training for Systems Integrators

Skills or Interests	Related Job Descriptions
designing complex systems	Systems Analyst; Systems Consultant
sales	Sales Representative (Computer Products and Services)

Unions and Associations

Systems Integrators do not normally belong to a labor union. They may belong to a variety of industry associations or consultant organizations, some of which are listed in Appendix 2, parts 2 and 3.

Tips for Entry

1. Take courses in major operating systems such as Windows XP or Linux, and familiarize yourself with the use of setup, configuration, and batch or script files.
2. If you have a PC, learn everything about what makes it tick.
3. Consider starting as a salesperson in a computer store to gain some experience dealing with customers and installing or demonstrating systems.
4. Look for opportunities for volunteer work or internship with a nonprofit organization or school that needs help setting up their computer system.
5. Subscribe to industry periodicals such as *PC Magazine* and *Info World.*

COMPUTER STORE OWNER OR MANAGER

CAREER PROFILE

Duties: Runs a retail computer hardware or software store; makes stocking decisions; does advertising and promotion; keeps accounts; trains and supervises clerks, technicians, or other employees

Alternate Title(s): None

Salary Range: $35,000 to $50,000 (managers)

Employment Prospects: Fair

Advancement Prospect: Fair

Prerequisites:

Education or Training—Community or four-year college recommended with basic computer and business-related courses

Experience—Retail sales or technical support

Special Skills and Personality Traits—Marketing; accounting; managing stock; training and supervising employees; needs to be an energetic risk taker (particularly for independents) but also well organized

CAREER LADDER

```
┌─────────────────────────────────────────┐
│   Computer Store Manager (or Owner)      │
└─────────────────────────────────────────┘

┌─────────────────────────────────────────┐
│      Assistant Manager or Buyer          │
└─────────────────────────────────────────┘

┌─────────────────────────────────────────┐
│      Retail Clerk, Computer Store        │
└─────────────────────────────────────────┘
```

Position Description

Computer stores come in a variety of sizes and types. There are nationwide chain computer stores that offer mainly software and accessories, and others that stock a selection of both computer systems and software. General consumer electronics or office supply chains may have computers and software in one of their departments, with a department Manager. There are also independently owned local stores that put together computers from generic components and offer a limited selection of software. Towns too small to have chain stores may have local stores that provide everything—computers, system integration, software, consulting, and repairs. In independent stores the Owner and Manager are generally the same person.

Regardless of the kind of store, the Manager is the person responsible for making decisions about its operation and for training and supervising employees. The Manager, perhaps with the assistance of a buyer, must select what brands of equipment or software to stock. This involves dealing with vendors or distributors and keeping track of such things as release dates for computer games or the latest version for business software, and monitoring sales so that the most popular products are always in stock. The Manager

or buyer must also be aware of special promotions or offers and be able to negotiate for the best wholesale price.

Once stock is obtained, determining the best retail price is also a challenge. Prices must be low enough to be competitive, and competitors are always changing their own prices. Pricing too low means the store won't be able to meet its expenses and make a profit.

For independent stores, decisions must also be made about advertising—how much, what kind, and in what medium, print or broadcast. Having a website is also an increasingly popular option.

Managers in chain stores make fewer of these decisions because the parent company often arranges for distribution and even pricing, and sets other policies. The Manager concentrates on meeting sales goals. Owner-Managers must take full responsibility and accept the risk of business failure in exchange for the chance to keep more of the profits.

Hiring, training, and supervision are essential parts of the Store Manager's work. A rude sales clerk or one who doesn't know details about products can drive customers away from the store. Because sales clerks have poorly paid entry-level jobs, turnover tends to be high. Motivating employees to take a genuine interest in their work can be difficult.

Salaries

Store Managers in chains may make salaries up to approximately the level of corporate middle managers. Owner-managers may make little profit until the store is established, and have to put their own money at risk. A successful Owner may eventually do better than his or her corporate counterpart.

Employment Prospects

Sales of computers and software over the Internet are putting great pressure on traditional storefront businesses. Together with the big chains and their ability to slash prices, these trends have driven many small, independently owned computer or software stores out of business.

Employment prospects are still fairly good with the chains, due to high turnover. The best prospects for Owner-Managers are in remote areas that have enough people to support a small store but not enough to attract a chain, or for businesses that can create "added value" by marketing to particular kinds of customers (such as schools) and offering training, systems integration, and superior support.

Advancement Prospects

Advancement possibilities in chains are limited, since Store Manager is already on the top rung within the store. An individual who makes the right contacts may be able to move from Store Manager to a position at the parent corporation's headquarters.

Owner/Managers of local stores tend to advance by increasing their store's sales, creating new lines of business (such as service and repair or network consulting), or by being able to open branch stores in other communities.

Education and Training

Chains generally require that Store Managers have a four-year college degree in a business-related field with courses in retail, marketing, and management. Independents who have the money can go into business without any formal qualifications, but they should seek training or help if they don't have small business experience or sufficient technical knowledge.

Experience, Skills, and Personality Traits

Most Manager candidates will have worked for a few years as a retail clerk, support representative, or assistant manager. Mastery of general computer hardware and software skills is important, although an individual who is highly motivated can learn much of this on the job. Understanding of the computer hardware and software industry market is essential and should be combined with general knowledge of marketing, inventory, and bookkeeping techniques. The "people side" of the job requires the ability to select, train, supervise and motivate employees, many of whom will be at entry level and with limited skills.

Cross-Training for Computer Store Managers/Owners

Interests	Related Job Descriptions
representing hardware or software manufacturers	Sales Representative, Computer Products
advertising	Advertising Account Executive; Advertising Manager
matching computer systems to users' needs	Systems Integrator

Unions and Associations

Independent store owners often belong to local chambers of commerce and small business associations. Joining groups devoted to marketing, management, and other business activities can be helpful for making contacts and picking up useful tips.

Tips for Entry

1. Get some retail experience, perhaps through a part-time job at a chain computer store. On the job, look for opportunities to help with a variety of tasks such as software buying, inventory, or customer support.
2. If there is an independently owned local computer store in your area, ask the owner if he or she needs some part-time help.
3. In high school, take introductory business-related courses. At community or four-year college, consider a major in marketing or retail management.
4 If you are considering starting a computer store, try to make sure there are enough potential customers and not too much competition. Federal and state small business agencies can provide much helpful information.

SALES REPRESENTATIVE, COMPUTER PRODUCTS

CAREER PROFILE

Duties: Deals with businesses or other organizations that want to buy a vendor's computer hardware or software product; promotes the product line; helps customers with selection, configuration, and support

Alternate Title(s): Customer Account Executive

Salary Range: $45,000 to $75,000 or more

Employment Prospects: Good

Advancement Prospects: Good

Prerequisites:

    Education or Training—College degree with business-related courses preferred

    Experience—Sales or customer support experience

    Special Skills and Personality Traits—Mastery of technical details; understanding of business needs; outgoing personality; ability to inspire confidence; adaptability

CAREER LADDER

> Sales Manager, Computer Products

> Sales Representative, Computer Products

> Sales Assistant, Computer Products

Position Description

Individuals and families often buy a computer system or software at a local store. Large businesses, schools, and government agencies, however, must buy hundreds or even thousands of systems at a time or license software to be provided to users on a network. The computer hardware and software manufacturers or vendors need to establish long-term relationships with the large customers who are so important to their success. The key person in establishing and maintaining such customer relationships is the Sales Representative.

The Sales Representative works with "leads" or inquiries that the vendor has received through advertising, trade shows, or other sources. He or she also develops contacts through recommendations from satisfied customers. After contacting a prospective customer, the Sales Representative asks questions about that person's business or organization. Based on the answers, the representative can recommend the type or model of hardware or software that will best satisfy the customer's needs. Since the typical computing needs of a school, a retail store chain, an accounting firm, and a factory will all be quite different, representatives tend to specialize in working with customers in a particular kind

of business or industry. This enables them to gain more detailed knowledge of how particular kinds of customers use their computers and software.

The Sales Representative must be familiar with the details of the vendor's products, how they work with other products, and how businesses use them. He or she must also keep track of competing products, understand their advantages and disadvantages, and understand the strategy the vendor has developed for convincing customers that its product is better. Within the pricing guidelines set by the vendor, the Sales Representative tries to come up with the most attractive discount, terms of payment, delivery schedule, and service contract.

In addition to mastering all these details, the representative must of course have strong selling skills. He or she must be able to identify with the customer's needs and problems and reassure the customer that the vendor's products are the best possible and most attractively priced solution, and that the company will offer reliable service and support.

Sometimes the representative will go to the customer's place of business and demonstrate and introduce the equipment or software to the manager or executive who will make the purchase decision. He or she will supply the information needed for purchase recommendations or bids. After the sale, the representative often provides introductory training and support to get users up to speed.

The work of a Sales Representative can be hectic and often requires travel to customer sites and trade shows. The work week can be considerably longer than the standard 40 hours. Because there are always more opportunities than time, the successful representative learns how to prioritize and balance the maintenance of existing customers with the pursuit of new contacts.

Salaries

Sales Representatives can be paid in a variety of ways. One common package is a base salary plus a bonus based on meeting or exceeding a sales quota. Some Representatives may work entirely on salary, while others are paid on commission (a percentage of the value of sales made). Because pay is often tied to sales success, annual pay can range from low to spectacular depending on sales opportunities and ability.

Employment Prospects

Since late 2000 the computer industry, along with the economy as a whole, has suffered from a slowdown, leading in turn to businesses being more reluctant to invest heavily in computer equipment and software. While the economy will eventually recover, it is unlikely that the growth in "generic" computer products will return to previous levels. Rather, businesses (and thus prospective Sales Representatives) need to look for specific application areas where demand is strong and sustained growth seems likely. Such areas might include health care, biotech, security systems, and advanced telecommunications and networking.

Advancement Prospects

A Sales Representative who posts good sales totals and shows good leadership skills can become a branch or district manager in charge of all salespeople for a vendor in a particular area or for a particular industry. Becoming an independent sales or marketing consultant is also a possibility.

Education and Training

Most large vendors require a college degree in a computer-related field, particularly if the equipment or software to be sold is highly technical or specialized. Many manufacturers conduct special training courses for Representatives.

Experience, Skills, and Personality Traits

Employers are looking for sales experience and ability together with adequate technical knowledge. Sales work rewards an outgoing personality and the ability to understand people's needs and concerns. Because the computer industry changes at such a rapid pace, adaptability and the ability to learn new material quickly are also important.

Cross-Training for Sales Representatives

Skills or Interests	Related Job Descriptions
selling products in a store	Retail Clerk, Computer Products
advertising	Advertising Account Executive; Advertising Manager
finding customers	Marketing Specialist

Unions and Associations

Sales Representatives can join sales or marketing organizations to compare notes and learn about new sales or promotional techniques.

Tips for Entry

1. Consider whether you like both the technical side of computing *and* sales work. You'll need both to succeed in this field.
2. While in school, try to combine a technical degree program with good introductory courses in marketing, retail sales, and management. Also look for opportunities to gain sales experience in computers or electronics, as in a retail clerk position in a computer store (though any sales experience is helpful).
3. Read industry journals and websites to find hardware and software vendors that are reported to be doing well, or that are about to introduce a new product line. These are the most likely to be looking for more Sales Representatives, and may be willing to provide training for entry-level employees. Your research will also prepare you to answer interview questions in a way that shows your knowledge and interest in the business.

SALES MANAGER, COMPUTER PRODUCTS

CAREER PROFILE

Duties: Supervises the sales operation for a computer product manufacturer or vendor; trains and develops sales representatives; supports representatives by running promotions and gathering sales leads

Alternate Title(s): District Sales Manager; Regional Sales Manager; National Sales Manager; Product Manager

Salary Range: $50,000 to $100,000

Employment Prospects: Good

Advancement Prospects: Fair

Prerequisites:

Education or Training—Four-year technical degree plus business courses; MBA helpful for higher positions

Experience—Several years of sales or marketing experience

Special Skills and Personality Traits—Ability to extract key information from details; prioritization scheduling; supervision and motivation/leadership skills; personal drive and energy

CAREER LADDER

```
┌─────────────────────────────────┐
│      National Sales Manager     │
└─────────────────────────────────┘

┌─────────────────────────────────┐
│      Regional Sales Manager     │
└─────────────────────────────────┘

┌─────────────────────────────────┐
│   District (Local) Sales Manager │
└─────────────────────────────────┘

┌─────────────────────────────────┐
│      Assistant Sales Manager    │
└─────────────────────────────────┘
```

Position Description

Nothing stands still in the highly competitive computer industry. Manufacturers of computer systems, peripheral devices, and software must continually reach out to potential customers while building long-term relationships with existing customers. Competitors are always coming out with new products and launching their advertising campaigns, so companies must continually "resell" the advantages of their own products.

The person who coordinates sales operations is the Sales Manager. Depending on the size of the company and the complexity of its product line, the Sales Manager may be assigned a particular product (or kind of product), a geographic area, or a particular kind of customer (such as educational institutions). His or her duties include:

- getting reports from marketers that identify areas where there are potential customers
- being briefed on the details of new or upcoming products or new models or releases of existing products
- meeting with the sales representatives and giving them both information and motivation

- bringing new sales representatives up to speed and continuing the training of existing ones
- coordinating the gathering of sales leads (potential customers) from advertising campaigns, trade shows, and other sources
- giving leads to sales representatives, and establishing sales targets or quotas
- monitoring the performance of representatives and doing periodic evaluations

Sales Managers are nearly always busy, but the approach of a new product "launch" or trade show brings additional pressure as the company seeks to take maximum advantage of publicity.

Salaries

Sales Managers in small companies that produce only one basic product will be at the low end of the salary scale. In larger companies there will be several layers of sales management with the local, regional, and national Sales Managers at different salary levels.

Employment Prospects

Contraction and mergers in the computer industry have reduced the growth in Sales Manager positions. In order to be competitive, candidates need strong sales experience and/or knowledge of specialized markets (such as biotech, medicine, or communications and networking). Beyond that, building a strong track record in sales (together with some patience) is the best route to success.

Advancement Prospects

As with sales representatives, the "bottom line"—total sales—is the most important factor in a Sales Manager's career. Success at the local level can lead to promotion to regional or national Sales Manager, or a "jump" to another, larger company.

Education and Training

Sales Managers generally need a four-year degree in a computer-related field plus strong preparation through business-related courses. For the upper rungs of the sales management ladder, employers often prefer individuals who have both a technical degree and an MBA. Individuals who have an entry-level position in sales management often continue their education at night or on-line to gain the qualifications for higher positions.

Experience, Skills, and Personality Traits

Sales Managers usually have several years of experience in sales, marketing, or a related field. The Sales Manager must have the ability to keep up with the many reports coming from marketing specialists and sales representatives, identifying the key facts and conclusions. He or she must be able to train, supervise, and motivate sales representatives and must work closely with the company's marketing or advertising managers. The successful individual is usually an outgoing personality with drive and personal energy, but also self-discipline and the ability to focus on details without losing track of the "big picture."

Cross-Training for Sales Managers

Interests	Related Job Descriptions
selling or cultivating customers	Sales Representative
creating sales campaigns	Advertising Manager

Unions and Associations

Sales Managers can belong to sales, marketing, or general management organizations. If the manager specializes in sales to a particular industry, he or she may also join trade organizations for that industry.

Tips for Energy

1. Are you interested in both selling and managing people? You will need both to be a successful Sales Manager.
2. Get sales experience as soon as possible, whether in a store or as a sales representative or sales trainee.
3. In college, work toward a technical degree (computer science or information systems) but include basic courses in marketing, retail sales, and business management.
4. Find a specialized area in which you have strong interest and that is likely to be in continued high demand. Try to select positions that will add to your knowledge and experience in that area, but do not focus so narrowly that you miss out on other opportunities.
5. Once you have an entry-level job, try to find time to work toward getting an MBA. It won't be easy to find time, but your track record plus that degree can open many doors.

ADVERTISING ACCOUNT EXECUTIVE OR MANAGER, COMPUTER PRODUCTS AND SERVICES

CAREER PROFILE

Duties: Creates and manages advertising campaigns for an advertising agency's client, or within a company's advertising department

Alternate Title(s): Account Representative; Advertising Manager

Salary Range: $35,000 to $80,000

Employment Prospects: Fair

Advancement Prospects: Good

Prerequisites:

    Education or Training—Four-year degree in business-related field plus computer-related courses

    Experience—Work as advertising assistant, designer, or writer

    Special Skills and Personality Traits—Imagination; knowledge of marketing and industry practices; writing and communication skills; combination of drive and discipline

CAREER LADDER

```
┌─────────────────────────────────────┐
│   Advertising Manager (in-house)     │
└─────────────────────────────────────┘

┌─────────────────────────────────────┐
│ Senior Account Executive (for agency)│
└─────────────────────────────────────┘

┌─────────────────────────────────────┐
│        Account Executive             │
└─────────────────────────────────────┘

┌─────────────────────────────────────┐
│        Advertising Trainee           │
└─────────────────────────────────────┘
```

Position Description

The complexity of the computer industry and its very competitive nature create a tremendous ongoing need for companies to keep customers (or potential customers) informed about products, and to persuade people to buy them. Some companies call on the services of an advertising agency to mastermind their advertising campaigns. The person assigned by the agency for this task is called an Account Executive.

Companies may also have an in-house Advertising Manager to coordinate advertising activities. Often both positions exist, with the Account Executive designing and overseeing advertising campaigns while the Advertising Manager coordinates in-house efforts. Since the duties of these positions overlap so much, they are discussed together here.

An advertising campaign generally begins with marketing or consumer research that uses surveys, promotions, or test campaigns to attempt to identify the kinds of people most likely to want to buy a particular product. The Account Executive, working with marketing specialists and advertising designers, then comes up with a theme for the advertising campaign. For example, if a company has created a handheld computer the size of a small notebook that travelers can use to access their e-mail and manage their contacts, the theme might be something like "Your Pocket Office" or "The Great Communicator."

In addition to the theme, the advertising team identifies the key points the advertising will try to get across such as the portability and ease of use of the product and that this product can connect in so many ways (by regular phone lines, radio, or cell phone) that the user will never be out of touch with his or her office.

The Account Executive and the advertising team must decide which media and advertising methods to use, and how much to spend on each. (The final budget decision is usually made by the Advertising Manager.)

Some of the possibilities include:

- print ads in the trade press (computer or business magazines)
- newspaper and general magazine ads
- TV and radio commercials
- creating a website (or enhancing the advertising on an existing one)
- a booth at a trade show, and related activities (such as demonstrations or parties)
- press conferences and product announcements
- designing slogans and visual design themes or logos

Throughout the process, the Account Executive and Advertising Manager will need to keep in touch with marketing specialists and researchers and media relations experts (who deal with reporters and product reviewers). The campaign must also be kept within budget.

A full-blown advertising campaign is a major investment. The Account Executive must be able to show a company's executives that a campaign is getting results, either directly in sales or indirectly in terms of favorable public awareness of the company and product. The long-term success is measured in terms of the company's market share, or the proportion of all users of a particular kind of product that use the company's product.

An Account Executive may work on only one large campaign for a big company, or may work on several smaller campaigns, perhaps researching one, launching another, and evaluating the results of a third. The pressure can be intense, and the best-designed campaign can get into trouble if a product ships late or turns out to have significant "bugs," or if a competing product with impressive features hits the market.

Advertising Managers may have a somewhat more stable situation, since they work only for one company and can be more familiar with that company and have better long-term working relationship. But this doesn't mean there is no pressure, and the Advertising Manager may have to keep the agency and Account Executive focused and on budget.

People in the advertising field must keep in touch with changes in how the various media are used. In particular, the growing corporate presence on the Internet means that familiarity with tools for advertising and marketing on the World Wide Web is increasingly required.

Salaries

At entry level, a trainee or account assistant may make about $35,000. As an individual gains experience and takes full charge of campaigns, salaries can rise into the $50,000 to $60,000 range. "Hot-shot" executives with big accounts can make considerably more.

Employment Prospects

Advertising is an exciting field that attracts many applicants, so competition for entry-level jobs is high. Applicants who have specialized industry knowledge and technical knowl-

edge (such as Internet site development) have an edge. Given the relative stagnation of the "core" computer industry in the 2000–03 period, it might be a good idea to look "outside the box" for opportunities involving other technologies (such as wireless communications) or other industries (such as health care or security.)

Advancement Prospects

Prospects are excellent for motivated individuals with the right skills and a good track record. In an agency, Account Executives advance by taking on bigger campaigns successfully, and by building long-term relationships with clients. In-house Advertising Managers can move up the management ladder (such as from regional to national level) or can get a position at a larger company.

Education and Training

A four-year degree with a business major is preferred, but liberal arts graduates with good communication skills and some business knowledge can also get entry-level jobs.

Experience, Skills, and Personality Traits

Experience as an ad designer, writer, or advertising assistant is very helpful. Writing skills are essential, because the Account Executive will be creating proposals that must favorably impress the client. Personal communication skills are equally important, because advertising is a team effort and the Account Executive must work both with team members and the executives of the client company, who will often ask tough questions about a campaign and its potential for success. Other necessary skills include familiarity with the use of different media (print, broadcast, or Internet) and with the way reporters and reviewers cover the industry.

A confident, outgoing, even driven personality that thrives on intensity is necessary to reach the top on this field. A mix of characteristics, such as self-discipline, focus, and pacing is also important.

Cross-Training for Account Executives or Advertising Managers

Skills or Interests	Related Job Descriptions
dealing with the media	Media Specialist, Computer Products and Services
designing Web advertising	Webpage Designer; Web Developer
doing market research	Marketing Specialist, Computer Products and Services

Unions and Associations

Advertising Managers and Account Representatives can join many advertising-related organizations. Joining industry or trade groups can also be a useful way to keep in touch with product trends.

Tips for Entry

1. While in high school, look for opportunities to work with advertisers, such as a school paper or yearbook.
2. For college, look for a business curriculum that is strong in courses in marketing and advertising. Don't neglect courses in writing, communications, and media.
3. Learn about the computer industry by reading the trade press and reading books or taking courses that cover major sectors of the industry, such as databases, networking, and multimedia.
4. When looking for an entry-level job or internship at an agency, look for agencies that have high-tech clients whose campaigns may need skills you possess, such as Internet-based advertising.

MARKETING SPECIALIST, COMPUTER PRODUCTS AND SERVICES

CAREER PROFILE

Duties: Does research to help determine the marketing opportunities for a computer product or service; helps design and prepare marketing campaigns and promotions

Alternate Title(s): Product Manager; Marketing Manager; Marketing Researcher

Salary Range: $35,000 to $80,000 (managers)

Employment Prospects: Fair

Advancement Prospects: Good

Prerequisites:

Education or Training—Four-year degree with emphasis on business and marketing and computer-related concentration; MBA a plus

Experience—Experience as marketing assistant preparing materials or helping conduct research

Special Skills and Personality Traits—Analysis; understanding of economics and marketing principles; communications and media; good interpersonal and management skills

CAREER LADDER

```
┌─────────────────────────────────┐
│      Marketing Manager          │
└─────────────────────────────────┘

┌─────────────────────────────────┐
│   Assistant Marketing Manager   │
│      or Product Manager         │
└─────────────────────────────────┘

┌─────────────────────────────────┐
│ Marketing Specialist or Researcher │
└─────────────────────────────────┘

┌─────────────────────────────────┐
│      Marketing Assistant        │
└─────────────────────────────────┘
```

Position Description

The essence of marketing is creating the best possible match between a product and the needs of the target customer group or "market"—the people most likely to be interested in buying that product. Success means increased sales and revenue, and the resources needed to do further product development. Failure threatens to put a company further behind its competition because it no longer has the ability to keep up with the "state of the art." This can lead to a downward spiral that can put a once dominant company out of business. Because it is so critical to corporate success, marketing is often considered to be as important as technical excellence: Indeed, critics sometimes complain that companies that win a huge share of the market don't necessarily have the best products. But marketers can genuinely improve products by making engineers and developers pay attention to users' needs.

An entry-level Marketing Specialist may do tasks like these:

- prepare brochures and store displays to call public attention to the product
- create product demonstrations for trade shows or stores
- do research to identify possible new markets for a product (that is, kinds of people or businesses that are likely to be interested)
- use surveys or on-line feedback to get comments and suggestions for improvement from existing users of the product

A Marketing Specialist who focuses on gathering data about customers and product use and analyzing market trends is called a marketing researcher. In small companies this work is often not a separate job, but in larger companies marketing researchers can pursue a career in that specialty.

A Specialist who has gained several years' experience in such tasks can move into a managerial position. The first rungs on the management ladder may involve supervising survey takers or data coders. In higher management, a larger company may have a separate product manager for each product or line of products, under the direction of an overall marketing manager. A marketing manager is concerned with directing research, coordinating marketing efforts, and with giving feedback to the product developers about features that should be included. He or she may:

- help the development team incorporate desirable features into the product design
- conduct user tests of prototype, or "beta," products still in development
- prepare for the "launch," or public introduction, of a product, often in connection with a trade show
- prepare marketing and promotional efforts at trade shows—either computer trade shows or trade shows for the industry where the product will be used
- prepare market analysis reports using materials gathered by market researchers to analyze how well a product is doing against its competition in the current market, or highlight potential new markets
- give the company's executives predictions of future sales—a key to corporate financial planning
- hire, train, and supervise marketing assistants and researchers

A small start-up company may have only one person who performs all these functions, perhaps with the aid of an assistant or two. A large company will have a whole marketing department with a marketing manager and managers who deal with particular geographic or industrial areas. Alternatively, Marketing Specialists can work for public relations or market consulting firms that provide services to companies in the computer industry.

Like advertising specialists, Marketing Specialists must be aware of changing trends in the use of different forms of media. For example, use of the World Wide Web and on-line catalogs and ordering systems means that marketers must be familiar with and comfortable with the Internet while remaining aware of its limitations. Understanding changing demographics (such as growing populations of older persons and minorities) can also be important.

Salaries

An entry-level Marketing Specialist or marketing researcher can start around $25,000 to $30,000. An assistant marketing manager or senior marketing researcher can make around $50,000, and upper-level managers (such as marketing or product managers) can earn upward of $80,000.

Employment Prospects

The highly competitive nature of the computer hardware and software industry creates a strong demand for skilled Marketing Specialists, researchers, and managers. Some

large companies offer internships or training for new graduates. A smaller company can offer more challenge and faster advancement, but is less likely to offer training. The recent computer industry contraction may make it harder for new graduates to find work.

Advancement Prospects

Marketing researchers can advance to senior status, work for a firm that offers market consulting, or become independent consultants. The other route to advancement is by way of management, working toward product manager or marketing manager positions.

Education and Training

Most people entering this field have a four-year degree in business, with emphasis on marketing. Courses in economics, mathematics (for analysis), communications, and media are also helpful. The concentration or sub-major should be computer-related, such as information systems or (for hardware companies) engineering. An MBA is a strong plus for the marketing manager career track.

Experience, Skills, and Personality Traits

Work as an assistant in preparing marketing materials or doing surveys or other research is helpful. The needed skills include mastery of analytical tools (such as statistical and survey techniques), understanding of economic principles, and familiarity with the typical practices of the industry. Report writing requires good writing skills. Interpersonal communication skills are also very important, because a marketing manager must be able to communicate the marketing strategy both to coworkers and higher management. The individual should be both visionary and able to master details, imaginative but down to earth when "bottom line" questions come up.

Cross-Training for Marketing Specialists

Interests	Related Job Descriptions
advertising	Account Executive; Advertising Manager
product development	Project Manager

Unions and Associations

The Computer and Electronics Marketing Association and the Sales and Marketing Management Research Center offer information and links to resources for individuals interested in a marketing career.

Tips for Entry

1. Consider your role as a consumer and the ways in which marketers try to reach you—direct mail,

printed ads, commercials, promotions or contests, and so on. Think about why the marketers may have "targeted" you for their product, and why they think you may be interested.

2. In high school, help with promotions such as sales to raise money for clubs or sports. Consider whom you are trying to reach and how you might appeal to them.

3. In college, get a broad business background but focus especially on marketing, communications, and media. Look at case studies or simulations that can help give you a feel for how marketing works.

4. Read the computer or industry press and websites to find companies that seem to be growing rapidly or start-ups with exciting new products. They may have opportunities for marketing assistants.

PUBLIC RELATIONS SPECIALIST, COMPUTER PRODUCTS AND SERVICES

CAREER PROFILE

Duties: Deals with inquiries from the press and tries to protect or build up the company's public image

Alternate Title(s): Media Relations Specialist; Public Affairs Counsel

Salary Range: $30,000 to $80,000

Employment Prospects: Good

Advancement Prospects: Fair

Prerequisites:

    Education and Training—Four-year degree, usually in journalism or communications; business-related courses

    Experience—Work dealing with the public or preparing materials for the media

    Special Skills and Personality Traits—Excellent written and spoken communications; poise; ability to relate to technical people and the media

CAREER LADDER

```
┌─────────────────────────────────┐
│     Public Relations Manager    │
└─────────────────────────────────┘

┌─────────────────────────────────┐
│    Public Relations Specialist  │
│         (or Consultant)         │
└─────────────────────────────────┘

┌─────────────────────────────────┐
│    Public Relations Assistant   │
└─────────────────────────────────┘
```

Position Description

How a company and its products are seen by the public is very important to corporate success. The Public Relations Specialist tries to manage contacts with the media and the general public in a way that creates a favorable image.

In the computer industry, most contact is with the trade or industry press—computer magazines such as *InfoWorld* or *PC Magazine*—and, increasingly, with Web-based news services and reviewers. Suppose, for example, that a rumor surfaces that a much anticipated new product from the company is going to miss its shipping deadline. This rumor can be quite damaging to sales, because it might lead prospective customers to buy competing products rather than wait, and it might convey an image that the company is in trouble and can't properly manage its software development. This in turn might cast doubt on the company's future as a reliable supplier of software.

In response, the Public Relations Specialist may issue a press release or offer interviews with reporters. If the rumor is actually false, he or she will assure the press that there is no delay in the shipping schedule and that everything is on track. If there really *is* a delay, a "damage control" approach

will be taken, trying to minimize the length of the delay or its importance, or possibly giving some "spin" by saying something like, "We wanted to make sure this was a really solid product, so we've taken a bit more time to make sure everything is just right."

In addition to technical matters dealt with in the trade press, the Public Relations Specialist for a computer-related company must sometimes deal with crises common to all companies that can surface in the general or business press, such as lawsuits, charges of such offenses as sexual harassment or environmental violation, and so on. Dealing with the press during a crisis can be like walking a tightrope. Lying to the press or misleading them can easily backfire and make it very hard to get a fair hearing in the future. Cooperating with the press can bring a more sympathetic response, but not all questions can be answered, for legal or corporate policy reasons.

The Public Relations Specialist does not just respond to crises or routine queries, however. His or her role is "proactive"—always looking for opportunities to get the company favorable publicity. Some activities that can promote this objective include:

- preparing press releases and media kits to accompany product announcements
- giving background interviews or arranging interviews with top company executives
- making sure trade press editors and reviewers are supplied with copies of software plus detailed review guides
- highlighting ways in which the company is helping the community, ranging from recycling and other "ecofriendly" practices in manufacturing to things like scholarships and internships for students or outreach to minorities

A Public Relations Specialist who has an interest in management and appropriate skills can work toward becoming a public relations manager. In addition to being responsible for all the kinds of tasks given above, the manager of the public relations department must prepare a budget for the department's activities, hire and train assistants, and keep in touch with the managers of other departments, including development (or production), marketing, and legal.

In larger companies public relations and media relations may be separate functions, with the latter being handled by a media specialist or media spokesperson. Smaller companies will have one person or a small staff that handles both the general public and the media. Larger companies also usually have a full department (and manager) devoted to public relations.

Public Relations or media relations Specialists can also work for public relations consulting firms, where they are assigned to client companies.

Salaries

Entry-level Media Relations Specialists will start around $30,000 a year, with experience bringing salaries toward $40,000. Managers or experienced specialists for larger companies can make more than $80,000.

Employment Prospects

Most companies small or large are acutely aware of the importance of good public relations in an age when the media aggressively seek to uncover information and when news, good or bad, travels at the speed of light. As a result, demand is strong for people in this specialty, but so is the competition for top positions.

Advancement Prospects

Skilled and experienced public relations or media professionals can move into management within medium- to large-sized companies, or can become top specialists or management specialists in a public relations firm.

Education and Training

A four-year college degree is required, but it can be in one of several different fields, such as journalism, communica-

tions, or media. Computer-related courses are not particularly necessary, though the individual needs to become familiar with how the computer industry operates.

Experience, Skills, and Personality Traits

Experience dealing with the public or working as an assistant in a media organization is helpful. Good written and oral communication skills are a must. The individual must be articulate and adaptable enough to come up with a good answer even when thrown off balance by an interviewer's question. This kind of poise must extend to dealings inside the company as well. The media seem to be by nature suspicious, and technical people in turn distrust the media, believing they often distort facts or do not understand the technology. The media specialist must try to get technical people to cooperate with the needs of public relations and help the media to understand technical details.

Cross-Training for Public Relations Specialists

Interests	Related Job Descriptions
devising advertising campaigns	Advertising Account Executive
getting people interested in a company's products	Marketing Specialist

Unions and Associations

Public Relations Specialists can belong to a variety of organizations devoted to media and public relations. Joining computer industry organizations and reading the trade press are also important ways to keep in touch with industry trends and practices.

Tips for Entry

1. When you take journalism classes, also look at the reporting process from the point of view of the people being reported on. How do they try to manage the media, "plant" favorable ideas, or minimize damage?
2. Study how the different kinds of media work and how dealing with them may be different—how broadcast media or the Internet differ from printed media, and how trade media differ from the general media.
3. Practice public relations skills by volunteering to publicize school events or acting as "media contact" for a campus organization.
4. When looking for an entry-level job, find out how the prospective employer has been covered in the media. This can help you answer questions about how you would handle various situations.

INDUSTRY ANALYST, COMPUTER PRODUCTS AND SERVICES

CAREER PROFILE

Duties: Reports on industry trends and specific companies for industry or investment publications or brokers; analyzes the market performance of companies and makes recommendations for investment

Alternate Title(s): Investment Analyst

Salary Range: $50,000 to $85,000

Employment Prospects: Fair

Advancement Prospects: Good

Prerequisites:

Education or Training—Four-year degree in business-related field; courses in communications and technology

Experience—Work as research assistant in marketing, computer trade press, or investment industry

Special Skills and Personality Traits—Analytical skills; practical psychology; written and oral communications; ability to get along with a variety of people

CAREER LADDER

```
┌─────────────────────────────────────┐
│     Manager, Investment Research     │
└─────────────────────────────────────┘

┌─────────────────────────────────────┐
│ Senior Industry Analyst or "Pundit"  │
└─────────────────────────────────────┘

┌─────────────────────────────────────┐
│          Industry Analyst            │
└─────────────────────────────────────┘

┌─────────────────────────────────────┐
│           Assistant Analyst          │
└─────────────────────────────────────┘
```

Position Description

Computer-related companies and other forms of "high-tech" businesses have been a hot investment area in recent years (although there has been a downturn recently). Investors need to decide how much of their funds should go into this sector, what companies to invest in, and whether to buy more stock in a given company, hold what they have, or sell. Industry (or investment) Analysts gather information about how specific companies and whole industries are doing, and draw conclusions that are used by investors, companies that serve the computer industry (such as banks), economic planners, and government agencies.

Analysts generally look for investment opportunities or problem areas. For example, a start-up company claims to have a unique product that meets an unfilled need. The Analyst may be intrigued by the company, but he or she needs answers to questions such as:

- Does the company have enough financing to develop and market the product?
- Does their marketing plan make sense? Are the potential customers really there?

- Are the executives and managers experienced, or are they long on ideas but short on business sense?
- Is a large, established company likely to come out with a competing product and use its superior marketing resources to dominate the market?
- Are there large companies that may seek to buy out the small company?

Besides seeking investment opportunities in start-ups, the Industry Analyst also seeks to warn about potential problems. For example, a large, established company may have too much of its resources tied up in an older technology and have no new products in the pipeline. While the company's annual balance sheet still looks impressive, its market share may be going down, and investors may need to look elsewhere.

Industry Analysts work in a variety of settings. Some work in-house for a company, analyzing its industry and the competition for the benefit of marketers: Their information is usually confidential. Others work for the trade press, writing columns in publications such as *InfoWorld* or *Computer Week.* The investment industry (stockbrokers and investment research companies like Dow Jones) also hire Industry Analysts to prepare reports for brokers and their clients. There are also investment newsletters.

An Industry Analyst can lead a pretty hectic life. There are plenty of phone calls to and from industry contacts and corporate media people. The Analyst often attends special briefings where a company tries to create the most favorable possible impression of its present or future performance—and possibly make subtle digs at competitors. Trade shows like Comdex and the more specialized meetings and conferences are all opportunities to find tidbits of information. But the Analyst, like the journalist, must check facts and take people's motivations into account.

When a start-up company is ready to issue stock to the public it has an IPO (Initial Public Offering). This is an especially important challenge to the Analyst, who must make recommendations about purchasing the company's stock while the shares are still available. The corporate public relations and media people will be trying to flood the media with favorable stories, and the Analyst will have to sift through the information to get answers to his or her questions. Analysts also face pressure because whether they are right or wrong about a key development will affect their reputation and chances for future employment. Recent corporate accounting scandals have brought the role of the Investment Analyst into question. Analysts must be aware of possible conflicts of interest (such as their reporting on companies with whom they have or have had business relationships). Evolving ethical standards and proposed legislation are moving toward requiring greater "transparency" and full disclosure by Analysts so investors will better understand the factors that might influence an Analyst's opinions. Meanwhile, Industry Analysts must examine more closely the accounting of the companies they report about, to ensure that reported revenues or profits are real.

Salaries

Entry-level Industry Analysts working in-house at computer companies or brokerage firms may start around $50,000. As they move up to senior positions the salary can go up to $75,000 or so, with managers possibly making even more.

Analysts working as columnists in the trade press may be salaried or paid by the column. They tend to make less than in-house people unless they achieve a "name" or reputation. Analysts serving as consultants can do best of all, making $200 to a few thousand dollars a day if they have a top reputation. With the downturn in the stock market and the recent corporate scandals, investors today are demanding more complete and accurate information from Analysts and looking more closely at Analysts' experience and track record. At the same time that the bar to entry in this field is being set higher, the number of positions available has declined because of a decrease in the number of business publications (particularly on-line ones).

Employment Prospects

Job security is fairly low, and the best way to guard against unemployment is to develop good contacts in the industry, a good track record, and specialized knowledge of particular parts of the industry.

Advancement Prospects

Prospects for advancement are fairly good, either in-house or as a consultant. The same strategy that makes it easier to find new jobs also helps find better ones. The in-house route to advancement usually lies along the management track. This can be management either in an investment or research firm, or in the computer industry itself, since the broad-based knowledge gained by the Analyst can be very valuable for product development and marketing departments.

Education and Training

To do the job, the Industry Analyst needs both a general understanding of economics, investment, and market psychology and specific knowledge about the computer industry. This usually translates to a four-year degree in a business-related field (economics, business administration, accounting, finance, or management), as well as basic courses in computer technology and information systems.

Experience, Skills, and Personality Traits

As the name suggests, the key skill for this position is analytical—the ability to determine the significance of data from corporate reports, economic and industry statistics, and reports by other Analysts. The results are conclusions that identify opportunities and problems, as well as long-term trends. Since Analysts write reports and make presentations, good writing and speaking skills and organization are also important.

A variety of work experiences can help prepare an individual to become an Industry Analyst: work in market research, trade journalism, and the investment industry are all applicable. He or she must have a good working knowledge of the stock market, corporate finance and accounting, and the effects of government policies, taxes, and regulations on the industry.

The personality of the Analyst must combine concentration and thoughtfulness with the ability to get along with a variety of other professionals while maintaining a critical attitude to what they say.

Cross-Training for Industry Analysts

Interests	Related Job Descriptions
marketing	Marketing Specialist
journalism	Reporter, Computer-Related Publications
public relations	Public Relations Specialist

Unions and Associations

The Association for Investment Management and Research is a professional organization that includes Industry Analysts.

Tips for Entry

1. Read the business section of your local newspaper and publications such as the *Wall Street Journal*. Observe how commentators present their conclusions and the evidence they base them on.
2. Practice your analytical skills by picking a company and trying to learn as much as possible about it. Try to predict its performance over the coming year.
3. Be sure to keep in touch with overall trends in the economy. These will not only affect the computer and related industries—they may also impact your work and role as an Industry Analyst.
4. In college, make sure your curriculum includes courses in economic analysis, business, communication skills, and computer-related subjects.
5. Look for internships in areas such as business journalism and venture capital or investment banking firms. A market research position might also provide valuable insight and experience.

REPORTER, COMPUTER-RELATED PUBLICATIONS

CAREER PROFILE

Duties: Gathers facts on people and events in the computer industry; interviews people for background or because they are important or interesting; writes news stories for computer magazines or the Internet

Alternate Title(s): Journalist; Trade Reporter

Salary Range: $25,000 to $50,000

Employment Prospects: Fair

Advancement Prospects: Fair

Prerequisites:

Education or Training—Four-year journalism or liberal arts degree with technical courses or technical major with writing courses

Experience—Writing, reporting, or research experience such as for a school or local publication

Special Skills and Personality Traits—Ability to organize details; analysis; clear writing; ability to get along with people while sometimes asking pointed questions

CAREER LADDER

```
┌─────────────────────────────────┐
│   Senior Reporter or Columnist  │
└─────────────────────────────────┘

┌─────────────────────────────────┐
│         Staff Reporter          │
└─────────────────────────────────┘

┌─────────────────────────────────┐
│       Assistant Reporter        │
└─────────────────────────────────┘
```

Position Description

The computer industry has a number of newspapers (such as *InfoWorld* and *PC Week*) and magazines (such as *PC Magazine*) that report on new technological developments and the companies and people involved with them. The Reporter can be assigned all kinds of stories, ranging from coverage of a product "roll-out," to reports from trade shows, to interviews with key people in the industry. An individual with technical knowledge and good writing skills can also write summaries of new products or reviews in which a new software package is put through its paces.

An individual usually starts out as a "general assignment" Reporter who gets the basic information on the assigned story and writes it up. More experienced Reporters can do in-depth interviews or analyses of markets or industry trends. (The latter is similar to the work of an industry analyst, except it is for publication, not for the private use of clients.)

A Reporter who develops expertise in a particular area of the industry or who has a lively, distinctive writing style can become a columnist. Columnists have more freedom to choose what they will write about than do Reporters. Suc-

cessful columnists can syndicate or sell their column to more than one publication.

Reporters must develop long-term relationships with contacts—such as corporate media representatives who can provide timely information and an extra tidbit or two, or people working in the industry who will provide information "off the record" that gives insights into what is really going on inside a company. The Reporter must be careful to protect the identity of confidential sources, while seeking other sources to cross-check the information. Inaccurate information can damage a company, hurt the publication's reputation, or even lead to a lawsuit.

Reporters must finish their work in time for each publication deadline, and the pressure can get intense when a big story is breaking and the publication has to go to press in just a few hours.

Reporters must keep up with changes in the media. In particular, they must learn how to search the Internet for useful information while realizing that much information found there may not be reliable. Reporters may have to write supplementary material for their publication's website, such as details that won't fit in the printed story or late-breaking developments that arrived after press time. Some Reporters may even specialize in Web-based publications.

Salaries

Entry-level Reporters start out in the $20,000 range and can move up to $40,000 or more with experience and specialized knowledge. A columnist who develops a reputation as an industry "pundit" can make considerably more.

Employment Prospects

The face of the computer trade press has been changing in recent years. Some monthly computer magazines have gone out of business, merged with others, or gotten slimmer. The weekly newspaper-format publications are still going strong, but there are only a few of them and opportunities are thus limited. Many Web-based publications have also fallen on hard times because of their inability to generate revenue through advertising or subscriptions. Probably the most reliable employers are printed industry or business publications seeking on-line Reporters for their websites, but competition will be intense for these jobs. (For more about writing or editing for on-line publications, see the related entry, On-line Writer/Editor.) An individual can increase employment opportunities by developing special expertise in a particular area such as networking or graphics, and contacting specialized industry newsletters and technical journals.

Advancement Prospects

Advancement as a Reporter is reflected in increasingly important assignments and in becoming a "beat reporter" who specializes in a particular aspect of the industry. Individuals can advance further by becoming managers of news operations. Another possibility is to use the knowledge and contacts gained from reporting to move into the industry as a marketing or public relations specialist or to become an industry analyst within the computer or investment industries.

Education and Training

Most individuals in this field have a four-year degree in journalism or another media-related field, although media-savvy liberal arts graduates can also get entry-level positions. A technical background is not always necessary, though it helps, and a person with a technical degree and good writing skills can cross over into journalism.

Experience, Skills, and Personality Traits

General journalism (newspaper or magazine) experience is helpful, as is work in marketing research or media relations. The key skills involve communications—writing, interviewing, and asking questions, along with the ability to do research (including on-line research) and to "pitch" story ideas to editors. The individual should be able to work under pressure, adapt to changing circumstances, and get along well with people from different backgrounds.

Cross-Training for Reporters

Skills or Interests	Related Job Descriptions
on-line writing	On-line Writer/Editor
analyzing company and industry trends	Marketing Specialist; Industry Analyst
relating to media and the public	Public Relations Specialist

Unions and Associations

Reporters can belong to both journalistic and trade organizations. (See Appendix II, parts 3 and 4 for examples.)

Tips for Entry

1. Get journalism experience through your school paper or other campus publications or through part-time work with a local news organization. Most journalism programs try to help students find suitable internships. Also, many Web-based news services are seeking product reviews (such as game reviews). You probably won't get paid anything, but it can be good experience.
2. Consider experiencing the other side of the coin by getting an internship working in public relations or marketing for a computer-related business.
3. Read both computer industry publications and media-related publications. Keep an eye on trends such as the growing use of the Internet by corporate public relations people and the media.
4. You may be able to work your way into an entry-level position by showing writing samples to a publication and perhaps offering to do a trial assignment, or by selling articles to magazines.

COMPUTER-RELATED
OFFICE POSITIONS

DATA ENTRY OPERATOR

CAREER PROFILE

Duties: Enters data into computer programs; fills out on-screen forms; verifies accuracy of data

Alternate Title(s): Data Entry Keyer; Input Operator

Salary Range: $16,000 to $25,000

Employment Prospects: Poor

Advancement Prospects: Fair

Prerequisites:

Education or Training—High school diploma generally required; vocational classes or employer training

Experience—General office/clerical experience; typing

Special Skills and Personality Traits—General literacy; fast, accurate typing skills; attention to detail; ability to perform repetitious work

CAREER LADDER

```
┌─────────────────────────────────┐
│  Office Manager or Manager,      │
│  Data Entry Department           │
└─────────────────────────────────┘

┌─────────────────────────────────┐
│  Senior or Experienced           │
│  Data Entry Operator             │
└─────────────────────────────────┘

┌─────────────────────────────────┐
│  Data Entry Operator             │
└─────────────────────────────────┘

┌─────────────────────────────────┐
│  Trainee                         │
└─────────────────────────────────┘
```

Position Description

Data Entry Operators use computer terminals or special-purpose machines (such as 10-key adding machines or cash registers) to type in data to be stored by a computer program. Usually the data is stored on a computer disk, but some machines store keyed material on magnetic type. Some typical applications include:

- typing in data from cancelled checks, time cards, receipts, and similar sources
- taking information from applicants (such as for a driver's license or library card) and typing it into the computer
- retail clerk jobs that involve computerized cash registers (often a separate job classification, but similar to data entry)

The Data Entry Operator must be able to maintain a fast, steady pace with good accuracy. More experienced operators may work with more complex data that might have to be interpreted in some way (such as deciding the category in a computerized form that corresponds to the input data). Operators may have to verify or check data.

Salaries

Data Entry Operator is a low-paid job that tends to pay minimum wage in the corporate world. Government agencies tend to pay somewhat more. Unionized employees also tend to make more.

Employment Prospects

The use of Data Entry Operators is steadily declining. Most retail transactions now use bar code scanners to enter data automatically, and financial transactions (such as check processing) are increasingly all-electronic with no manual keying from paper documents. Some data entry jobs, however, will continue to be available.

Advancement Prospects

An experienced operator who shows initiative and learns more about computers can work toward becoming a supervisory operator, assistant manager, or office manager.

Education and Training

Most employers require a high school diploma or equivalent.

Experience, Skills, and Personality Traits

Previous clerical experience and familiarity with office machines and routines are helpful. Many employers will train individuals who have sufficient typing skills. The individual must be comfortable doing routine work for many hours each day.

Cross-Training for Data Entry Operators

Interests	Related Job Descriptions
working with documents	Word Processor
designing or creating text	Desktop Publisher; Computer Typesetter

Unions and Associations

Data Entry Operators may belong to clerical worker unions.

Tips for Entry

1. Students working toward a technical career may be tempted to take a Data Entry Operator job simply as a way to earn some money while going to school, but it is probably better to look for a job in which one can learn new technical or creative skills.

2. If you do work as a Data Entry Operator, try to learn more about the computer software and systems being used. You may be able to help set up the equipment, troubleshoot the problems, or manage the workflow in the office.

WORD PROCESSOR

Duties: Creates or revises documents using word processing software, often with the aid of forms or templates; formats and prints documents

Alternate Title(s): Word Processing Technician; Word Processing Operator; Typist; Clerk-typist

Salary Range: $18,000 to $25,000

Employment Prospects: Good

Advancement Prospects: Fair

Prerequisites:

Education or Training—High school diploma; business or vocational school certificate helpful

Experience—General clerical/office experience

Special Skills and Personality Traits—Fast, accurate typing; knowledge of grammar and proofreading; knowledge of major word processing software; comfortable with doing routine work

```
┌─────────────────────────────┐
│   Supervisor or Manager,    │
│      Word Processing        │
└─────────────────────────────┘

┌─────────────────────────────┐
│      Word Processor         │
└─────────────────────────────┘

┌─────────────────────────────┐
│   Word Processing Trainee   │
└─────────────────────────────┘
```

Position Description

The creation of documents (letters, memos, reports, etc.) is a major part of work in offices of all kinds. Starting in the 1970s, word processing machines and, later, desktop computers replaced the typewriter in most offices. The typist was replaced by a skilled document creator who has mastered complex word processing software (such as Microsoft Word or WordPerfect). This person is often called a Word Processor.

Some Word Processors create letters and other documents as part of general clerical or secretarial duties, including filing, answering the telephone, or serving as a receptionist. Other Word Processors work in specialized word processing centers or secretarial pools where they do only word processing.

As they gain experience, Word Processors can perform more complex or creative tasks. For example, they can use their specialized knowledge of legal or medical terminology to transcribe dictation from tape, create documents that include more elaborate formatting or graphics, or use their writing skills to create documents from a sketchy outline or a few notes.

Word Processors must become familiar with the major features of the software they are using, such as navigating around the screen, editing text, checking spelling and grammar, selecting and applying styles, and formatting the document for printing. They must also be familiar with general computer tasks such as loading, saving, and copying files. Modern word processing programs have a facility for templates that allows creation of standard documents simply by typing information into fields on the screen. Experienced Word Processors can modify templates to meet special needs, or even create new templates.

Salaries

Entry-level salaries for Word Processors tend to be fairly low (under $20,000). Individuals working for the government or a large company may receive substantial benefits (vacation, medical, etc.). Experience and specialized skills bring higher salaries.

Employment Prospects

The traditional role of the secretary has diminished because computers allow many mid-level managers, who previously had secretaries, to handle their own correspondence. Voice-recognition software that turns spoken words directly into text may also reduce the need for keyboarders, although at present such software is not very accurate. Meanwhile, there continues to be a strong demand for individuals who have good word processing and related skills.

Advancement Prospects

Some advancement is possible simply by gaining experience and being assigned more complex tasks. An individual can go further, however, by acquiring specialized knowledge or skills, such as legal or medical transcription or knowledge of advanced software features and desktop publishing or graphics programs. Another route to advancement is to work toward becoming office supervisor or manager.

Education and Training

A high school diploma is generally required, with good general literacy (reading, grammar, and writing). High school students interested in word processing should take classes in keyboarding, office skills, and use of popular software packages. This training is also available at many community colleges and vocational schools.

Experience, Skills, and Personality Traits

A Word Processor needs to be familiar with general office procedures, so some experience working as a clerk or office assistant is helpful. In addition to literacy, typing, and software skills, the individual should be able to look up material in reference books (dictionaries or directories, for example), write or rewrite material in "business English," proofread and correct grammar, and work well with other members of the office staff. Ability to use Internet resources may also be needed.

Cross-Training for Word Processors

Interests	Related Job Descriptions
creating documents with complex formatting	Desktop Publisher
setting type	Computer Typesetter
doing on-line research	On-line Researcher; Legal Researcher
working with graphics	Computer Graphics Technician

Unions and Associations

Some Word Processors may belong to clerical unions. This is particularly true of government workers.

Tips for Entry

1. If you can't find a suitable course, you can still learn word processing software on your school or home PC. There are many books and training videos available for most popular software packages.
2. Use a part-time or summer job to gain experience as an office assistant. This will help you get used to the workplace, and make future employers more confident that you'll fit in.
3. If you are working as a Word Processor, look for ways to upgrade your skills (perhaps in night school). Also look for opportunities to help coordinate work, supervise, or train people. This experience will make you a better candidate for office manager openings.
4. Long hours of typing can cause serious health problems such as carpal tunnel syndrome and eyestrain. Try to obtain a suitable chair, use proper posture and hand position, and take "stretch breaks" regularly. Your company or the state can supply more information.

DESKTOP PUBLISHER

CAREER PROFILE

Duties: Designs and creates documents, brochures, and publications using sophisticated page layout software; prints out documents or creates slides, transparencies, and other formats

Alternate Title(s): Document Designer

Salary Range: $22,000 to $45,000

Employment Prospects: Good

Advancement Prospects: Good

Prerequisites:

Education or Training—Four-year degree emphasizing graphic arts, communications, or writing; also general computer operations and use of major office software packages

Experience—Several years of experience creating documents such as brochures and newsletters

Special Skills and Personality Traits—Page design and layout; understanding of impact of design and typography on reading; detailed familiarity with major desktop publishing software; ability to understand clients' needs and work with them; attention to detail; ability to work under deadline pressure

CAREER LADDER

```
┌─────────────────────────────────┐
│  Manager (publications department│
│         or print shop)          │
└─────────────────────────────────┘

┌─────────────────────────────────┐
│  Desktop Publishing Specialist  │
└─────────────────────────────────┘

┌─────────────────────────────────┐
│   Word Processor or Assistant   │
│   (publications department)     │
└─────────────────────────────────┘
```

Position Description

Roughly speaking, Desktop Publishers are to word processors what architects are to carpenters. Desktop Publishers design documents as a whole, while word processing staff supplies the text itself. The term Desktop Publisher covers a variety of professionals who design and create documents ranging from simple reports or brochures to page layouts for magazines and books of many different types.

The Desktop Publisher must consider a number of aspects of document design, including:

- text layout (margins, use of columns, tables, etc.)
- typography (the selection of fonts, or type faces of characters, and their size and "weight" or thickness)
- integration of illustrations (photos, graphics, diagrams, etc.) into the text; includes understanding of file formats and image editing tools
- general readability (making it easy to identify important text and accommodating auxiliary text such as sidebars and footnotes without causing eyestrain)

- suitability to readership (design elements used in reference books are unlikely to work in popular magazine articles, and vice versa)

The Desktop Publisher job category is not always well defined. Experienced Word Processors are also familiar with the use of fonts, headings, columns, and typography, and may perform many of the simpler functions of the Desktop Publisher. In smaller organizations, one person may be both architect and carpenter, moving back and forth between considering design and writing the text. Larger organizations tend to separate the design and text creation functions, however.

One way to distinguish the two job categories is by the software typically used. Word Processors use word processing software such as Microsoft Word or WordPerfect. Desktop Publishers use page design software such as Quark and PageMaker. Page design software tends to be more complex and to require more experience than word processing software.

Salaries

Entry-level Desktop Publishers start around the $25,000 to $30,000 range, near the top end for experienced Word Processors. Experienced Desktop Publishers, particularly those with large companies, can approach $50,000 or more.

Employment Prospects

The demand for printed documents is declining in a few areas. For example, software today often comes with all the help text on-line and only a minimal printed manual (if any). Use of the Web (and intranets) may also reduce the creation of printed documents. But if true, this is a long-term trend, and there continues to be strong demand for people with good document design skills. Magazines, books, and glossy brochures aren't likely to go away soon.

Nationwide copy and print shop chains increasingly offer desktop-publishing services. A businessperson needing to distribute a document at a meeting can fly in the previous evening, send text by modem to the print shop, and pick up the finished brochure on the way to the meeting the next morning. People who can create documents on a "rush" basis with minimal supervision are always in demand.

Desktop Publishers with strong graphics and design skills are always in demand at advertising agencies and in corporate public relations departments.

Individuals can increase their job opportunities by mastering specialized skills such as creating slides, transparencies, and even Power Point presentations. And since many of the principles of Internet page design are similar to desktop publishing, it is possible to cross over into that growing field.

Advancement Prospects

Skilled Desktop Publishers can reach the senior level in a publisher's production department, or seek positions such as publications manager or manager of a print shop. Consulting (contracting) work is also available.

Education and Training

Most positions require a college degree, and course work in writing, graphic arts, and communications is helpful. Once past that threshold, employers are mainly interested in experience and skills, including detailed familiarity with the software to be used. Since this software is complicated, training provided by software vendors and commercial trainers can be helpful.

Experience, Skills, and Personality Traits

Experience working in a print shop or publisher's production department can be very helpful. The individual must combine good design skills, understanding of the purpose of different kinds of publications and the common style conventions used, and familiarity with the software and other tools used to create documents. Publications such as magazines and books involve a team effort where the desktop publishing specialist will be working with writers, editors, graphics specialists, advertising people, and printers. Good interpersonal communication skills are important, especially for individuals interested in extending their career into management.

Cross-Training for Desktop Publishers

Interests	Related Job Descriptions
creating text	Word Processor
designing webpages	Webpage Designer
multimedia	Multimedia Developer

Unions and Associations

Employees of copy or print shops and many small publications are not usually members of labor unions. Unions are more common in newspapers, large publishers, and government agencies.

Tips for Entry

1. You can practice some page layout and design skills using a word processor such as MS Word on your home and school PC. Look at the templates that come with the software and experiment with the use of headings, columns, and typefaces.
2. Look for local businesses or nonprofit organizations for which you can design simple flyers, brochures, or booklets. People who don't think they can afford professional printing may appreciate your help. Save the documents you create in a portfolio that you can use when job hunting.
3. Since desktop publishing software is expensive you will probably have to take a courses at a community college or vocational school to learn it. (However, less expensive educational versions of software may be available through your school.)
4. Another alternative is to look for a publisher who needs an office assistant. Besides giving you some experience in working in a production department, they may offer you more advanced training.
5. Consider learning webpage design while you are mastering desktop publishing. Many companies want to put their printed documents on the Web as well. Many software packages have built-in converters that output text in HTML, the language used to format Web pages, and you can use that to give you a head start.

COMPUTER TYPESETTER

CAREER PROFILE

Duties: Uses a computerized system to set type for printing newspapers and other publications; checks proofs and assembles page layouts

Alternate Title(s): Compositor; Typographer

Salary Range: $25,000 to $45,000

Employment Prospects: Fair

Advancement Prospects: Fair

Prerequisites:

Education or Training—High school diploma and apprenticeship or community college certificate or degree

Experience—General work with proofing, typesetting, layout (paste-up), and running printing equipment

Special Skills and Personality Traits—Basic computer skills, typing, proofreading, graphic arts and design; photography; steady work habits; ability to concentrate on details, sometimes under pressure

CAREER LADDER

```
┌─────────────────────────────────────┐
│      Supervisor or Manager           │
│  (printing department or shop)       │
└─────────────────────────────────────┘

┌─────────────────────────────────────┐
│   Senior Typesetter or Compositor    │
└─────────────────────────────────────┘

┌─────────────────────────────────────┐
│ Journeyman Typesetter or Compositor  │
└─────────────────────────────────────┘

┌─────────────────────────────────────┐
│       Apprentice (or Trainee)        │
└─────────────────────────────────────┘
```

Position Description

While the combination of desktop publishing software and a laser printer works well for producing a few copies of a brochure or pamphlet, newspapers and other publications that print thousands of copies approach things differently: Text must be set into type and printed. Traditionally type was set using a sort of overgrown typewriter called a linotype that inserted metal type into a frame for printing. Today the most common system uses special-purpose computer software that drives a phototypesetting machine. This device creates negative images of the type characters that are developed to create the printing plate.

At a newspaper or magazine, the Computer Typesetter works with copy (text to be typeset) that has been marked with special symbols by the proofreader. These symbols specify how text will be aligned, what kinds and sizes of typeface to use, and so on. The Computer Typesetter uses special control key codes to apply these specifications to the text as it is viewed on a screen. Once the text is input, the phototypesetter is set up to create the photographic output (the printing plate). (In large shops a lower-level operator or assistant may perform this task.) Finally, test copies called proofs are made from the printing plate and carefully examined for errors or problems. If any are found, the Computer Typesetter corrects the text or control codes and creates a new plate and proofs. It may take several cycles of proofing and correction before the plates are ready.

Meanwhile, the editorial staff has made a layout that shows where the different elements (headlines, news, ads, pictures, and so on) are to go on each page. The material from the phototypesetter must be carefully arranged to match the layout, proofed, and any layout errors corrected. Only then is the publication "ready for the press."

Print shops follow similar procedures to the above, except they are not tied to the daily or weekly cycle of newspaper production. Rather, they produce individual "jobs" such as advertising flyers or small press publications. A popular alternative to traditional computer typesetting is emerging in the form of "computer to plate" (CTP) systems. Here the printing plates are created directly from the digital files produced by desktop publishing or graphics programs. Although there can sometimes be problems with the "translation" of complex graphics or type formats, it is likely that the growth of CTP will mean that people interested in the printing field will move increasingly toward becoming desktop publishers rather than printing specialists.

Salaries

For newspapers and large print shops, the biggest determining factor is whether the workplace is unionized. Experienced nonunion workers start around $25,000, with unionized workers making about 25 percent to 50 percent higher wages. Employees of small print shops that are generally not unionized are likely to be near the low end of the wage scale.

Employment Prospects

There is a good demand for individuals who are fully up to speed on the technology of automated typesetting. There is little demand for the older manual or partially automated systems. As previously mentioned, technological change may require greater emphasis on desktop publishing or advanced graphics skills.

Advancement Prospects

In newspapers and large shops individuals may be able to advance into supervisory or management positions. Advancement in small shops tends to be limited (since the owner is also the manager). Individuals who have the drive and acquire the necessary business and management skills (and money) may be able to start their own print shop.

Education and Training

High school graduates who have gained experience and training can qualify for entry-level (trainee) positions. Useful courses include keyboarding, basic computer operation, graphic arts, print shop, and journalism. Many community colleges offer degrees or certificates in graphic arts or printing technology.

Experience, Skills, and Personality Traits

Employers generally prefer applicants who have experience with the model or type of equipment that they are using. However, they are often willing to train applicants who have a broad mix of skills—both typography and graphic arts—so they can do both typesetting and paste-up work.

Cross-Training for Computer Typesetters

Interests	Related Job Descriptions
creating documents on a PC	Desktop Publisher
editing complex text	Technical Editor

Unions and Associations

Many Computer Typesetters, particularly those working in metropolitan areas, belong to the Communications Workers of America. Workers in shops that use lithography (offset printing) may belong to the Graphic Communications International Union.

Tips for Entry

1. If you're in high school, check out the school newspaper—it's a good place to learn proofing and layout skills, even if they don't do their own typesetting.
2. Local branches of the Communications Workers of America or other printers' unions are a good source for apprenticeship programs.
3. Find out which community colleges in your area have degrees or certificates in printing, graphic arts, or related fields. Night school may be a possibility.
4. Also check for local "full service" print shops that do offset or lithographic printing (not just desktop publishing on a laser printer). You may be able to use a part-time job to build your skills.

BOOKKEEPER/ACCOUNTING ASSISTANT

CAREER PROFILE

Duties: Uses traditional or computerized procedures to gather financial data; performs calculations; balances accounts and compiles reports

Alternate Title(s): Bookkeeping Clerk; Accounting Clerk

Salary Range: $22,000 to $40,000

Employment Prospects: Fair

Advancement Prospects: Fair

Prerequisites:

Education or Training—High school; business courses; two-year college or business school preferred

Experience—General office experience; clerical and bookkeeping work

Special Skills and Personality Traits—Following procedures; attention to detail; arithmetic; use of accounting and spreadsheet software; writing; steady, methodical work habits

CAREER LADDER

```
┌─────────────────────────────────────┐
│            Accountant                │
└─────────────────────────────────────┘

┌─────────────────────────────────────┐
│       Full-Charge Bookkeeper         │
└─────────────────────────────────────┘

┌─────────────────────────────────────┐
│ Accounting or Bookkeeping Assistant  │
│             or Clerk                 │
└─────────────────────────────────────┘
```

Position Description

Any activity of a business that involves money has to account for that money in some way. This includes sales and money due from customers (accounts receivable), purchases from vendors (accounts payable), inventory, payroll, internal budgeting, taxes, and much more. Bookkeeping or Accounting Assistants do the detail work needed to keep up with all these transactions. Examples of duties can include:

- entering transactions into journal records in accounting software
- running routine spreadsheets and financial reports for each period (week, month, or quarter) of data
- generating or checking invoices or bills
- maintaining inventory records and reports
- processing payroll checks
- making bank transactions
- running routine audits (checking for accuracy and consistency)

A Bookkeeping or Accounting Assistant working in a large corporation will probably work in a particular department such as accounts receivable or payroll. In a small business, he or she may keep all the accounts for the owner.

Although the individual should know how to use a 10-key adding machine, most data is now entered at a standard PC keyboard or numeric keypad. A variety of accounting software may be used. Small businesses often buy commercial packages (such as Quicken or AccPac) that provide modules for each function such as inventory, accounts payable, accounts receivable, and payroll. Large corporations often have complex specialized accounting software—either commercial packages that have been extensively customized or programs developed in-house.

In addition to accounting software, Bookkeeping or Accounting Clerks often use spreadsheet software such as Excel or 1-2-3 to perform calculations and create reports. Familiarity with word processing (and often e-mail and networking) is also required.

Salaries

Experienced individuals can make around $30,000 to $50,000 or more if they have supervisory duties. Large businesses and businesses in metropolitan areas tend to pay more.

Employment Prospects

The increasing automation of bookkeeping and accounting functions is reducing the demand for lower-level clerks and assistants. For example, many stores and warehouses have inventory systems that track products by bar code and automatically generate orders for replacement merchandise. User-friendly small business accounting software allows many small business owners to do their own bookkeeping without assistance. Nevertheless, there is still a reasonable demand for Bookkeepers or Accounting Assistants in large businesses.

Advancement Prospects

Individuals who get an entry-level position and improve their skills have a reasonable chance of advancement to such positions as chief (or "full charge") bookkeeper or office manager.

Another possibility is to take courses leading to a degree in accounting, a career that is considered professional. Salaries for accountants tend to start about where bookkeepers top out.

Education and Training

A high school diploma with business-related courses is the minimum requirement. A community college or business school certificate or degree is desirable. Subjects that should be covered include business mathematics, keyboarding, computer operations, popular accounting and spreadsheet software, and principles of accounting.

Experience, Skills, and Personality Traits

General office experience is very helpful because it introduces standard business practices and procedures. The individual must be able to interpret and carry out fairly complex procedures, enter data quickly and accurately, perform calculations and recognize possible errors, and write clearly. Good communication skills are helpful for explaining problems and asking for needed information. A steady, methodical personality is probably most suited for this kind of work.

Cross-Training for Bookkeepers or Accounting Assistants

Interests	Related Job Descriptions
analyzing numeric data	Statistician
checking accuracy of programs and procedures	EDP Auditor

Unions and Associations

Bookkeeping or Accounting Assistants in larger corporations may belong to clerical worker unions. Those working in small businesses are unlikely to be unionized.

Tips for Entry

1. There are several inexpensive home or small business accounting programs for PCs. You can use one to familiarize yourself with general principles. Once you've learned how to use the program, you may be able to help your family or a local business with their accounts.
2. "Program Suites" like Microsoft Works can give you more software to try out, including simple database and spreadsheet functions.
3. Check for community college programs in bookkeeping or accounting. Before enrolling, find out what software and equipment they teach, and compare it to requirements in job ads.
4. Government agencies are a good source for entry-level jobs. You can also register with a temporary employment agency. There may be a need for temporary workers for seasonal businesses (such as department stores around Christmastime or tourist resorts during the summer).

STATISTICIAN

Duties: Analyzes numeric data to draw conclusions useful for science, business, or public policy; helps designs computer simulations; uses special software and mathematical techniques to create reports with tables and charts

Alternate Title(s): Statistical Analyst; Numerical Analyst; Demographer; Survey Researcher

Salary Range: $30,000 to $60,000

Employment Prospects: Fair

Advancement Prospects: Good

Prerequisites:

Education or Training—Minimum four-year college degree in statistics; science or business courses depending on application interest

Experience—Work with scientific tests, marketing surveys or polls, and so on as appropriate for specialty

Special Skills and Personality Traits—Understanding of mathematical relationships and possibilities of error; computer programming and use of statistical software; writing and communication skills; personality combining curiosity with methodical work habits

```
┌─────────────────────────────────────┐
│   Statistical Research Director      │
│      or Statistics Professor         │
└─────────────────────────────────────┘

┌─────────────────────────────────────┐
│        Senior Statistician           │
│      or Statistics Instructor        │
└─────────────────────────────────────┘

┌─────────────────────────────────────┐
│           Statistician               │
└─────────────────────────────────────┘

┌─────────────────────────────────────┐
│      Assistant or Trainee,           │
│       Statistical Research           │
└─────────────────────────────────────┘
```

Position Description

"Nine out of 10 doctors recommend XYZ pills."

"Economic growth last quarter was the slowest in 20 years."

"Sixty-four percent of the respondents supported war with Iraq."

"Smoking is by far the single most important risk factor for lung cancer."

Statements like these are part of the news and advertising that fills the daily media. They all represent claims based on statistics.

Statisticians attempt to draw conclusions based on numeric data. The data can come from a variety of sources such as polls and surveys, economic indicators, scientific experiments, medical studies, and product test results. The questions to be answered depend on the needs of the researchers, managers, or policy makers. Some typical questions might include:

- Which of several factors is most important in predicting whether a programmer trainee will be successful on the job?

- What age group buys the most computer games? What kinds of games do they like best?

- How do the salaries of men and women in the computer industry (with similar education and experience) compare? Does this relationship change with increased work experience?

- What is the relationship (if any) between the climate phenomenon called El Niño and shorebird populations? Salmon? Crop yields?

- Does this experimental drug work better than a placebo (sugar pill)?

Questions like these are answered by applying accepted methods of statistical analysis to the data. Working with other researchers, the Statistician designs an experiment, survey, or data-gathering plan that will provide the raw material for analysis.

The Statistician must be very careful to minimize error. He or she must look at the sample data (whether polling results or temperature measurements) to make sure that some sort of bias has not entered into the selection process. In a famous pre–World War II example, a pollster predicted a Republican victory in a presidential election, based on a poll conducted by telephone. The problem was that in the 1930s most of the poorer people who were inclined to vote Democrat did not own phones and were thus not represented in the sample. Part of the Statistician's responsibility is to estimate the amount of error (the "error bar") in the results, and to help users avoid drawing inappropriate conclusions from the data.

Another technique used by Statisticians is computer simulation. For example, a program can attempt to simulate (or "model") the behavior of customers faced with competing choices for long distance phone service or of wolves preying on deer in a national forest. The simulation results can be compared with real-world results and variables can be "tweaked" in an attempt to make the simulation a better predictor of the future. Scientists ranging from physicists to biologists often use simulation programs to gain insight into phenomena when it is impractical to perform actual experiments. Although simulation is a powerful tool, a simulation is only as good as the assumptions made by its designers. Statisticians must clarify these assumptions.

Statistics play an important part in economic planning by both business and government. Most people are familiar with terms such as GDP (Gross Domestic Product), the unemployment rate, and the Dow Jones stock average. These are all calculated by statisticians using formulas of varying complexity. Politicians, advertisers, and the media often use (or abuse) statistics for their own purposes.

Some Statisticians do theoretical rather than applied work. These "Mathematical Statisticians" try to improve the tools or methods used by applied Statisticians. Theoretical Statisticians tend to work in universities or research labs.

While some statistics can be calculated using commercial spreadsheet programs (or even a calculator), most Statisticians work with powerful software packages such as SPSS. There is also specialized software for polling and survey taking, and for recording data from scientific instruments. Statisticians often use their programming skills to write programs in languages such as Fortran or C++, or use the specialized macro languages included in software packages. The Statistician must be able to choose the appropriate software tools and move the data between them as necessary. Statistical reports are usually presented in the form of charts and tables together with explanatory text.

Salaries

An entry-level Statistician with a four-year degree and little experience may earn around $30,000. A graduate degree and appropriate experience can bring salaries above $50,000, with the highest salaries going to advanced researchers or individuals who exercise managerial functions. Private industry tends to pay more than government; and larger firms pay more than smaller ones.

Employment Prospects

Demand for Statisticians is reasonably good. The arrival of easier-to-use statistics packages and the increased training of managers and MBAs in statistics may be reducing the need for lower-level Statisticians. An alternative career path is to become an instructor or professor in statistics at a community college or university.

Advancement Prospects

Individuals with advanced mathematical and statistical skills can become consultants. Consultants are often hired for special projects, such as to design a customer survey for a new product line. Another possibility is to work toward management of a research department.

Education and Training

The minimum requirement is a four-year college degree with a major in statistics and a strong mathematics background as well as some courses in information processing and programming. Advanced positions (and college teaching positions) require a master's or doctoral degree. The individual will probably have a sub-major or second degree in a particular applications area such as economics, sociology, environmental science, marketing, or political science. For working in the corporate world, some solid course work in economics, marketing, and business administration is very helpful.

Experience, Skills, and Personality Traits

Experience applying mathematical skills (such as laboratory assistant or working with an opinion survey or marketing firm) is helpful. Important skills include the ability to visualize the relationships between variables, "number sense" and the ability to recognize likely error; general computer use and use of specialized software; good knowledge of programming languages (such as SPSS or Fortran) or macro languages used in software. Since information must be presented in a way that makes it useful and accessible, writing and graphics skills are also important. A personality that combines curiosity with methodical attention to detail is ideal. The individual should be able to work well with other researchers and with people who will be using the results.

Cross-Training for Statisticians

Interests	Related Job Descriptions
working with financial data	Bookkeeping or Accounting Assistant
analyzing databases	Database Analyst; Data Miner
programming for mathematical or scientific applications	Scientific or Engineering Programmer; Researcher, Computer Science
marketing	Marketing Researcher
teaching	Professor, Computer Science

Unions and Associations

Statisticians are considered professional employees and do not normally belong to labor unions. They can join organizations such as the Mathematical Association of America and the American Statistical Association, as well as organizations relating to the area of science or industry in which they are employed.

Tips for Entry

1. "Writing up" experiments in a school science lab or entering mathematically oriented projects in a science fair are good ways to get experience using statistical methods.

2. Some statistical or mathematical software vendors offer special academic or educational versions of the software at much lower prices than the commercial version.

3. Marketing research companies may need assistants for a survey being conducted in your area: Watch for notices in newspapers or local Internet newsgroups. The U.S. Census is another possibility.

4. Membership in professional organizations and reading technical journals can provide contacts or job leads. Campus recruiters may also offer interviews.

ON-LINE RESEARCHER

CAREER PROFILE

Duties: Retrieves data and answers questions using databases or the Internet; usually specializes in a particular field

Alternate Title(s): Data Retrieval Specialist; Research Assistant; Database Assistant; specialized areas such as Legal Assistant or Medical Research Assistant

Salary Range: $30,000 to $50,000

Employment Prospects: Good

Advancement Prospects: Fair

Prerequisites:

Education or Training—Four-year college degree in computer science or information systems preferred

Experience—Database assistant or on-line research experience

Special Skills and Personality Traits—Familiarity with Internet and specialized databases; programming and use of search languages; persistence; ability to try varied approaches to information retrieval; keeping up to date on sources; adaptability; good communication skills

CAREER LADDER

```
┌─────────────────────────────────────┐
│   Manager, Research Department       │
└─────────────────────────────────────┘

┌─────────────────────────────────────┐
│ Senior On-line or Database Specialist│
└─────────────────────────────────────┘

┌─────────────────────────────────────┐
│       On-line Researcher             │
└─────────────────────────────────────┘

┌─────────────────────────────────────┐
│   Database or On-line Trainee        │
└─────────────────────────────────────┘
```

Position Description

On-line Researchers (and people with similar job titles) specialize in retrieving and compiling information from databases. Some common types of databases include:

- a corporation's databases containing financial records, product specifications, contracts, or other documents
- bibliographic databases (containing author, title, and subject information about books or periodicals)
- specialized legal (LexisNexis) or medical (MedLine) databases containing case citations, papers, and studies
- scientific databases (such as data on chemical molecules, weather and climate information, or human genetic structure)
- databases containing the full text of articles from general publications such as the *New York Times* or industry publications such as *PC Magazine*

On-line Researchers work in a variety of settings and generally specialize in particular kinds of information. For example, a legal researcher may be asked to find all cases in the federal courts that deal with a particular legal issue. This mate-rial will be used by lawyers to prepare legal briefs or pleadings where previous decisions by judges are cited. A researcher for a pharmaceutical company may use a special database to find molecules that are similar in structure to those of a drug being tested, in the hope of finding a more effective or safer version. In a newsroom, On-line Researchers may provide reporters with news stories that contain useful background information for the latest Washington scandal.

Not all data searches involve in-house or commercial databases. The explosive growth of the Internet provides online researchers with many other possible sources of information. For example, preliminary versions of scientific papers are sometimes published on-line before they are printed in the traditional journals. Many newspapers and other publications put selected stories on their website. Familiarity with the Internet and the use of search engines such as Google and directories such as Yahoo! are now necessary parts of the on-line researcher's tool kit.

Specialized On-line Researchers often have additional job duties. For example, legal assistants often use the information they retrieve to prepare and file routine legal paperwork.

On-line Researchers in all specialties must keep up with new features that may be implemented for particular databases, and with new sources that pop up on the Internet. Compiling and maintaining a good set of links or "bookmarks" to available information sources can be helpful.

Salaries

Salaries vary with the size of the organization and the degree of complexity and specialization. Individuals skilled in the use of commercial databases such as Dialog and LexisNexis often hold specialized job titles (such as legal assistant) and are paid more highly than researchers who work mainly with bibliographic data, news articles, or the Internet.

Employment Prospects

Demand is high for individuals who have both good general research skills (including the Internet) and specialized skills in the legal, medical, or scientific area. Eventually search engines with natural language processing and artificial intelligence may replace on-line researchers for the more routine sorts of queries.

Advancement Prospects

As they gain more experience and specialized skills, On-line Researchers can earn higher pay. There is also considerable opportunity for independent contractors or "information brokers" who can connect users to the information sources they need. Another career possibility is to get a library science degree and become a reference librarian, an area where on-line research skills are also very important.

Education and Training

Many On-line Researchers have a four-year college degree in a computer-related field such as information systems. Liberal arts graduates who have taken appropriate computer-related courses and can demonstrate skills also have a shot at entry-level jobs. Specialized researchers often have graduate degrees or additional training in fields such as law, marketing, medicine, or a scientific field.

Experience, Skills, and Personality Traits

The individual must have a good general background in computing, with emphasis on database structure, networking, and the Internet. Programming experience is a plus;

knowledge of search techniques (including use of Boolean terms and SQL, or Structured Query Language) is also important. An On-line Researcher must have good communication skills: first, to help the information user determine what precisely is needed, and later, to be able to present the information in the most useful form.

Searching for information can be time consuming. Often several different kinds of queries will fail to retrieve a useful result, and the researcher must try a different approach. Persistence, patience, and adaptability are all important.

Cross-Training for On-line Researchers

Interests	Related Job Descriptions
answer queries in a library	Reference or Special Librarian
work with bibliographic data	Reference Librarian; Technical Services Librarian; Library Assistant
analyze numeric data	Statistician
write on-line articles	On-line Writer/Editor

Unions and Associations

Some On-line Researchers may be classified as clerical employees and belong to clerical worker unions.

Tips for Entry

1. Hone your on-line research skills by using the Internet, library book or magazine catalogs, or commercial information services when researching school papers or projects.
2. Think about a field where you would like to do research (such as law, science, medicine, or a particular kind of business or industry). Search the Internet and compile a guide to sites and sources that relate to that field.
3. For college, consider a major in information science or library science (if available)—both emphasize information retrieval skills. Don't neglect getting a good background in database software and use of query languages and search engines.
4. You may have to be creative in finding entry-level positions. You may be able to use your search skills in a position that includes other duties, such as research assistant, legal assistant, or library assistant.

COMPUTER CARTOGRAPHER

CAREER PROFILE

Duties: Creates maps from data stored in databases or obtained in the field; integrates maps with GPS (Global Positioning System) applications

Alternate Title(s): GIS (Geographic Information Systems) Specialist; Cartographic Technician

Salary Range: $30,000 to $50,000

Employment Prospects: Good

Advancement Prospects: Fair

Prerequisites:

Education or Training—Two-year college degree with computer database and graphics skills, mathematics (geometry and trigonometry), and principles of geography; four-year degree or graduate study required for many positions

Experience—Computer graphics and CAD experience helpful

Special Skills and Personality Traits—Spatial perception and visualization; database use, graphics, and CAD; advanced mathematics (topology and mapping theory); should be able to concentrate for long periods and like to work with details

CAREER LADDER

```
┌─────────────────────────────────────┐
│   Director, Cartographic Services    │
└─────────────────────────────────────┘

┌─────────────────────────────────────┐
│        Senior Cartographer           │
└─────────────────────────────────────┘

┌─────────────────────────────────────┐
│        GPS or GIS Specialist         │
└─────────────────────────────────────┘

┌─────────────────────────────────────┐
│   Trainee or Technician, Cartography │
└─────────────────────────────────────┘
```

Position Description

Maps and mapping software are used in a variety of applications by workers known as Cartographers or GIS (Geographic Information Systems) Specialists.

A common application of GIS is to plot data from a database on a map to show geographic concentration. For example, a map of a metropolitan area can have dots or shading layered on it to show criminal activity, the location of toxic waste dumps, or the degree of earthquake hazard. On a more positive note, maps can show areas where the greatest number of new jobs are being created or the kinds of trees growing in a forest.

The Computer Cartographer can create new maps using coordinates that are keyed in or obtained from surveying instruments or sensors. He or she must be familiar both with database retrieval and with different kinds of computer graphics programs that plot the data, such as those based on rasters (or pixel dots) and those based on vectors (lines). Maps are often stored as a series of layers that show different kinds of data such as elevation and vegeta-

tion type. The maps can be manipulated to show different scales or graphic resolutions, and printed on special plotters or printers.

Many Computer Cartographers work for government agencies that manage demographic information—data about what kinds of people live where, the distribution of economic activity, and so on. Highway and mass transit agencies must map their transportation systems. Utility companies use mapping software to keep track of power and sewer lines. Many kinds of scientists use map information, ranging from weather and climate forecasting to geology and seismology (earthquake faults). Businesses can use mapping information to target marketing campaigns or to manage the delivery of goods.

The growing use of GPS (Global Positioning System) technology has added a new dimension to the use of maps. GPS uses portable receivers that pick up signals from a system of satellites. Calculations based on the signals allows the GPS device to determine the receiver's location on the earth's surface to within a couple of hundred feet or less.

Computer Cartographers can work for manufacturers of GPS devices to create the stored maps and databases that the device uses to translate the set of coordinates it has calculated into a "you are here" display that can show a pilot, truck driver, or ordinary motorist his or her current map location. When combined with a database and sophisticated software, the system can even tell a driver what turns to make or exits to take to get to a desired destination.

Cartographers also create original maps and mapping databases from the "raw data" gathered by surveyors, aerial photography, satellites, or other means. These specialists must understand advanced mathematics such as topology (the study of surfaces) and use a technique called photogrammetrics to measure areas that cannot be accessed physically or for military or intelligence agency use. The maps are drawn using special CAM (Computer-aided Mapping) programs that simplify the task of map drawing.

Salaries

Salaries vary with the kind of cartography being used and the kind of organization. Entry-level positions involving routine tasks such as maintenance of GPS databases start around $30,000, with experience and specialized skills bringing higher salaries into the $40,000 range or more. Specialists in remote sensing or Cartographers who do original mapping work can make up to $50,000 or more. Many of the higher-paying jobs are with government agencies.

Employment Prospects

The growth of GPS applications has led to a fairly strong demand for Computer Cartographers. The need to manage environmental and land-use problems has also led to new applications for Cartographers. As the U.S. military continues to fight terrorism and intervene in various parts of the world, it is likely that there will be strong demand for military applications of cartography and GPS systems, such as surveillance and reconnaissance by satellites and remotely piloted drones, as well as in creating map displays for soldiers on the ground. Job seekers should read industry publications to learn about areas of high demand.

Advancement Prospects

One way individuals can advance in this field is by getting an advanced degree in geography or a related subject, learning the advanced mathematical skills needed for designing new kinds of maps, or becoming a specialist in the use of maps for particular industrial needs. Going into management is also a possibility, particularly in government agencies that do extensive mapping such as the U.S. Geological Survey, Meteorological Service (Weather Bureau), or naval or oceanographic offices.

Education and Training

Individuals with a two-year college degree with courses in computer graphics and CAD, database use, geography, and mathematics (especially geometry and trigonometry) may qualify for entry-level positions as cartographic aides or technicians. A four-year or graduate degree in geography with advanced mathematics is generally required for positions involving map design.

Experience, Skills, and Personality Traits

While experience in cartography is not always needed for entry-level positions, experience that shows computer skills (databases, graphics, and CAD) and knowledge of mathematical principles (particularly geometry and trigonometry) is important to most employers. In addition to computer and mathematics skills, individuals need good vision and the ability to visualize spatial relationships. The ability to concentrate for long periods of time and to organize details is also important.

Cross-Training for Computer Cartographers

Interests	Related Job Descriptions
creating design drawings	CAD Technician
analyzing demographic data	Statistician

Unions and Associations

Some low-level cartographic employees may belong to clerical workers' unions. Professionals can join organizations such as the American Society for Photogrammetry and Remote Sensing and the American Congress on Surveying and Mapping.

Tips for Entry

1. If you're the kind of person who likes to map out all the dungeons in a computer role-playing game, cartography may be the job for you. You can find many other kinds of maps on the Internet, including weather maps and maps of Mars or the moon. Try to identify the techniques the map makers uses to represent information.

2. People can often combine cartography with other interests, such as environmental studies, land use, history, geology, and transportation. Your interests can help you find an area in which to specialize as you acquire the computer and mathematics skills.

3. See if your college has a major in geography. The department may be able to give you more information about courses and areas of specialization.

4. The growth of GPS has resulted in many start-up companies marketing products that use the technology for innovative applications. Find out if they have

part-time or temporary positions that can use your computer and map skills.

5. Other organizations that may hire Computer Cartographers include government planning agencies, defense contractors, news media, reference book publishers, transportation companies, and companies involved with natural resources such as oil or gas.

ACADEMIC INFORMATION SCIENCE PROFESSIONS

PROFESSOR, COMPUTER SCIENCE

CAREER PROFILE

Duties: Teaches college courses in computer science theory and information management; performs research and supervises student research; can serve as consultant to government or business

Alternate Title(s): Professor, MIS (Management Information Science)

Salary Range: $50,000 to $90,000

Employment Prospects: Fair

Advancement Prospects: Fair

Prerequisites:

Education or Training—Minimum of master's degree; doctoral degree for full-time university professorship

Experience—Experience as research or teaching assistant

Special Skills and Personality Traits—Ability to handle theory and abstractions; teaching ability; mastery of research methodology; good writing and communication skills; interest in learning and intellectual challenges; creativity

CAREER LADDER

```
┌─────────────────────────────────────┐
│   Full Professor, Computer Science   │
└─────────────────────────────────────┘

┌─────────────────────────────────────┐
│ Associate Professor, Computer Science│
└─────────────────────────────────────┘

┌─────────────────────────────────────┐
│       Instructor or Lecturer,        │
│          Computer Science            │
└─────────────────────────────────────┘
```

Position Description

Professors of Computer Science teach courses in a variety of computer-related fields in a community college or university. The traditional computer science curriculum includes courses involving:

- algorithms (procedures for manipulating data)
- data structures (arrays, lists, and other ways to represent data in the computer)
- object-oriented program design (breaking programs into manageable parts that contain data and procedures that fit together)
- software engineering (principles of program design, development, and testing)
- operating system design, network theory, compiler design, and computer architecture
- systems analysis (determining the needs and goals for software)
- computer graphics theory
- user interface design
- simulation and modeling
- artificial intelligence techniques (expert systems, neural networks, and so on)
- robotics

The computer science curriculum emphasizes theory rather than the practical considerations found in most business programming situations. Therefore many universities have an alternative curriculum and major: management information systems (MIS) or information systems (IS). This course of study also covers systems analysis and programming theory, but it is more practically oriented. Additional subjects in MIS might include:

- network administration
- database analysis and design
- computer security and auditing
- business applications programming and report generation
- systems integration

MIS students also take courses in management and business administration, or even work toward an MBA (master's in business administration) degree along with their computer studies. While computer science is normally in the science and technology part of the campus, MIS is often part of the business school, reflecting its different orientation.

Whether working in a computer science or MIS department, the Professor gives class lectures and seminars, advises students on their research projects, and conducts his or her own research (often with the aid of student assistants).

Recent developments in media, telecommunications, and the Internet offer alternatives to the traditional classroom setting. Professors can record classes on videotape, conduct seminars via Internet chat services, or develop joint courses with faculty in other institutions. A number of institutions now offer "distance learning" programs where students can take classes and even earn degrees without ever setting foot on campus.

Professors in research institutes may do little or no teaching. Professors who have established a reputation in a particular field can serve as consultants to business or government.

Salaries

The first teaching position after getting the master's degree is usually an instructorship or lectureship, which involves teaching or leading class sections under the supervision of a Professor. This pays around $25,000 to $30,000. Professors average from $40,000 (associate) to about $65,000 (full professor).

Employment Prospects

Consolidations and cutbacks in higher education have made it harder in general to get an entry level (associate) professorship. Individuals must often work on a part-time or temporary basis as a lecturer or instructor until they can build up their record by doing research and publishing papers. The strong demand for Computer Science and MIS graduates does give applicants in this field an advantage over those seeking jobs in many other campus departments.

Advancement Prospects

Because full professorship (which usually brings tenure, and thus job security) is so desirable, competition is vigorous for the relatively few positions available. Traditionally, individuals advance in the academic world more by research (leading projects and publishing papers) than by teaching skill. Individuals who are willing to give up the quest for academic job security can seek nontraditional ways in which to teach or become consultants to industry if they have specialized knowledge that is in demand.

Education and Training

A graduate (master's) degree in computer science or MIS is generally required for any teaching at the community (two-year) college level. Full-time professorships in a university require a doctoral (Ph.D.) degree.

Experience, Skills, and Personality Traits

Teaching experience is important, but the key to advancement as a Professor is usually research and publication. Professors are expected to spend a considerable portion of their time seeking to create new theories in information science or to devise new techniques that will eventually become part of the toolbox of the working programmer. In addition to teaching and research skills, Professors need good writing and communication skills and the self-discipline to work on long-term projects without supervision. The best Professors inspire students with their genuine love of learning and scientific exploration.

Cross-Training for Computer Science Professors

Interests	Related Job Descriptions
teaching computer skills in K–12 schools	Teacher of Computer Skills (K–12)
developing school computer courses	Curriculum Specialist, Educational Computing
teaching applications software	Trainer, Computer Applications

Unions and Associations

Computer science and MIS Professors normally belong to faculty organizations on campus, national academic organizations, and leading professional organizations such as the Association for Computing Machinery (ACM) and Institute of Electrical and Electronics Engineers (IEEE). Professors in MIS may also belong to professional management organizations.

Tips for Entry

1. The academic life can be attractive, but the goal of becoming a Professor is long-term and will take considerable time and money. If possible, talk to a favorite college teacher or professor about what his or her working life is like. This can help you decide whether you want to commit yourself to an academic career.

2. Try to decide whether you prefer teaching or research. If the latter, you may want to look for positions in laboratories or industry that don't require teaching. Also think about whether you prefer exploring theory to devising practical applications. This can help you choose between computer science and MIS as a specialty.

3. In addition to applying for teaching assistant positions on campus, you may be able to get some teaching experience by volunteering to help teach computer skills in a school or community center.

4. Educators will have to deal with the growing shortage of qualified graduates for computer fields, and technology is making new ways of teaching possible. Keep in touch with these trends and look for them to bring new job opportunities.

5. Many large companies offer continuing education and training for their programmers and other MIS personnel, or even programs designed to bring in talented

people who lack formal education. This may offer you additional opportunities to teach courses in MIS or computer science outside the university.

6. If you gain special expertise, writing articles or books might become an additional source of income.

7. Keep up with new developments in education, such as Web-based "distance learning" courses.

8. The demand for technical expertise in developing countries may provide employment opportunities abroad.

LIBRARY ASSISTANT

CAREER PROFILE

Duties: Works in library circulation, reference, or technical service departments under supervision of a librarian; can check books in or out, answer simple questions from library users, or help catalog books or periodicals

Alternate Title(s): Library Clerk; Library Technician; Library Paraprofessional

Salary Range: $15,000 to $35,000

Employment Prospects: Fair

Advancement Prospects: Fair

Prerequisites:

Education or Training—Minimum of high school diploma; two-year college degree or certificate preferred

Experience—General clerical experience that brings familiarity with filing and indexing procedures; work dealing with the public

Special Skills and Personality Traits—General literacy; familiarity with use of reference books; general computer skills; typing; knowledge of cataloging procedures; good communication skills; must like to work with details; circulation and reference staff must be comfortable working with the general public

CAREER LADDER

```
┌─────────────────────────────────┐
│   Senior Library Assistant      │
│   or Paraprofessional           │
└─────────────────────────────────┘

┌─────────────────────────────────┐
│      Library Assistant          │
└─────────────────────────────────┘

┌─────────────────────────────────┐
│       Library Clerk             │
└─────────────────────────────────┘
```

Position Description

The category of Library Assistant as discussed here covers a variety of positions. Library clerk positions generally involve routine clerical tasks such as checking books in and out, renewing and reserving books, issuing or renewing library cards, shelving books, helping with acquisition (purchase of new books), typing, and filing.

The Library Assistant job title generally involves individuals who have more extensive training in library procedures such as through a community college program in library science. Typical Library Assistant tasks include:

- supervising clerks in the circulation department and dealing with user complaints or disruptive users
- running small branch or mobile libraries under supervision of a librarian
- answering basic reference questions by phone or in person, and referring more complex questions to a reference librarian

- teaching library users how to use the catalog and reference materials
- looking up cataloging and other bibliographic records from on-line library catalog databases such as OCLC
- checking or revising descriptive cataloging (the part of the catalog card that describes the author, title, publisher, and so on)
- helping design or prepare displays or other special programs
- assisting with computer-related services such as the Internet and multimedia
- helping users with special needs, such as non-English speakers and the disabled

As this list suggests, the Library Assistant can be called upon to provide a number of services. While an individual may be hired specifically for a particular function, changing needs may lead to training or reassignment to other areas.

By the early 1990s most libraries had abandoned their traditional card catalogs in favor of computerized catalogs in which library users look up books and magazines at computer terminals. The new catalogs provide better access to library materials because there are more ways to look things up than the limited number of headings on the old cards. Cataloging, too, has become more efficient because work done by one library is made available to many others.

Libraries are also increasingly called upon to provide public access to on-line databases and the Internet, particularly serving people who lack the skills or financial resources to have their own PCs.

As a result of these trends, library workers (including Library Assistants) must use computers for many job functions. Computer literacy has joined general literacy as a basic job requirement.

Many Library Assistant functions involve dealing with the public in the circulation and reference departments. This requires the ability to relate to people with different ages, backgrounds, and needs, as well as the sometimes difficult challenge of dealing with disruptive people.

Specialized libraries (such as those associated with museums or scientific institutions) may require Assistants who are familiar with their speciality. For example, an Assistant in an art library may need to be familiar with art history or the display and preservation of art works.

Salaries

Clerical and entry-level positions start at around $15,000—more in big cities. Experienced Library Assistants performing complex or supervisory duties can earn around $30,000. University libraries tend to pay more than public libraries.

Employment Prospects

Concern about poor literacy in America has led to some improvement and growth in public libraries and reasonable demand for library clerks and Assistants. Most jobs are in urban public library systems and university libraries, although private and specialized libraries are also possibilities. Individuals who have skills in high demand have an easier time finding employment. Such skills include database operations and use of the Internet, as well as Spanish or Asian languages in areas where large populations speak them.

Advancement Prospects

Library clerks can take courses or receive training qualifying them for the more demanding Library Assistant position. Library Assistants generally progress along a series of salary "steps" as they gain experience. The top rank generally goes to those who act as supervisors, such as in the circulation department. Beyond that, advancement generally requires getting a master's degree in library science (MLS) and becoming a professional librarian.

Education and Training

Clerical positions can be filled by individuals who have a high school diploma, good grades, and basic computer and clerical skills. Many employers want Library Assistants to be at least two-year college graduates; some colleges offer an associate in arts degree (AA) in library technology that is preferred by many employers. Individuals who have skills in high demand may be able to bypass these requirements.

Experience, Skills, and Personality Traits

General clerical (office) experience and experience dealing with the public (such as retail sales) are viewed positively by employers. Important skills include computer literacy; familiarity with databases and the Internet; basic knowledge of library filing and classification systems; good communication skills; and the ability to deal with the general public. Libraries offer job possibilities for a variety of personalities. An introverted book lover may do well in cataloging, while an outgoing problem solver may become a good reference assistant, and a person who likes to work with and manage people may thrive in the circulation department.

Cross-Training for Library Assistants

Interests	Related Job Descriptions
working with the public	Retail Sales Clerk, Computer Products
managing a school library	Media Specialist (School Libraries)
working professionally with library science	Reference or Special Librarian; Librarian (Technical Services)

Unions and Associations

Library clerks and Assistants in public or university libraries may belong to clerical worker unions.

Tips for Entry

1. Many public libraries use volunteers to help with tasks such as shelving books or conducting children's "story time." This can be a good opportunity to learn something about library work while developing contacts that could lead to a job.
2. Look for community college programs in library technology. You can also broaden your background with courses that emphasize multimedia, foreign languages, and working with children.
3. Take a personal skills inventory. If you have good computer or language skills, look for library jobs that emphasize them. The same goes for special interests such as art, music, or archaeology.
4. Remember that many library skills are transferable to other kinds of work, such as working in a corporate library, information center, archive, or help desk.

REFERENCE OR SPECIAL LIBRARIAN

CAREER PROFILE

Duties: Answers questions from library users; helps users plan their library research; does general reference work or works as a Special Librarian in an academic or business setting

Alternate Title(s): None

Salary Range: $30,000 to $55,000

Employment Prospects: Fair

Advancement Prospects: Fair

Prerequisites:

Education or Training—Master's degree in library science; subject area expertise or additional degree for Special Librarians

Experience—Work with on-line catalogs, databases, and reference sources; work with public

Special Skills and Personality Traits—Comprehensive understanding of the structure, uses, and retrieval of information sources; ability to use a variety of databases and media; ability to clarify users' information needs and to instruct them in research techniques; excellent communication skills; willingness to cope with limited resources and a heavy workload

CAREER LADDER

```
┌─────────────────────────────────────┐
│           Library Director           │
└─────────────────────────────────────┘

┌─────────────────────────────────────┐
│     Director or Chief, User Services │
└─────────────────────────────────────┘

┌─────────────────────────────────────┐
│         Reference Librarian          │
└─────────────────────────────────────┘

┌─────────────────────────────────────┐
│    Associate Reference Librarian     │
└─────────────────────────────────────┘
```

Position Description

The modern library has much more than just books, periodicals, sound recordings, and videos. It contains powerful tools people can use to find information. The Reference Librarian is the person who provides answers to questions on a variety of subjects and helps library users master tools such as reference books, catalogs and indexes, CD-ROM databases, on-line information services, and the Internet.

Reference Librarians are library scientists who have studied the structure of information and methods for its retrieval. They are familiar with a variety of traditional, multimedia, and on-line information sources. Some types of information library users seek include:

- bibliographic tools (such as catalogs and magazine indexes) used to find books or articles in magazines or newspapers
- encyclopedias (general or specialized, printed, multimedia, or on-line)
- atlases and statistical information (including government publications)
- general handbooks or guidebooks on a variety of subjects
- reference books (on specialized subjects)
- on-line databases containing the text of magazine articles, scientific papers, legal decisions, medical studies, and other documents
- career resources (job listings, information about employers, and so on)
- community resources (contact information for social and health agencies, training programs, and so on)

Some questions handled by the Reference Librarian are straightforward or have specific answers. Questions about numbers (the population of Boston), historical dates (when Massachusetts was founded), and so on can be looked up and provided on the spot. Requests for introductory material can also be handled easily. For example, if a user asks for basic information about the country of Luxembourg, he or she can be directed to an encyclopedia or an on-line source such as the *CIA World Factbook*.

But the Reference Librarian often has to ask some questions in order to determine what kind of information the library user really needs. If someone asks the Librarian for information about whales, the Librarian may ask whether the inquirer wants to know about whales in general, or about a particular kind of whale, or an aspect of whales such as their endangered species status or their intelligence.

The Librarian also takes the user's age, background, and likely purposes into account. A third grader probably wants a general introduction to whales, while a high school biology student may need a more detailed textbook or help in finding websites or magazine articles about whales or marine biology. If the user is doing a paper or research project, the Librarian may show him or her how to use catalogs, indexes, and perhaps the Internet to find more information.

Many Reference Librarians work in public libraries answering general questions, but public libraries also have specialized services such as children's departments, libraries with literature in non-English languages, or branches designed primarily to serve businesses. While the general principles remain the same, the Reference Librarian working in these areas will also apply specialized knowledge.

Reference Librarians in university libraries are also likely to be more specialized, and many corporations have their own in-house libraries that provide reference service to managers and others working in the company. Corporate Librarians must become "information entrepreneurs" who can not only provide information service, but also demonstrate its value to the company when annual budgets are set.

The Reference Librarian and specialized librarians strive to connect people to the information and resources they need. Once considered a quiet place that changed little over decades, the library continues to undergo rapid technological change. Libraries, together with schools, are in the front lines of the effort to make information technology and literacy accessible to everyone.

Salaries

As with teachers, salaries for Librarians of all types have improved in recent years, although they remain less than those earned by people with comparable skills in the corporate world. Public libraries in large cities and university libraries tend to pay more.

Employment Prospects

Competition for entry-level Librarian positions in attractive urban areas tends to be vigorous. Individuals can improve their chances by acquiring specialized skills (such as business databases or the Internet), being willing to work evenings or weekends, and considering positions in more remote areas.

Individuals who have a special area of interest (such as archaeology, art, or music) should also consider special libraries such as those attached to museums or research institutes. Job seekers with business experience and knowledge of a particular industry can seek employment in corporate libraries. Individuals with programming and other computer-related skills may be able to cross over into such areas as database analysis or multimedia development.

Advancement Prospects

Advancement can come from increased specialization, becoming a consultant in some area of library work, or going into library management with the goal of becoming chief of a library department or Library Director.

Education and Training

All professional librarians must have a master's in library science (MLS) degree. The curriculum provides training in all aspects of library work, but individuals who want to become Reference Librarians will concentrate on the use of reference sources and databases as well as the "reference interview" or techniques for helping library users clarify their needs.

Experience, Skills, and Personality Traits

Experience as a library intern or assistant is helpful, as is experience with the Internet and on-line databases. Important skills include the ability to organize and extract information, communication and interviewing skills, willingness to work odd hours or with limited resources, persistence, and love of public service.

Cross-Training for Reference Librarians

Interests	Related Job Descriptions
working in library cataloging department	Librarian, Technical Services
running a high school library	Media Specialist (School Libraries)
teaching computer skills	Teacher, Computer Skills

Unions and Associations

The American Library Association (ALA) is the main professional organization for Librarians. It has affiliated state organizations. Librarians in special libraries often belong to the Special Libraries Association (SLA); there are also specialized organizations for particular kinds of special libraries.

Tips for Entry

1. Roughly speaking, if you find you are more interested in organizing information, you should look into technical services (cataloging). If you are more interested in using tools to help people find information, you may be interested in becoming a Reference Librarian.

2. When investigating college library science programs, make sure they are up to date in their approach to computer technology and the Internet. Also ask about internships and job placement help.

3. Keep up with periodicals such as *American Libraries* and *Library Journal* for job notices and tips. The Special Libraries Association website also has listings for nontraditional positions that use librarian skills.

4. When looking for a job, don't forget to keep in mind any particular skills you may have (such as webpage design or multimedia authoring) that might match the needs of libraries that are trying to expand their coverage of the Internet and new media technology.

5. Libraries are increasingly interested in serving people with special needs. Your language skills and ability to relate to people from different cultures may be a plus for you in job interviews.

CATALOGER (LIBRARIAN)

CAREER PROFILE

Duties: Assigns subject headings to books and other library materials; verifies or establishes the standard form of names of authors and institutions; classifies materials to establish their shelving location

Alternate Title(s): Subject Cataloger; Classifier

Salary Range: $30,000 to $50,000

Employment Prospects: Fair

Advancement Prospects: Fair

Prerequisites:

Education or Training—Master's in library science (MLS) degree from ALA-accredited library school

Experience—Experience working with library catalog records and on-line cataloging systems

Special Skills and Personality Traits—Excellent reading skills and ability to characterize what a book is about; mastery of complex classification systems; attention to detail; ability to work without much contact with the public

CAREER LADDER

```
┌─────────────────────────────┐
│      Head Cataloger         │
└─────────────────────────────┘

┌─────────────────────────────┐
│      Senior Cataloger       │
└─────────────────────────────┘

┌─────────────────────────────┐
│        Cataloger            │
└─────────────────────────────┘
```

Position Description

Few library users take the time to wonder how a library is able to keep track of the hundreds of thousands of books, periodicals, videos, sound recordings, computer disks, and other materials on its shelves. The electronic catalogs in most libraries today make it easier than ever before for people to find the materials they want. It is the Library Catalogers who make all this organization and retrieval possible.

When a book or other item arrives at the library, Catalogers must determine several things:

- the correct name of the author or authors (many people with similar names have written books in the last 500 years, and the same person can publish under several versions of his or her name). Catalogers create an "authority file" with the established entry form for each person or organization.
- the correct description of the item (including author, title, publisher, publication date, any series the item belongs to, and so on)
- which Library of Congress subject headings best describe the contents of the item. There are many kinds of subheadings that break down subjects into more specific aspects.

- the classification number that will determine where the book will be shelved. (Most public libraries use the venerable Dewey Decimal numeric classifications, while many university libraries use the Library of Congress A-Z classifications).

Generally, professional librarians do the subject cataloging and classification. The descriptive cataloging is often done by library assistants.

The Library of Congress prepares millions of catalog records for the materials it adds to its collection. In addition, most libraries belong to cooperative on-line catalogs such as OCLC. Since many materials acquired by a library have already been cataloged by the Library of Congress or another library in the on-line system, catalogers can use these existing catalog records as the basis for their own cataloging. Library assistants can prepare these modified cataloging records, which are then checked by a professional Cataloger. This use of automation gives the Cataloger more time to do "original cataloging"—that is, cataloging and classification of materials that have no existing cataloging records or that are unusual or specialized. For example, a library that has a collection of local history materials or small press publications will probably have to create its own cataloging records for them.

Catalogers can also specialize in cataloging periodicals and other serial publications. Periodicals bring their own challenges: They frequently change names or cease publication only to reappear under a different title. And while computers have aided Catalogers tremendously, the new media of the information age (computer software and CD-ROM publications) also stretch the traditional cataloging rules.

Salaries
Entry-level Catalogers generally start in the high $20,000 range. Experience or specialization can bring higher salaries of $40,000 or more.

Employment Prospects
The work of the Library of Congress and the on-line catalog databases such as OCLC has reduced the need for most libraries to do their own cataloging of most books and other materials. The Library of Congress is of course itself a major employer of Catalogers. Libraries that focus on rare or specialized materials in fields such as science, the arts, law, and medicine are also a good source of employment for Catalogers who have good knowledge of the subject.

Advancement Prospects
Catalogers can move into management as head of the cataloging department or of technical services (a library division that includes cataloging and other functions involving processing of materials). An individual who also has interest in and experience with management can seek the top position of director of the library.

Education and Training
Like all professional librarians, the Cataloger must nearly always have a master's degree in library science (MLS) from an ALA-accredited institution. This program includes all aspects of library work, but an individual interested in cataloging will probably focus on the use of authority records, subject headings, classification schedules, and other tools.

Experience, Skills, and Personality Traits
Library school students normally serve as interns or library associates to get hands-on experience of library operations. Important skills for Catalogers include the ability to quickly get a sense of the key subjects or topics covered by a book or other item; mastery of the details of the complex subject heading and classification system; consistency; and organization. Since Catalogers do not have much direct contact with library users they do not need "people skills" as much as do library managers or reference librarians, but communication skills are still important. The individual should be comfortable with working many hours at a computer terminal.

Cross-Training for Catalogers

Interests	Related Job Descriptions
helping users find library materials	Reference or Special Librarian
organizing materials for school libraries	Media Specialist (School Libraries)

Unions and Associations
Catalogers belong to the American Library Association (ALA), their state library association, the Special Libraries Association (SLA), and various professional "roundtables" or other groups devoted to cataloging issues.

Tips for Entry
1. If you are the kind of person who is fascinated by information in all its complexity and variety, cataloging may be for you. If you are more interested in helping people find information, you should consider becoming a reference or special librarian.
2. In your undergraduate years, take introductory courses in subjects such as bibliography, use of reference sources, and research techniques. Make sure you are familiar with basic computer operations, the use of databases, and the Internet. Don't forget, however, that a broad education that introduces many aspects of the physical and social sciences and arts will help you deal with the many kinds of materials you will be cataloging.
3. A part-time or temporary library assistant job may be a good way to get some experience and to find out whether you really like library work.
4. When choosing a library school, try to determine if their program is technologically up to date. Since the job market in this field is always competitive, you should think about special skill areas (such as foreign languages, special subject knowledge, or computer expertise) that might give you an edge.

MEDIA OR CURRICULUM SPECIALIST (SCHOOL LIBRARIES)

CAREER PROFILE

Duties: Manages all aspects of a school library, combining educational and librarian functions; selects and organizes materials; trains teachers and students in the use of multimedia and on-line resources

Alternate Title(s): School Librarian

Salary Range: $30,000 to $45,000

Employment Prospects: Good

Advancement Prospects: Fair

Prerequisites:

Education or Training—Master's degree in library science for individuals based in school libraries; master's in education and credentials for individuals working as classroom teachers; coursework in computer skills, multimedia, and networks

Experience—Experience in teaching or library work with emphasis on multimedia and the Internet

Special Skills and Personality Traits—Ability to quickly master new technology; thorough understanding of education and needs of teachers and students; excellent communication and managerial skills

CAREER LADDER

```
┌─────────────────────────────────┐
│   Director, Media or Curriculum │
│     Development Department       │
└─────────────────────────────────┘

┌─────────────────────────────────┐
│  Media or Curriculum Specialist │
└─────────────────────────────────┘

┌─────────────────────────────────┐
│   Assistant, Aide, or Instructor,│
│         Media Center             │
└─────────────────────────────────┘
```

Position Description

Unlike the case with large public and university libraries, the average high school library has just one person who combines the functions of library manager, collection developer, cataloger, reference librarian, and teacher of computer and media skills. This versatile, busy person is the Media Specialist.

As manager, the Media Specialist must supervise employees or volunteers, schedule class visits to the library and other activities, and handle budgeting and other paperwork. The Media Specialist must also select materials (books, periodicals, CD-ROM references, educational software, videos, and so on). He or she will often consult with teachers to determine what materials will best support the needs of their students.

Sometimes there are tough issues involving selection. It's seldom possible to get everything everyone wants. For example, given limited funds, should the library purchase an extensive (but expensive) multimedia package that will help the environmental science class with its projects, or spend the money on several subscriptions to magazines that can help students and teachers interested in the Internet and Web design?

Sometimes the school library can become the focus of controversy when some parents object to materials being in the library—for example, because they feel they are too sexually explicit or do not sufficiently recognize the contributions of minorities.

The Media Specialist must maintain a catalog of the library and keep track of materials borrowed from the library. Fortunately, much of the tedium of routine processing can be relieved by integrated software packages that can handle acquisition (adding an item to the collection), cataloging (using Library of Congress or other records), and circulation.

The Media Specialist spends considerable time introducing each class to the library and showing students how to use reference books, multimedia computers, and other resources.

A related position is that of Curriculum Specialist. While the Media Specialist is usually based in the library, the Curriculum Specialist is more directly involved in the development of teaching skills. For example, the Curriculum Specialist can advise teachers on new products and other resources that might be of interest to their classes. He or she may hold workshops to train teachers in the use of multimedia and the Internet. Knowledge of the teaching process and the needs of teachers and students is thus very important for this position.

The growth of the Internet and the nationwide effort to link schools to the Net presents an exciting challenge to the Media Specialist. Many teachers were trained before the Internet became widely available, and they need to be brought up to speed before they can supervise their students' use of the Internet. While the Internet is a marvelous educational resource, it also contains materials considered inappropriate for young people. The Media Specialist often has the job of creating guidelines for use of the Internet. Blocking software may be used to screen out objectionable material, but it is not a substitute for keeping in close touch with what students are doing. (The Media Specialist as a librarian must also be concerned with free speech and free access, rights stoutly defended by the American Library Association. Balancing these two concerns can be quite a challenge.)

Salaries

The positions of Media Specialist and Curriculum Specialist are still evolving, and salaries depend a lot on the job description and responsibilities. Media Specialists working in school libraries start at about $30,000. Curriculum Specialists who work for state departments of education and conduct workshops for teachers tend to make higher salaries.

Employment Prospects

Because of the new emphasis on multimedia and the Internet in the educational system there is a growing demand for Media Specialists, especially for individuals who have strong Internet and multimedia skills. These positions are exciting and desirable and tend to be very competitive.

Advancement Prospects

A Media Specialist in a school library can probably advance only by getting a job in a larger school or by going into administration or management. Curriculum Specialists can advance by becoming directors of special projects or going into management in the department of education.

Education and Training

Media Specialists generally must have a master's of library science (MLS) degree. Curriculum Specialists often have a master's degree in education, though liberal arts graduates with strong skills may be able to enter the field.

Experience, Skills, and Personality Traits

Depending on the job description, employers will be looking for some combination of library, multimedia, or teaching experience. The variety of skills required make this a good position for a "Renaissance Person" who is fascinated both by technology and by the interaction of teachers and learners.

Cross-Training for Media or Curriculum Specialists

Interests	Related Job Descriptions
organizing library materials	Cataloger
helping library users find information	Reference Librarian
developing multimedia products	Multimedia Developer

Unions and Associations

Curriculum Specialists classified as teachers may belong to a teacher's union (the National Education Association or American Federation of Teachers). Media Specialists acting as librarians generally belong to the American Library Association.

Tips for Entry

1. Be flexible in assessing your interests and comparing them to job descriptions. Try to determine whether a particular position seems to call more for a librarian or for a teacher.
2. You can increase your employment possibilities by looking for other settings where your library and media skills can be used, such as church schools, computer camps, senior centers, adult or continuing education, corporate training programs, and so on.
3. Use the Internet both for job hunting and for keeping up with the many resources (including simulations, projects, and lesson plans) that you can use on the job.

APPENDIXES

APPENDIX I
USING THE WORLD WIDE WEB
FOR CAREER PLANNING

The Internet and the World Wide Web are changing the way people look for educational and employment opportunities. The websites for educational institutions can give useful information about the majors and courses offered. Many employers now list job openings on their websites, while prospective employees can post their résumés to be scanned by eager recruiters. There are also a number of sites that specialize in helping job seekers. What follows is a set of tips that combine traditional and on-line techniques for career development, accompanied by references to useful websites.

A Note on Websites and Addresses

> The World Wide Web is a constantly changing array of data sources. Some addresses given here may no longer be valid by the time you read about them. There will no doubt be many new sources of information and help appearing as more institutions move onto the Web. Use search techniques (see below) and lists of links on webpages to find more information.

Exploring Career Interests

1. Start by considering what areas or applications of computing interest you the most (such as artificial intelligence or database design or marketing computer products). Read the relevant job descriptions in this book and note the kinds of training and skills needed for a career in that area. Jot down some keywords from your reading—they will be helpful in doing Web searches later.

2. You can find more details and job descriptions on the Web. For example the on-line version of the *Occupational Outlook Handbook (www.bls.gov/oco)* lets you search by keyword to find matching job descriptions.

3. In addition to traditional personality and preference tests, you can use sites such as Career Key *(www. careerkey.org/english/)* to get suggestions for careers based on your personal talents and interests.

4. By now you have probably found a few kinds of work in the computer field that you want to pursue further.

Before you get too immersed in specific job descriptions, step back and explore your target profession as a whole. Check the appendixes in this book for organizations, periodicals, and books relating to your field of interest. Visit the websites of professional or industry organizations—they often have links to further information. Look through an introductory text or two—don't worry if the material is too advanced. Just get the big picture of what computer mapmakers (or statisticians, or desktop publishers . . .) are concerned with in their profession.

5. Find out what software engineers (or Web designers, computer technicians, or on-line marketers . . .) have to say about their professions and careers by borrowing a few issues of a professional or trade periodical at your local library.

6. As you become more focused on your goals, start creating a file with useful information and contacts. Free-form database or note-taking programs are ideal for this purpose. Also, use your Web browser's "bookmarks" facility to create folders (such as Career Research, Bibliography, Colleges, Job Listing Sites, and so on). This will help you organize the resources you are finding on the Web.

7. Comprehensive guides that bring together many kinds of resources available for your career search are starting to appear. One of the best-organized and most useful is the Riley Guide *(www.rileyguide.com)*. Use this and other sources to add to your collection of bookmarks.

8. There are two general tools that you can use to research anything on the World Wide Web. First, there are directory services such as Yahoo! *(www.yahoo.com)*. You can click on the Computers and the Internet category and then work your way down to listing of categories such as computer science, industry information, magazines, employment, organizations, and so on.

9. The way to cast the widest net is to use a search service such as Google *(www.google.com)* and give it keywords that describe what you are looking for. Since you can get thousands of "hits," it is important to be as specific as possible. Don't type "programming" when what you really want is "artificial intelligence programming."

Finding College and Vocational Programs

There are more than 1,200 colleges offering computer science majors and hundreds more with management information systems, information systems, multimedia studies, and other computer-related majors. This is far too many to list in an appendix, so instead, here are some tips for matching your interests in the computer field to college majors or community college or vocational certificate programs.

1. Printed guides to colleges are still one of the easiest ways to look up basic information about institutions. For example, the annual publication *Peterson's Four-Year Colleges* includes information about the programs and degrees offered by more than 2,000 U.S. and Canadian colleges. The accompanying CD lets you search using keywords such as "artificial intelligence" or "information systems." *Peterson's Two-Year Colleges* provides similar information for community colleges. Another good reference is Edward Fiske's *The Fiske Guide to Colleges,* which focuses on the top 300 institutions.

2. There are a number of resource guides for various colleges majors on the Web. For example, the University of North Carolina at Wilmington has a resource page on computer science at *http://www.uncwil.edu/stuaff/career/Majors/computer.htm.*

3. A keyword search in a search engine such as Google or HotBot *(www.hotbot.com)* can also help you find institutions associated with particular subjects. For example, a search for "multimedia studies" will pull up a number of pages relating to college programs in this field.

4. Suppose you want to find a specific institution that has been recommended to you from some other source. You can use Yahoo's organized listings of universities and colleges by region to locate colleges near you, or use this trick: In your Web browser's address box, type www. followed by the most likely initials for the college, followed by .edu—for example, *http://ww.cmu.edu* for Carnegie Mellon University. You may have to make a few guesses, but it usually works.

Evaluating Educational Programs

1. Try to get recommendations from people working in your intended career field. If you don't know anyone appropriate, newsgroups or chat rooms relating to your career field may be a good place to make such queries, but don't make decisions based on what any one person says on-line.

2. If possible, visit companies that do the kind of computer work you are pursuing. Ask them what colleges they think are doing a good job of preparing students for their workplace, and what kind of work experience they like applicants to have.

3. Compare the on-line or printed college catalogs with typical requirements listed in job descriptions in this book and in real employment ads.

4. If possible, visit several colleges that appear to be good possibilities. Ask them about work-study or internship programs, or cooperative efforts they may have with local computer companies.

5. Although it is important to plan an education that will give you the qualifications you will need to apply for work, try not to focus *too* narrowly, particularly in the first college years. A liberal and diverse education is an asset for many computer careers, particularly in areas such as teaching, multimedia, and library work. Business courses can provide a vital perspective for individuals who will be working in corporate computing departments. Remember that if you are just starting college, in two, four, or more years you will be entering a workplace in which the skills that are in most demand may have changed considerably. Versatility and the ability to make quick adjustments are vital in any computer-related field.

6. Increasingly, education does not end with entry into the workplace. Traditionally, once an individual was working full-time, continuing education was limited to night school (tiring and hard to schedule) or correspondence schools (not very interactive). Today, however, an increasing number of institutions offer "distance learning" programs where students can take courses and even earn a degree via the Internet. Class material is presented via videotape or websites, and discussion is carried on through e-mail and conferencing software. This flexibility means that students can do their work anywhere and anytime. Many distance learning programs are offered by fully accredited, prestigious universities, but it is important to check with state or regional accrediting agencies before enrolling.

7. Industry certifications in operating systems, programming facilities, and hardware are increasingly important for assuring prospective employers that you have mastered certain skills. Information about dozens of certification programs can be found at *http://www.certcities.com.*

Searching for Job Openings

1. Once you have the necessary education and, hopefully, some work experience, it is time to enter the job market. There are several traditional sources for job listings, including newspapers, trade journals, and college or state employment centers. Many of these listings are now appearing on the World Wide Web, where you can easily search them for suitable positions.

2. There are a variety of sites that specialize in job listings. Some include the full Help Wanted ads from daily newspapers, while others compile listings

submitted directly by employers or from other sources such as newsgroups. Here are some examples of popular "megasites."·

America's Job Bank lists nearly a million jobs from thousands of employers and employment agencies. *(www.ajb.dni.us)*

Brass Ring allows jobseekers to research prospective employers, as well as providing the usual job search and résumé services. *(www.brassring.com)*

Career Magazine is a site with many job listings, news about trends in the job marketplace, and even a discussion forum where job hunters can compare notes. *(www.careermag.com)*

CareerBuilder has several types of job searches plus resources and on-line résumé posting. *(www.careerbuilder.com/)*

Computerjobs.com lists computer-related positions by location and type of work. The site includes free registration that allows you to match your current skills to possible jobs, as well as post your résumé on-line. *(www.computerjobs.com)*

DFW Job Search has a number of search facilities and other resources. *(www.jobcenter.com)*

Other megasites with job listings and other resources include:

HotJobs features company profiles and résumé help. *(www.hotjobs.com)*

JobBankUSA *(www.jobbankusa.com)*

The Monster Board *(www.monster.com)* is about as big as the name suggests.

There are many other sites that offer job listings and help for job seekers. Some specialize in particular regions or in helping women or minorities. Others are devoted to particular fields. Professional organizations often have job listing services for their members.

3. If you see an ad or other information about employment opportunities at a particular company, you can check its profile at some of the sites listed above. It's also a good idea to go directly to the company's website. After all, that's a place where the company is likely to describe things that it believes are most important about itself. If you don't have the Web address for a company, try typing www., the company name or initials, plus .com into your browser's address box. For example, for ABC Corp. you can try *http://www.abc.com,* while for Mega Promotions it might be *http://www.mega.com* or *http://www.megapromotions.com.* You may well find additional job listings at the corporate website.

Getting Salary Information

Salary is one of the trickiest issues in any job interview. To prepare yourself to make a realistic salary demand (or to evaluate an employer's offer), you should consult recent surveys of salaries in the computer field. There are a number of websites that can provide useful salary information.

The Riley Guide has pointers to salary surveys at *http://www.rileyguide.com/salguides.html.* Some of the leading salary survey resources include:

JobStar Central *(jobstar.org/tools/salary/index.cfm)*
Salary.com *(www.salary.com)*
WageWeb *(www.wageweb.com)*
Wall Street Journal Career Journal.com *(www.careerjournal. com)*

The federal Bureau of Labor Statistics (BLS) at *http://www.bls.gov* has government surveys on employment and wages.

Salaries must be viewed in relationship to the cost of living (food, rent, and so forth), which varies considerably between different parts of the country. A facility such as the Cost of Living and Salary Calculator at "Sperling's Best Places" *(www.bestplaces.net/html/cost_of_living.html)* can be helpful for comparing salaries in various places.

Advertising Yourself

You don't always have to go to where the jobs are—you can help the employers find you.

1. As noted above, some sites allow you to submit an electronic résumé. They may match it against the database, or recruiters may use the site to find résumés that match their needs. It's a good idea to read the résumé service's instructions and tips carefully so you can prepare the most effective résumé.

2. Many people are creating their own webpages to serve as dynamic résumés. There are services that will prepare a site for you, but if you learn how to use a program such as Microsoft FrontPage you can easily put together a site that better expresses your individuality. Recruiters using search engines will be able to find your résumé if you include keywords that match common descriptions of the job(s) you seek.

3. Newsgroups are another way to post your résumé. Most Web browsers can read newsgroups, or you can connect to a site such as Deja *(www.deja.com)* that provides free access to newsgroups.

APPENDIX II
PROFESSIONAL, INDUSTRY, AND TRADE ASSOCIATIONS

There are hundreds of organizations involved with various aspects of computer science, software and hardware engineering, information systems management, multimedia, education, marketing, and many other aspects of the computer industry.

The following listing of selected groups is divided into categories for convenience. Web addresses (URLs) are listed when available, since visiting an organization's website is often the most convenient way to learn about an organization and to contact it for further information. Note that when "Web form" is listed as the e-mail address it means that queries or requests can be sent to the organization by using a form on its website. The form can usually be reached through a "Contact," "Join," or "E-mail" link.

PART 1: COMPUTER SCIENCE AND ENGINEERING GROUPS

American Association for Artifical Intelligence
445 Burgess Drive
Menlo Park, CA 94025-3442
Phone: (650) 328-3123
E-mail: info@aaai.org
http://www.aaai.org/

American Society for Information Science and Technology
1320 Fenwick Lane
Suite 510
Silver Spring, MD 20910
Phone: (301) 495-0900
E-mail: asis@asis.org
http://www.asis.org/

Association for Computing Machinery (ACM)
One Astor Plaza
17th Floor
New York, NY 10036-5701
Phone: (212) 869-7440
E-mail: ACMHELP@acm.org
http://www.acm.org

Computing Research Association
1100 17th Street, NW
Suite 507
Washington, DC 20036-4632
Phone: (202) 667-1066
E-mail: info@cra.org
http://www.cra.org

Institute for Certification of Computing Professionals
2350 East Devon Avenue
Suite 115
Des Plaines, IL 60018-4610
Phone: (847) 299-4227
or (800) 843-8227
E-mail: office@iccp.org
http://www.iccp.org/

Institute of Electrical and Electronics Engineers (IEEE) Computer Society
1730 Massachusetts Avenue, NW
Washington, DC 20036-1992
Phone: (202) 371-0101
E-mail: membership@computer.org
http://www.computer.org

Mathematical Association of America
1529 18th Street, NW
Washington, DC 20036-1385
Phone: (800) 741-9415
E-mail: maahq@maa.org
http:/www.maa.org

National Center for Supercomputing Applications (NCSA)
University of Illinois at Urbana-Champaign
152 Computing Applications Building
605 East Springfield Avenue
Champaign, IL 61820-5518
Phone: (217) 244-0072
E-mail: kareng@ncsa.uiuc.edu
http://www.ncsa.uiuc.edu

National Telecommunications and Information Administration
U.S. Department of Commerce
1401 Constitution Avenue, NW
Washington, DC 20230
Phone: (202) 482-7002
E-mail: rdesilva@ntia.doc.gov
http://www.ntia.doc.gov

SIGGRAPH (Graphics Special Interest Group)
E-mail: enger@siggraph.org
http://www.siggraph.org
For additional contact information, see Association for Computing Machinery (ACM).

The Society for Computer Simulation International
P.O. Box 17900
San Diego, CA 92177-7900
Phone: (619) 277-3888
E-mail: info@scs.org
http://www.scs.org

Society for Industrial and Applied Mathematics
3600 University City Science Center
Philadelphia, PA 19104-2688
Phone: (215) 382-9800
E-mail: siam@siam.org
http://www.siam.org

Society of Manufacturing Engineers
One SME Drive
P.O. Box 930
Dearborn, MI 48121-0930
Phone: (313) 271-1500
E-mail: service@sme.org
http://www.sme.org

Software Engineering Institute
4500 Fifth Avenue
Pittsburgh, PA 15213-3890
Phone: (412) 268-5800
E-mail: Web form
http://www.sei.cmu.edu/

PART 2: ORGANIZATIONS FOR CONSULTANTS, PROFESSIONALS, AND OTHER WORKERS

American Home Business Association
4505 South Wasatch Boulevard
Suite 140
Salt Lake City, UT 84124
Phone: (800) 664-2422
E-mail: info@homebusiness.com
http://www.homebusiness.com/FLAX/

**Association of Independent
Information Professionals**
8550 United Plaza Boulevard
Suite 101
Baton Rouge, LA 70809
Phone: (225) 408-4400
E-mail: info@aiip.org
http://www.aiip.org/

**Association of Information System
Professionals**
c/o University of Wisconsin, Madison
School of Business
4267 Grainger Hall
Madison, WI 53706
Phone: (608) 263-2538
E-mail: aisp@bus.wisc.edu
http://www.aisp.bus.wisc.edu/

**Association of Information Technology
Professionals**
P.O. Box 809189
Chicago, IL 60680-9189
Phone: (800) 244-9371
E-mail: AITPHQ@aitp.org
http://www.aitp.org/

Association of Internet Professionals
4790 Irvine Boulevard
Suite 105-283
Irvine, CA 92620
Phone: (866) AIP-9700
E-mail: info@association.org
http://www.association.org/

Association of Support Professionals
1211 Barnard Avenue
Watertown, MA 02472-3414

Phone: (617) 924-3944
E-mail: jfarber@asponline.com
http://www.asponline.com/

Communications Workers of America
501 Third Street, NW
Washington, DC 20001-2797
Phone: (202) 434-1279
E-mail: cwaweb@cwa-union.org
http://www.cws-union.org

**Computer Professionals for Social
Responsibility**
P.O. Box 717
Palo Alto, CA 94302
Phone: (650) 322-3778
E-mail: cpsr@cpsr.org
http://www.cpsr.org

Electronics Technicians Association
5 Depot Street
Greencastle, IN 46135
Phone: (765) 653-4287
E-mail: eta@tds.net
http://www.eta-sda.com

**Independent Computer Consultants
Association**
11131 South Towne Square
Suite F
St. Louis, MO 63123
Phone: (800) 774-4222
     or (314) 892-1675
E-mail: info@icca.org
http://www.icca.org/index.htm

**International Society of Certified
Electronics Technicians**
3608 Pershing Avenue
Fort Worth, TX 76107-4527
Phone: (817) 921-9101
E-mail: info@iscet.org
http://www.iscet.org

**National Association for
the Self-Employed**
P.O. Box 612067
DFW Airport
Dallas, TX 75261-2067
Phone: (800) 232-6273
E-mail: Web form
http://www.nase.org/

**National Federation of Independent
Business**
3322 West End Avenue
Suite 700
Nashville, TN 37203
Phone: (800) NFIB-NOW
E-mail: Web form
http://www.nfib.com/

**Office and Professional Employees
International Union**
265 West 14th Street
6th Floor
New York, NY 10011
Phone: (800) 346-7348
E-mail: Web form
http://www.opeiu.org/

**Professional and Technical Consultants
Association**
543 Vista Mar Avenue
Pacifica, CA 94044
Phone: (408) 971-5902
E-mail: info@patca.org
http://www.patca.org

**Service and Support Professionals
Association**
11031 Via Frontera
Suite A
San Diego, CA 92127
Phone: (858) 674-5491
E-mail: Web form
http://www.thesspa.com/

**Society of Telecommunications
Consultants**
P.O. Box 416
Fall River Mills, CA 96028
Phone: (503) 336-7060
E-mail: stchdq@stcconsultants.org
http://www.stcconsultants.org

U.S. Small Business Administration
1441 L Street, NW
Washington, DC 20016
Phone: (800) 827-5722
E-mail: answerdesk@sba.gov
http://www.sba.gov

PART 3: INDUSTRY GROUPS

American Accounting Association
5717 Bessie Drive
Sarasota, FL 34233-2399
Phone: (941) 921-7747
E-mail: office@aaahq.org
http://accounting.rutgers.edu/raw/aaa/

**The American Congress on Surveying
and Mapping**
6 Montgomery Village Avenue
Suite 403
Gaithersburg, MD 20879
Phone: (240) 632-9716
E-mail: info@acsm.net
http://www.acsm.net

American Design Drafting Association
P.O. Box 11937
Columbia, SC 29211
Phone: (803) 771-4272
E-mail: national@adda.org
http://www.adda.org

American Electronics Association
P.O. Box 54990
Santa Clara, CA 95056-0990
Phone: (408) 987-4200
E-mail: csc@aeanet.org
http://www.aeanet.org

American Institute of Architects
1735 New York Avenue, NW
Washington, DC 20006
Phone: (800) AIA-3837
E-mail: infocentral@aia.org
http://www.aia.org

American National Standards Institute (ANSI)
1819 L Street, NW
6th Floor
Washington, DC 20036
Phone: (202) 293-8020
E-mail: info@ansi.org
http://web.ansi.org/default.htm

American Society for Photogrammetry and Remote Sensing
5410 Grosvenor Lane
Suite 210
Bethesda, MD 20814-2160
Phone: (310) 493-0290
E-mail: asprs@asprs.org
http://www.asprs.org

American Statistical Association
1429 Duke Street
Alexandria, VA 22314-3415
Phone: (703) 684-1221
   or (888) 231-3473
E-mail: asainfo@amstat.org
http://www.amstat.org

Association of American Geographers
1710 16th Street, NW
Washington, DC 20009-3198
Phone: (202) 234-1450
E-mail: gaia@aag.org
http://www.aag.org

Automated Imaging Association
900 Victors Way
Suite 140
P.O. Box 3724
Ann Arbor, MI 48106

Phone: (734) 994-8088
E-mail: hstraight@robotics.org
http://www.machinevisiononline.org

Computer-Aided Manufacturing International
3301 Airport Freeway
Suite 324
Bedford, TX 76021
Phone: (817) 860-1654
E-mail: webmaster@cami-i.org
http://www.cam-i.org

Computer Technology Industry Association (CompTIA)
B1815 S. Meyers Road
Suite 300
Lombard, IL 60148-6158
Phone: (630) 268-1818
E-mail: Web form
http://www.comptia.org

Electronics Industries Association
2500 Wilson Boulevard
Arlington, VA 22201
Phone: (703) 907-7500
E-mail: Web form
http://www.eia.org

Help Desk Institute
6385 Corporate Drive
Suite 301
Colorado Springs, CO 80919
Phone: (800) 248-5667
E-mail: sklossner@thinkhdi.com
http://www.thinkhdi.com

Information Technology Association of America
1401 Wilson Boulevard
Suite 1100
Arlington, VA 22209
Phone: (703) 522-5055
E-mail: webmaster@itaa.org
http://www.itaa.org

Office Automation Society International
5710 Meadow Wood Boulevard
Lyndhurst, OH 44124
Phone: (216) 461-4803
E-mail: JBDYKE@aol.com
http://www.pstcc.cc.tn.us/ost/oasi.html

Printing Industries of America
100 Dangerfield Road
Alexandria, VA 22314
Phone: (703) 519-8100
E-mail: gain@printing.org
http://www.gain.net

Robotics Industry Association
900 Victors Way
P.O. Box 3724
Ann Arbor, MI 48106
Phone: (734) 994-6088
E-mail: ria@robotics.org
http://www.robotics.org

Telecommunications Industry Association
2500 Wilson Boulevard
Suite 300
Arlington, VA 22201
Phone: (703) 907-7700
E-mail: tia@tiaonline.org
http://www.tiaonline.org

PART 4: SYSTEMS, MANAGEMENT, AND SECURITY ORGANIZATIONS

American Management Association
1601 Broadway
New York, NY 11019
Phone: (212) 586-8100
E-mail: customerservice@amanet.org
http://www.amanet.org/index.htm

American Society for Quality
600 North Plankinton Avenue
Milwaukee, WI 53203
Phone: (800) 248-1946
E-mail: help@asq.org
http://www.asq.org

Association for Information and Image Management
1100 Wayne Avenue
Suite 1100
Silver Spring, MD 20910
Phone: (800) 477-2446 or (301) 587-8202
E-mail: aiim@aiim.org
http://www.aiim.org

Association of Management Consulting Firms
380 Lexington Avenue
Suite 1700
New York, NY 10168
Phone: (212) 551-7887
E-mail: info@amcf.org
http://www.amcf.org

Computer Emergency Response Team
CERT Coordination Center
Software Engineering Institute
Carnegie Mellon University
Pittsburgh, PA 15213-3890
Phone: (412) 268-7090
E-mail: cert@cert.org
http://www.cert.org

Computer Security Institute
600 Harrison Street
San Francisco, CA 94107
Phone: (415) 947-6320
E-mail: csi@cmp.com
http://www.gocsi.com

**Information Systems Audit and
    Control Association**
3701 Algonquin Road
Suite 1010
Rolling Meadows, IL 60008
Phone: (847) 253-1545
E-mail: membership@isaca.org
http://www.isaca.org

**Information Systems Security
    Association**
7044 South 13th Street
Oak Creek, WI 53154
Phone: (414) 768-8000
E-mail: mbrship@issa.org
http://www.issa.org

**Institute for Operations Research
    and the Management Sciences
    (INFORMS)**
901 Elkridge Landing Road
Suite 400
Linthicum, MD 21090-2909
Phone: (800) 4INFORMS
E-mail: informs@informs.org
http://www.informs.org

Institute of Management Consultants
2025 M Street, NW
Suite 800
Washington, DC 20036-3309
Phone: (202) 367-1134
    or (800) 221-2567
E-mail: mika@imcusa.org
http://www.imcusa.org

National Management Association
2210 Arbor Boulevard
Dayton, OH 45439-1580
Phone: (937) 294-0421
E-mail: nma@nmal.org
http://www.nmal.org

**Product Development and
    Management Association**
17000 Commerce Parkway
Suite C
Mount Laurel, NJ 08054
Phone: (800) 232-5241
    or (856) 439-9052
E-mail: pdma@pdma.org
http://www.pdma.org

Quality Assurance Institute
7575 Dr. Phillips Boulevard
Suite 350
Orlando, FL 32819
Phone: (407) 363-1111
E-mail: Web form
http://wwwqaiusa.com

Society for Information Management
401 North Michigan Avenue
Chicago, IL 60611-4267
Phone: (800) 387-9746
    or (312) 527-6734
E-mail: info@simnet.org
http://www.simnet.org

**Urban and Regional Information
    Systems Association (URISA)**
1460 Renaissance Drive
Suite 305
Park Ridge, IL 60068
Phone: (847) 824-6300
E-mail: info@urisa.org
http://www.urisa.org

PART 5: GRAPHICS AND MULTIMEDIA

**Association for Multimedia
    Communications**
P.O. Box 10645
Chicago, IL 60610
Phone: (773) 276-9320
E-mail: Web form
http://www.amcomm.org

Graphic Arts Technical Foundation
200 Deer Run Road
Seawickley, PA 15143
Phone: (412) 741-6860
E-mail: info@gatf.org
http://www.gain.net

**Graphic Communications
    International Union**
1900 L Street, NW
Washington, DC 20036
Phone: (202) 462-1400
E-mail: Web form
http://www.gciu.org/index.shtml

**Interactive Digital Software
    Association**
1211 Connecticut Avenue, NW
Suite 600
Washington, DC 20036
E-mail: idsa@idsa.org
http://www.idsa.com

Interactive Media Alliance
GCATT Building
250 14th Street, NW
4th Floor
Atlanta, GA 30318-5394
E-mail: brian@tima.org
http://www.tima.org

**International Game Developers
    Association**
600 Harrison Street
San Francisco, CA 94107
Phone: (415) 947-6235
E-mail: info@igda.org
http://www.igda.org

**National Association of Schools
    of Art and Design**
11250 Roger Bacon Drive
Suite 21
Reston, VA 20190
Phone: (703) 437-0700
E-mail: info@arts-accredit.org
http://www.arts-accredit.org/nasad/
    default.htm

PART 6: INTERNET

Association of Internet Professionals
4790 Irvine Boulevard
Suite 105-283
Irvine, CA 92620
Phone: (866) AIP-9700
E-mail: info@association.org
http://www.association.org

International Webmasters Association
119 East Union Street
Suite F
Pasadena, CA 91103
Phone: (626) 449-3709
E-mail: Web form
http://www.iwanet.org

Internet Service Providers' Consortium
1301 Shiloh Road
Suite 702
P.O. Box 1086
Kennesaw, GA 30144-8086
Phone: (866) 533-6990
E-mail: office@ispc.org
http://www.ispc.org

Internet Society
1775 Wiehle Avenue
Suite 102
Reston, VA 20190-5108
Phone: (703) 326-9880
E-mail: info@isoc.org
http://www.isoc.org

Society of Internet Professionals
7321 Victoria Park Avenue
Suite 301
Markham, ON, L3R 2ZB, Canada
Phone: (416) 891-4937
E-mail: info@sipgroup.org
http://www.sipgroup.org

World Organization of Webmasters
9580 Oak Avenue Parkway
Suite 7-177
Folsom, CA 95630
Phone: (916) 608-1597
E-mail: info@joinwow.org
http://www.joinwow.org

PART 7: MARKETING, ADVERTISING, AND MEDIA

Advertising Club of New York
155 East 55th Street
Suite 202
New York, NY 10022
E-mail: Web form
http://www.theadvertisingclub.org

American Advertising Federation
1101 Vermont Avenue, NW
Suite 500
Washington, DC 20005-6306
Phone: (202) 898-0089
E-mail: aaf@aaf.org
http://www.aaf.org

**American Association
    of Advertising Agencies**
405 Lexington Avenue
New York, NY 10174-1801
Phone: (212) 682-2500
http://www.aaaa.org

American Marketing Association
311 South Wacker Drive
Suite 5800
Chicago, IL 60606
Phone: (800) AMA-1150
    or (312) 542-9000
E-mail: info@ama.org
http://www.marketingpower.com

International Advertising Associations
521 Fifth Avenue
Suite 1807
New York, NY 10175
Phone: (212) 557-1133
E-mail: iaa@iaaglobal.org
http://www.iaaglobal.org

Internet Advertising Bureau
1440 Broadway
21st Floor
New York, NY 10018
Phone: (212) 949-9030, ext. 206
E-mail: Web form
http://www.iab.net

Marketing Research Association
1344 Silas Deane Highway
Suite 306
P.O. Box 230
Rocky Hill, CT 06067-0230
E-mail: email@mra-net.org
http://www.mra-net.org

National Press Club
529 14th Street, NW
13th Floor
Washington, DC 20045
Phone: (202) 662-7500
http://npc.press.org

National Retail Federation
325 Seventh Street, NW
Suite 1100
Washington, DC 20004
Phone: (202) 783-7971
    or (800) NRF-HOW2
http://www.nrf.com

Online News Association
c/o Janice Castro
The Medill School of Journalism
1845 Sheridan Road
Evanston, IL 60208
E-mail: jcastro@northwestern.edu
http://www.onlinenewsassociation.org

Pi Sigma Epsilon
(Sales Fraternity Associated with Sales and
    Marketing Executives International)
427 East Stewart Street
Milwaukee, WI 53207
Phone: (414) 328-1952
E-mail: pse@pse.org
http://www.pisigmaepsilon.org

**Promotion Marketing Association
    of America**
257 Park Avenue South
Suite 1102
New York, NY 10010
Phone: (212) 420-1100
E-mail: Web form
http://www.pmalink.org

Public Relations Society of America
33 Irving Place
New York, NY 10003-2376
Phone: (212) 995-2230

E-mail: membership@prsa.org
http://www.prsa.org

**Sales and Marketing Executives
    International**
P.O. Box 1390
Sumas, WA 98295-1390
Phone: (770) 661-8500
E-mail: smei@earthlink.net
http://www.smei.org/users/sm

PART 8: ACADEMIC, TRAINING, AND LIBRARIES

**American Association for Adult
    and Continuing Education**
4380 Forbes Boulevard
Lanham, MD 20706
Phone: (301) 918-1913
E-mail: aacel10@aol.com
http://www.aaace.org

**American Association
    of Community Colleges**
One Dupont Circle, NW
Suite 410
Washington, DC 20036
Phone: (202) 728-0200
E-mail: Web form
http://www.aacc.nche.edu

**American Association
    of School Libraries**
50 East Huron Street
Chicago, IL 60611
Phone: (800) 545-2433
E-mail: AASL@ala.org
http://www.ala.org/aasl

American Federation of Teachers
555 New Jersey Avenue, NW
Washington, DC 20001
Phone: (202) 879-4400
E-mail: online@aft.org
http://www.aft.org

American Library Association
50 East Huron Street
Chicago, IL 60611
Phone: (800) 545-2433
E-mail: membership@ala.org
http://www.ala.org

**American Society for Training
    and Development**
1640 King Street
Alexandria, VA 22313-2043
Phone: (703) 683-8100
E-mail: Web form
http://www.astd.org/index_IE.html

Association for Career and Technical Education
1410 King Street
Alexandria, VA 22314
Phone: (703) 683-3111
E-mail: cwebb@acteonline.org
http://www.avaonline.org

Association for Computers in the Humanities
3060 JKHB Brigham Young University
Provo, Utah 84602
E-mail: ACHWeb@brown.edu
http://www.ach.org

Association for Educational Communications and Technology
1800 North Stonelake Drive
Suite Two
Bloomington, IN 47408
Phone: (877) 677-AECT
E-mail: aect@aect.org
http://www.aect.org

Association for Library and Information Science Education
11250 Roger Bacon Drive
Suite Eight
Reston, VA 20190-5202
Phone: (703) 234-4146
E-mail: Web form
http://www.alise.org/

Association for Supervision and Curriculum Development
1703 North Beauregard Street
Alexandria, VA 22311-1714
Phone: (800) 933-2723, press 2
E-mail: member@ascd.org
http://www.ascd.org

Association of Research Libraries
21 Dupont Circle
Suite 800
Washington, DC 20036
Phone: (202) 296-2296
E-mail: arlhq@arl.org
http://www.arl.org

Digital Library Federation
1755 Massachusetts Avenue, NW
Suite 500
Washington, DC 20036
Phone: (202) 939-4761
E-mail: dlf@clir.org
http://www.diglib.org

Educational Resources Information Center (ERIC)
2277 Research Boulevard M5 6M
Rockville, MD 20850
Phone: (800) 538-3742
E-mail: accesseric@accesseric.com
http://www.eric.ed.gov

Institute for the Certification of Computer Professionals
2350 East Devon Avenue
Suite 115
Des Plaines, IL 60018-4610
Phone: (847) 299-4227 or (800) 843-8227
E-mail: office@iccp.org
http://www.iccp.org

International Association of School Librarianship
Dept 962, Box 34069
Seattle, WA 98124-1069
E-mail: iasl@rockland.com
http://www.iasl-slo.org

International Society for Technology in Education
480 Charnelton Street
Eugene, OR 97401-2626
Phone: (800) 336-5191
E-mail: iste@iste.org
http://www.iste.org

Libraries for the Future
27 Union Square West
Suite 204
New York, NY 10003
Phone: (646) 336-6236
E-mail: lff@lff.org
http://www.lff.org

Library and Information Technology Association
50 East Huron Street
Chicago, IL 60611-2795
Phone: (800) 545-2433, ext. 4270
E-mail: lita@ala.org
http://www.lita.org

Library of Congress
101 Independence Avenue, SE
Washington, DC 20540
Phone: (202) 707-5000
E-mail: Web form
http://lcweb.loc.gov

National Educational Association
1201 16th Street, NW
Washington, DC 20036
Phone: (202) 833-4000
E-mail: Web form
http://www.nea.org

National Forum on Information Literacy
Patricia Senn Breivik, Chair
National Forum on Information Literacy
Dean of the University Library
San Jose State University
One Washington Square
San Jose, CA 95192-2419
Phone: (408) 924-2419
E-mail: pbreivik@email.sjsu.edu
http://www.infolit.org

Research Libraries Group
330 Madison Avenue
Sixth Floor
New York, NY 10017-5041
Phone: (800) 537-7546 or (650) 691-2333
E-mail: bl.ric@rlg.org
http://www.rlg.org

Resource Center for Cyberculture Studies
E-mail: dsilver@u.washington.edu
http://www.com.washington.edu/rccs/

Society for Technical Communications
901 North Stuart Street
Arlington, VA 22203-1823
Phone: (703) 522-4114
E-mail: stc@stc.org
http://www.stc.org

Special Libraries Association
1700 Eighteenth Street, NW
Washington, DC 20009-2514
Phone: (202) 234-4700
E-mail: sla@sla.org
http://www.sla.org

University Continuing Education Association
One Dupont Circle, NW
Suite 615
Washington, DC 20036-1168
Phone: (202) 659-3130
E-mail: Web form
http://www.ucea.edu

PART 9: WOMEN AND MINORITIES IN COMPUTING

American Indian Science and Engineering Society
P.O. Box 9828
Albuquerque, NM 87119-9828
Phone: (505) 765-1052
E-mail: info@aises.org
http://www.aises.org

Association for Women in Computing
41 Sutter Street
Suite 1006
San Francisco, CA 94104
Phone: (415) 905-4663
E-mail: awc@awc-hq.org
http://www.awc-hq.org

Association for Women in Science
1200 New York Avenue, NW
Suite 650
Washington, DC 20005
Phone: (202) 326-8940
E-mail: awis@awis.org
http://www.serve.com/awis/

Black Data Processing Association
6301 Ivy Lane
Suite 700
Greenbelt, MD 20770
Phone: (800) 727-BDPA
    or (301) 220-2180
E-mail: Web form
http://www.bdpa.org

National Action Council
    for Minorities in Engineering
Empire State Building
350 Fifth Avenue
Suite 2212
New York, NY 10118-2299

Phone: (212) 279-2626
E-mail: webmaster@nacme.org
http://www.nacme.org

National Association for Female
    Executives
P.O. Box 469031
Escondido, CA 92046-9925
Phone: (800) 927-NAFE
E-mail: nafe@nafe.com
http://www.nafe.com

National Association of Women
    Business Owners
8405 Greensboro Drive
Suite 800
McLean, VA 22102
Phone: (703) 506-3268
E-mail: national@nawbo.org
http://www.nawbo.org

National Society of Black Engineers
1454 Duke Street
Alexandria, VA 22314
Phone: (703) 549-2207
E-mail: info@nsbe.org
http://www.nsbe.org

Society of Hispanic Professional
    Engineers
5400 East Olympic Boulevard
Suite 210
Los Angeles, CA 90022

Phone: (323) 725-3970
E-mail: shpenational@shpe.org
http://www.shpe.org

Society of Women Engineers
1444 I Street, NW
Suite 700
Washington, DC 20005-2210
Phone: (202) 712-9043
E-mail: hq@swe.org
http://www.swe.org

Women in Management
P.O. Box 9560
Springfield, IL 62791-9560
Phone: (877) 946-6285
E-mail: nationalwim@aol.com
http://www.wimonline.org

Women in Technology International
6345 Balboa Boulevard
Suite 257
Encino, CA 91316
Phone: (800) 334-WITI
    or (818) 342-9746
E-mail: membership@corp.witi.com
http://www.witi.org/

APPENDIX III
SELECTED PROFESSIONAL
AND TRADE PERIODICALS

The following is a list of selected periodicals about various aspects of computing or the computer industry. Many periodicals' websites include on-line subscription forms for the print magazine, as well as the opportunity to subscribe to various newsletters that are distributed by e-mail. (In some cases, print publications have been turned into on-line-only publications.)

ACM Computing Surveys
ACM
One Astor Plaza
17th Floor
New York, NY 10036-5701
Phone: (212) 869-7440
E-mail: agha@cs.uiuc.edu
http://www.acm.org/surveys/

Advertising Age
711 Third Avenue
New York, NY 10017-4036
Phone: (212) 210-0100
E-mail: editor@adage.com
http://www.adage.com

Bioinformatics
Journals Customer Services
Oxford University Press
2001 Evans Road
Cary, NC 27513
Phone: (800) 852-7323
E-mail: Query form at
        http://www3.oup.co.uk/cgi-bin/cs/cs
http://bioinformatics.oupjournals.org

Boardwatch Magazine
1300 East Ninth Street
Cleveland, OH 44144
Phone: (216) 696-7000
E-mail: information@penton.com
http://www.boardwatch.com

Byte.com
[On-line-only publication]
E-mail: webmaster@byte.com
http://www.byte.com

*CADAlyst: the Newsletter
    of the AutoCad Users' Group*
One Phoenix Mill Lane
Suite 401
Peterborough, NH 03458

Phone: (603) 924-5400
E-mail: editors@cadalyst.com
http://www.cadalyst.com

Cadence Magazine
600 Harrison Street
San Francisco, CA 94107
Phone: (415) 947-6141
E-mail: awilliams@cmp.com
http://www.cadenceweb.com

Communication Systems Design
600 Harrison Street
San Francisco, CA 94107
Phone: (415) 947-6141
E-mail: dblaza@cmp.com
http://www.commsdesign.com/csd/issue

Communications of the ACM
Association for Computing Machinery
One Astor Plaza
17th Floor
New York, NY 10036-5701
Phone: (212) 869-7440
E-mail: ACMHELP@acm.org
http://www.acm.org

*Communications Technology: Official
    Trade Journal of the Society of Cable
    Television Engineers*
1201 Seven Locks Road
Potomac, MD 20854
Phone: (800) 777-5006 or (301) 424-3338
E-mail: clientservices@pbimedia.com
http://www.pbimedia.com

Computer Gaming World
Ziff-Davis
28 East 28th Street
New York, NY 10016-7930
Phone: (212) 503-3500
E-mail: cgwletters@ziffdavis.com
http://www.gamers.com/cgw/index.jsp

Computer Graphics World
PennWell
98 Spit Brook Road
Nashua, NH 03062
Phone: (603) 891-0123
E-mail: Web form
http://cgw.pennet.com/home.cfm

Cutter IT Journal (formerly *American
    Programmer*)
Cutter Information Corporation
37 Broadway
Suite One
Arlington, MA 02474
Phone: (800) 964-5118
E-mail: sales@cutter.com
http://www.cutter.com

Data Communications International
1221 Avenue of the Americas
New York, NY 10020
Phone: (800) 525-5003
    or (212) 904-6410

Data Mining and Knowledge Discovery
Editorial Office, Kluwer Academic
    Publishers
101 Philip Drive
Norwell, MA 02061
Phone: (781) 871-6600, ×245
E-mail: cheryl.knight@wkap.com
http://www.digimine.com/usama/datamine/

Datamation
[Formerly printed magazine; now
    on-line only]
Jupitermedia
23 Old Kings Highway South
Darien, CT 06820
Phone: (203) 662-2800
E-mail: Web form
http://itmanagement.earthweb.com

Diagnostic Imaging
600 Harrison Street
Fourth Floor
San Francisco, CA 94107
Phone: (415) 947-6000
E-mail: jhayes@cmp.com
http://www.diagnosticimaging.com

DM Review
[On-line publication on data mining
  and data warehousing]
240 Regency Court
Suite 201
Brookfield, WI 53045
E-mail: Web form
http://www.dmreview.com

Dr. Dobbs' Journal
2800 Campus Drive
San Mateo, CA 94403
Phone: (650) 513-4300
E-mail: editors@ddj.com
http://www.ddj.com

EETimes
P.O. Box 3095
Northbrook, IL 60065-3095
Phone: (847) 291-5215
E-mail: rkeane@cmp.com
http://www.eet.com

Electronic Design
Penton Media
1300 East Ninth Street
Cleveland, OH 44114
Phone: (216) 696-7000
E-mail: information@penton.com
  and Web subscription form
http://www.elecdesign.com

Embedded Systems
CMP
600 Harrison Street
San Francisco, CA 94107
Phone: (415) 947-6669
E-mail: eoconnell@cmp.com
http://www.embedded.com/mag.htm

Game Developer
P.O. Box 1274
Skokie, IL 60076-8274
Phone: (800) 250-2429
E-mail: gamedeveloper@alldata.com
http://www.gdmag.com/homepage.htm

InfoWorld
501 Second Street
San Francisco, CA 94107
Phone: (402) 292-5688

E-mail: customerservice@
  infoworld.com
http://www.infoworld.com

Information Today
143 Old Marlton Pike
Medford, NJ 08055
Phone: (609) 654-6266
E-mail: custserve@infotoday.com
http://www.infotoday.com/default.shtml

Information Week
600 Community Drive
Manhasset, NY 11030
Phone: (516) 562-7911
E-mail: llally@cmp.com
http://www.informationweek.com

Intelligent Enterprise
2800 Campus Drive
San Mateo, CA 94403
Phone: (847) 647-5928
E-mail: IntelligentEnterprise@
  halldata.com
http://www.intelligentcrm.com

Internet Week
CMP Media LLC
600 Community Drive
Manhasset, NY 11030
Phone: (516) 562-5000
E-mail: feedback@internetweek.com
http://www.internetweek.com

Internet World
[Formerly printed magazine; now
  on-line only]
16 Thorndal Circle
Darien, CT 06820-5421
Phone: (203) 559-2864
E-mail: information@penton.com
  and Web subscription form
http:/www.internetworld.com

Journal of Systems and Software
360 Park Avenue South
New York, NY 10010-1710
Phone: (888) 437-4636
E-mail: usinfo@elsevier.com
http://www.elsevier.com

Linux Journal
P.O. Box 55549
Seattle, WA 98155-0549
Phone: (206) 297-7514
E-mail: subs@ssc.com
http://www.linuxjournal.com

M-Business
[Print magazine discontinued; on-line
  publication only]
CMP Media LLC
600 Community Drive
Manhasset, NY 11030
Phone: (516) 562-5000
E-mail: Web form
http://www.mbusinessdaily.com

MIS Quarterly
Carlson School of Management
University of Minnesota
321 19th Avenue South
Suite 3-306
Minneapolis, MN 55455
E-mail: misq@csom.umn.edu
http://www.misq.org/

Network Magazine
CMP Media LLC
600 Community Drive
Manhasset, N.Y. 11030
Phone: (800) 577-5356 or (847) 647-6834
E-mail: NetworkMagazine@
  halldata.com
http://www.networkmagazine.com

PC Magazine
P.O. Box 54070
Boulder, CO 80322-4070
Phone: (212) 503-3500 or (415) 547-8000
E-mail: subhelp@pcmag.com
http://www.pcmag.com

PC World
501 Second Street
San Francisco, CA 94107
Phone: (415) 243-0500
E-mail: Web form
http://www.pcworld.com/magazine

School Library Media Research
American Association of School Libraries
50 East Huron Street
Chicago, IL 60611
Phone: (800) 545-2433
E-mail: AASL@ala.org
http://www.ala.org/aasl/SLMR/

Silicon Strategies
CMP Media LLC
600 Community Drive
Manhasset, NY 11030
Phone: (516) 562-5000
E-mail: mlapedus@cmp.com
  and Web form
http://www.siliconstrategies.com

Slashdot
[On-line-only publication]
E-mail: Web form
http://slashdot.org

Software Development
CMP Media LLC
600 Harrison Street
San Francisco, CA 94107
E-mail: Web form and
    swd@halldata.com
http://www.sdmagazine.com

Solid State Technology
PennWell
98 Spit Brook Road
Nashua, NH 03062
Phone: (603) 891-0123
E-mail: Web form
http://sst.pennet.com/home.cfm

SysAdmin
1601 West 23rd Street
Suite 200
Lawrence, KS 66046
Phone: (785) 841-1631
E-mail: cs@cmp.com and Web form
http://www.sysadminmag.com

Technology and Learning
CMP Media LLC
600 Harrison Street
San Francisco, CA 94107
Phone: (415) 947-6746 or (800) 607-4410
E-mail: jvconover@cmp.com
http://www.techlearning.com

Unix Review
CMP Media LLC
600 Harrison Street
San Francisco, CA 94107
Phone: (415) 947-6746
E-mail: Web form
http://www.unixreview.com

Windows Developer Magazine
CMP Media LLC
600 Harrison Street
San Francisco, CA 94107
Phone: (415) 947-6914
E-mail: Web form
http://www.windevnet.com

Wired Magazine
660 Third Street
First Floor
San Francisco, CA 94107
Phone: (800) 769-4733 or (415) 276-8400
E-mail: subscriptions@wired.com and
    Web form
http://www.wired.com

BIBLIOGRAPHY

The following bibliography is divided into four categories for convenience. The intention of these selections is to provide a variety for up-to-date, comprehensive, and inspirational starting points for exploring a career in computing.

JOB SEARCH AND CAREER DEVELOPMENT

There are many books that provide useful information for job seeking and career development. The following titles focus on employment opportunities and careers in computer-related fields or on the use of the Internet for career research. A few general references are also included.

Ackley, Kristina M. *100 Top Internet Job Sites: Get Wired, Get Hired in Today's New Job Market.* Manassas Park, Va.: Impact Publications, 2000.

Adams Jobs Almanac. 8th ed. Avon, Mass.: Adams Media Corporation, 2000.

Basta, Nicholas. *Opportunities in Engineering Careers.* Rev. ed. Chicago: VGM Career Books, 2003.

Bredin, Alice, and Kirsten M. Lagatree. *The Home Office Solution: How to Balance Your Professional and Personal Lives While Working at Home.* New York: Wiley, 1998.

Brown, Mark. *Opportunities in Technical Sales Careers.* Chicago: VGM Career Books, 2002.

Brown, Sheldon, and Mark Rowh. *Opportunities in Biotechnology Careers* Rev. ed. Chicago: VGM Career Books, 2001.

Burnett, Rebecca E. *Careers for Number Crunchers and Other Quantitative Types.* 2d ed. Chicago: VGM Career Books, 2002.

Burns, Julie Kling. *Opportunities in Computer Careers.* Chicago: VGM Career Books, 2002.

Careers in Focus: Business Managers. New York: Ferguson, 2003.

Careers in Focus: Engineering. 2d ed. New York: Ferguson, 2003.

Careers in Focus: Internet. 2d ed. New York: Ferguson, 2002.

Careers in Focus: Writing. 2d ed. New York: Ferguson, 2002.

College Board Index of Majors & Graduate Degrees 2003. New York: College Board, 2002.

Dikel, Margaret Riley, and Frances E. Roehm. *Guide to Internet Job Searching, 2002–2003.* New York: McGraw-Hill, 2002.

Dixon, Pam. *Job Searching Online for Dummies.* Foster City, Calif.: IDG Books Worldwide, 2000.

Eberts, Marjorie, and Margaret Gisler. *Careers for Computer Buffs & Other Technological Types.* 2d ed. Chicago: VGM Career Books, 1998.

Eberts, Marjorie, and Rachel Kelsey. *Careers for Cybersurfers and Other Online Types.* Chicago: VGM Career Books, 1997.

Echaore-McDavid, Susan. *Career Opportunities in Education.* New York: Facts On File, 2000.

Encyclopedia of Careers and Vocational Guidance. 12th ed. New York: Ferguson, 2002.

Ferguson, Donald L. *Opportunities in Journalism Careers.* Rev. ed. Chicago: VGM Career Books, 2001.

Farr, Michael [and others], editors, and U.S. Department of Labor. *The Enhanced Occupational Outlook Handbook, 2000–2001.* 3d ed. Indianapolis, Ind.: Jist Works, 2000.

Gabler, Laura R. *Career Exploration on the Internet: A Student's Guide to More than 500 Web Sites.* Chicago: Ferguson Publishing, 2000.

Gardner, Garth. *Careers in Computer Graphics & Animation.* Fairfax, Va.: GGC, 2001.

———. *Gardner's Guide to Colleges for Multimedia & Animation, 2003.* 3d ed. Washington, DC: GGC, 2002.

———. *Gardner's Guide to Internships in New Media, 2004:* Computer Graphics, Animation, Multimedia. 2d ed. Washington, DC: GGC, 2002.

Garner, Geraldine O. *Careers in Engineering.* Chicago: VGM Career Books, 2003.

———. *Great Jobs for Engineering Majors.* 2d ed. Chicago: VGM Career Books, 2002.

Goldberg, Jan, and Mark Rowh. *Great Jobs for Computer Science Majors.* Chicago: VGM Career Books, 2003.

Guiley, Rosemary Ellen, and Janet Frick. *Career Opportunities for Writers.* New York: Facts On File, 2000.

The JobBank Guide to Computer and High-Tech Companies. 2d ed. Avon, Mass.: Adams Media Corporation, 1999.

Keyes, Jessica. *How to Be a Successful Internet Consultant.* New York: AMACOM, 2002.

McCook, Kathleen de la Peña. *Opportunities in Library and Information Science Careers.* Chicago: VGM Career Books, 2002.

Meyer, Peter. *Getting Started in Computer Consulting.* New York: Wiley, 2000.

Morris, Mary S.E., and Paul Massie. *Cybercareers.* Upper Saddle River, NJ: Prentice Hall Computer Books, 1997.

Munday, Marianne, and Margaret Gisler. *Opportunities in Data and Word Processing Careers.* Chicago: VGM Career Books, 2002.

Peterson's Internships 2003. Lawrenceville, NJ: Peterson's/Thomson Learning, 2002.

Profiles of American Colleges with CD-ROM (2003 Edition). Woodbury, NY: Barron's Educational Series, 2002.

Resumes for Computer Careers. 2d ed. VGM Career Books, 2002.

Rotman, Morris B. *Opportunities in Public Relations Careers.* Rev. ed. Chicago: VGM Career Books, 2001.

Rowh, Mark. *Opportunities in Educational Support Careers.* Chicago: VGM Career Books, 2001.

Salmon, Mark. *Opportunities in Visual Arts Careers.* Rev. ed. Chicago: VGM Career Books, 2001.

Smith, Rebecca. *Electronic Resumes and Online Networking.* 2d ed. Franklin Lakes, N.J.: Career Press, 2000.

Stair, Lila, and Leslie Stair. *Careers in Computers.* 3d ed. Chicago: VGM Career Books, 2002.

———. *Careers in Marketing.* 3d ed. Chicago: VGM Career Books, 2002.

United States Department of Labor. *Occupational Outlook Handbook, 2002–2003.* Indianapolis, Ind.: Jist Works, 2002. [Also available on-line at *http://www.bls.gov/oco/home.htm*]

Wright, John. *The American Almanac of Jobs and Salaries, 2000–2001.* New York: Avon Books, 2000.

INSIGHTS INTO COMPUTER WORK AND THE COMPUTER INDUSTRY

The following biographies and historical overviews explore the work of significant individuals and the emergence of trends in computer science and the computer industry.

Berlinksi, David. *The Advent of the Algorithm: The Idea that Rules the World.* New York: Harcourt, 2000.

Brooks, Frederick. *The Mythical Man-Month, Anniversary Edition: Essays on Software Engineering.* Reading, Mass.: Addison-Wesley, 1995.

Cringely, R. X. *Accidental Empires.* New York: Harper, 1997.

Feigenbaum, E., P. McCorduck, and H.P. Nii. *The Rise of the Expert Company.* New York: Times Books, 1988.

Freiberger, Paul, and Michael Swaine. *Fire in the Valley: The Making of the Personal Computer.* New York: McGraw-Hill, 1999.

Grove, Andrew. *Only the Paranoid Survive.* New York: Currency Doubleday, 1996.

Hafner, K., and M. Lyon. *Where Wizards Stay Up Late: The Origins of the Internet.* New York: Simon & Schuster, 1996.

Henderson, Harry. *A to Z Biographical Dictionary of Computer Science and Technology.* New York: Facts On File, 2002.

———. *Pioneers of the Internet.* San Diego, Calif.: Lucent Books, 2002.

Jager, Rama Dev, and Rafael Ortiz. *In the Company of Giants.* New York: McGraw-Hill, 1997.

Kidder, Tracy. *The Soul of a New Machine.* New York: Modern Library, 1997.

Kohanski, Daniel. *The Philosophical Programmer: Reflections on the Month in the Machine.* New York: St. Martin's Press, 1998.

Levy, Steven. *Insanely Great: The Life and Times of the Macintosh, the Computer that Changed Everything.* New York: Penguin Books, 2000.

Lohr, Steve. *Go To.* New York: Basic Books, 2001.

Reid, R. H. *Architects of the Web.* New York: John Wiley, 1997.

Segaller, S. *Nerds 2.0.1: A Brief History of the Internet.* New York: TV Books, 1998.

Shasha, Dennis, and Cathy Lazere. *Out of the Minds: the Lives and Discoveries of 15 Great Computer Scientists.* New York: Springer-Verlag, 1995.

Slater, Robert. *Portraits in Silicon.* Cambridge, Mass.: MIT Press, 1987.

Spector, Robert. *Amazon.com: Get Big Fast.* New York: HarperBusiness, 2000.

Torvalds, Linus. *Just for Fun: the Story of an Accidental Revolutionary.* New York: HarperBusiness, 2001.

Ullmann, Ellen. *Close to the Machine: Technophilia and Its Discontents.* San Francisco: City Lights Books, 1997.

Waldrop, M. Mitchell. *The Dream Machine: J. C. Licklider and the Revolution that Made Computing Personal.* New York: Viking, 2001.

Yount, Lisa. *A–Z of Women in Science and Mathematics.* New York: Facts On File, 1999.

OVERVIEWS OF APPLICATIONS

The titles in this section are introductions or surveys of various applications of computer science and technology.

Ackermann, Ernest, and Karen Hartman. *The Information Searcher's Guide to Searching and Researching on the Internet and World Wide Web.* 2d ed. Wilsonville, Ore.: ABF Content, 2000.

Aho, Alfred V., Ravi Sethi, and Jeffrey D. Ullman. *Compiler Design: Principles, Techniques, and Tools.* Reading, Mass.: Addison-Wesley, 1985.

Allen, J. *Natural Language Understanding.* 2d ed. Reading, Mass.: Addison-Wesley, 1995.

Ambler, Scott W. *The Object Primer.* 2d ed. Cambridge University Press, 2001.

Arnold, Ken, and James Gosling. *The Java Programming Language.* 2d. ed. Reading, Mass.: Addison-Wesley, 1997.

Bach, Maurice J. *Design of the UNIX Operating System.* Englewood Cliffs, N.J.: Prentice Hall, 1987.

Back, T. *Evolutionary Algorithms in Theory and Practice: Evolution Strategies, Evolutionary Programming, Genetic Algorithms.* Oxford: Oxford University Press, 1996.

Baron, C., J. C. Geffory, and G. Motet, eds. *Embedded Systems Applications.* New York: Kluwer Academic Press, 1997.

Bates, Bob. *Game Design: The Art & Business of Creating Games.* Roseville, Calif.: Prima Tech, 2001.

Bates, Regis J. *Broadband Telecommunications Handbook.* New York: McGraw Hill, 1999.

Belew, Richard K., and C. J. van Rijsbergen. *Finding Out About: A Cognitive Perspective on Search Engine Technology and the WWW.* New York: Cambridge University Press, 2001.

Bentley, Jon. *Programming Pearls.* 2d ed. Reading, Mass.: Addison-Wesley, 1999.

Bergin, Thomas J., and Richard G. Gibson, eds. *History of Programming Languages—II.* Reading, Mass.: Addison-Wesley/ACM Press, 1996.

Biermann, Alan W. *Great Ideas in Computer Science: a Gentle Introduction.* 2d ed. Cambridge, Mass.: MIT Press, 1997.

Blanding, Stephen F. *Enterprise Operations Management Handbook, Second Edition.* Grand Rapids, Mich.: CRC Press, 1999.

Bremer, Michael. *The User Manual Manual: How to Research, Write, Test, Edit & Produce a Software Manual.* Concord, Calif.: UnTechnical Press, 1999.

Brookshear, J. Glenn. *Computer Science: An Overview.* 6th ed. Reading, Mass.: Addison-Wesley, 2000.

Burke, John J. *Neal-Schuman Library Technology Companion: A Basic Guide for the Library Staff.* New York: Neal Schuman Publishers, 2001.

Buyens, J. *Web Database Development: Step by Step.* Redmond, Wash.: Microsoft Press, 2000.

Carrano, Frank, and Janet J. Pritchard. *Data Abstraction and Problem Solving with C++: Walls and Mirrors.* 3d ed. Reading, Mass.: Addison-Wesley, 2001.

Colby, Clifford [and others], eds. *The Macintosh Bible.* 8th ed. Berkeley, Calif.: Peachpit Press, 2001.

Cook, Tony. *The ABC's of Mechanical Drafting with an Introduction to AutoCAD®.* Upper Saddle River, N.J.: Prentice Hall, 2001.

Crawford, Chris. *The Art of Computer Game Design.* Berkeley, Calif.: Osborne-McGraw Hill, 1982.

De Leeuw, B. *Digital Cinematography.* New York: Academic Press, 1997.

Dennis, Alan, and Barbara Wixom. *System Analysis and Design.* New York: Wiley, 2000.

Elsmari, R., and S. Navathe. *Fundamentals of Database Systems.* Redwood City, Calif.: Benjamin Cummings, 2000.

Evans, James R., and David Louis Olson. *Introduction to Simulation and Risk Analysis.* Upper Saddle River, N.J.: Prentice-Hall, 2001.

Forouzan, Behrouz. *Data Communications and Networking.* New York: McGraw Hill, 2001.

Fuller, J. L. *Robotics: Introduction, Programming, and Projects.* Upper Saddle River, N.J.: Prentice Hall, 1998.

Gookin, Dan. *PCs for Dummies.* 8th ed. New York: Hungry Minds, 2001.

Hall, James A. *Information Systems Auditing and Assurance.* Cincinnati, Ohio: South Western College, 2000.

Hall, Jim. *Online Journalism: A Critical Primer.* Sterling, Va.: Pluto Press, 2001.

Han, Jiawei, and Micheline Kamber. *Data Mining: Concepts and Techniques.* San Francisco: Morgan Kaufmann, 2000.

Hane, Paula J. *Super Searchers in the News: The Online Secrets of Journalists and News Researchers.* Medford, N.J.: Information Today, 2000.

Harvey, Brian. *Computer Science Logo Style.* 3 vols. 2d ed. Cambridge, Mass.: MIT Press, 1997.

Heath, Michael T. *Scientific Computing: An Introductory Survey.* 2d ed. New York: McGraw-Hill, 2002.

Hernandez, Michael J. *Database Design for Mere Mortals: A Hands-On Guide to Relational Database Design.* Reading, Mass.: Addison-Wesley, 1997.

Hillis, Daniel W. *The Pattern on the Stone: The Simple Ideas that Make Computers Work.* New York: Basic Books, 1998.

Huang, Xuedong [and others]. *Spoken Language Processing: A Guide to Theory, Algorithm and System Development.* Upper Saddle River, N.J.: Prentice Hall, 2001.

Johnson, Jeff. *GUI Bloopers: Don'ts and Do's for Software Developers and Web Designers.* San Francisco: Morgan Kaufmann, 2000.

Kernighan, Brian W., and P. J. Plauger. *The Elements of Programming Style.* 2d ed. New York: McGraw-Hill, 1978.

———. *Software Tools in Pascal.* Reading, Mass.: Addison-Wesley, 1981.

Kernighan, Brian W., and Rob Pike. *The UNIX Programming Environment.* Englewood Cliffs, N.J.: Prentice Hall, 1984.

Kershner, H. G. *Computer Literacy.* 3d ed. Dubuque, Iowa: Kendall/Hunt, 1998.

Kleitz, William. *Digital and Microprocessor Fundamentals: Theory and Applications.* Upper Saddle River, N.J.: Prentice Hall, 1999.

Knuth, Donald E. *The Art of Computer Programming.* Vol. 1: Fundamental Algorithms. 3d ed. Addison-Wesley, 1997. Vol. 2: Seminumerical Algorithms. 3d ed. Addison-Wesley, 1997. Vol. 3: Searching and Sorting. 2d ed. Addison-Wesley, 1998.

Kovel, Ralph M., and Terry H. Kovel. *Kovels's Bid, Buy, and Sell Online : Basic Auction Information and Tricks of the Trade.* New York: Three Rivers Press, 2001.

Langtangen, Hans Petter, Are Magnus Bruaset, and Ewald Quak, eds. *Advances in Software Tools for Scientific Computing.* New York: Springer-Verlag, 2000.

Laudon, K. C., and J. P. Laudon. *Management Information Systems: New Approaches to Organization and Technology.* Upper Saddle River, N.J.: Prentice-Hall, 1999.

Law, A., and W. Kelton. *Simulation Modeling and Analysis.* 3d ed. New York: McGraw-Hill, Hill, 1999.

Longley, P.A. (and others), eds. *Geographical Information Systems: Principles, Techniques, Management and Applications.* New York: Wiley, 1998.

Makedon, Fillia, and Samuel A. Rebelsky, eds. *Electronic Multimedia Publishing: Enabling Technologies and Authoring Issues.* Boston: Kluwer Academic, 1998.

McCorduck, Pamela. *Machines Who Think.* San Francisco: W. H. Freeman, 1979.

Mano, M. Morris, and Charles R. Kime. *Logic and Computer Design Fundamentals.* 2d ed. Upper Saddle River, N.J.: Prentice Hall, 2000.

Misener, Stephen, and Stephen A. Krawetz, eds. *Bioinformatics: Methods and Protocols.* Totowa, N.J.: Humana Press, 2000.

Moore, F. Richard. *Elements of Computer Music.* Upper Saddle River, N.J.: Prentice Hall, 1998.

Neumann, Peter G. *Computer-Related Risks.* Reading, Mass: Addison-Wesley, 1995.

Niederst, Jennifer. *Web Design in a Nutshell.* 2d ed. Sebastopol, Calif.: O'Reilly, 2001.

O'Brien, James A. *Introduction to Information Systems.* New York: McGraw Hill, 2000.

Packer, Randal, and Ken Jordan, eds. *Multimedia: From Wagner to Virtual Reality.* New York: Norton, 2002.

Parent, Rick. *Computer Animation: Algorithms and Techniques.* San Francisco: Morgan Kaufmann, 2002.

Parker, Roger C. *Web Design and Desktop Publishing for Dummies.* 2d ed. New York: Hungry Minds, 1997.

Patterson, D. A., and J. L. Hennessy. *Computer Organization and Design.* 2d ed. San Francisco: Morgan Kaufmann, 1998.

Pavlik, John V. *New Media Technology: Cultural and Commercial Perspectives.* Needham Heights, Mass.: Allyn and Bacon, 1998.

Rashidi, Hooman H., and Lukas K. Buehler. *Bioinformatics Basics: Applications in Biological Science and Medicine.* Grand Rapids, Mich.: CRC Press, 1999.

Raskin, Jef. *The Humane Interface: New Directions for Designing Interactive Systems.* Reading, Mass.: Addison-Wesley, 2000.

Ray, Erik T. *Learning XML.* Sebastopol, Calif.: O'Reilly, 2001.

Reddick, Randy, and Elliot King. *The Online Journalist: Using the Internet and Other Resources.* 3d ed. Belmont, Calif.: Wadsworth, 2000.

Rogers, Pauline B. *The Art of Visual Effects: Interviews on the Tools of the Trade.* Boston: Focal Press, 1999.

Russ, J. C. *The Image Processing Handbook.* 3d ed. Boca Raton, Fla.: CRC Press, 1999.

Sammes, Tony, Brian Jenkinson, and A. J. Sammes. *Forensic Computing: A Practitioner's Guide.* New York: Springer Verlag, 2000.

Schulmeyer, G., Gordon and James L. MacManus, eds. *Handbook of Software Quality Assurance.* 3d ed. Upper Saddle River, N.J.: Prentice Hall, 1999.

Sebesta, Robert W. *Concepts of Programming Languages.* 4th ed. Reading, Mass.: Addison-Wesley, 1999.

Semerson, J., and K. Curran. *Computer Numerical Control: Operation and Programming.* Upper Saddle River, N.J.: Prentice-Hall, 1996.

Shapiro, Stuart C. *Encyclopedia of Artificial Intelligence.* 2d ed. New York: Wiley, 1992.

Shortliffe, Edward H., ed. [and others] *Medical Informatics: Computer Applications in Health Care and Biomedicine.* 2d ed. Springer-Verlag, 2000.

Sipser, Michael. *Introduction to the Theory of Computation.* Boston: PWS Pub. Co., 1997.

Sommerville, Ian. *Software Engineering.* 6th ed. Reading, Mass.: Addison-Wesley, 2000.

Spainhour, Stephen, and Robert Eckstein. *Webmaster in a Nutshell.* 2d ed. Sebastopol, Calif.: O'Reilly, 1999.

Stefik, M. *Introduction to Knowledge Systems.* San Francisco: Morgan Kaufmann, 1995.

Stevens, Roger. *Computer Graphics Dictionary: Including Animation, Game Development, and Photorealism.* Hingham, Mass.: Charles River Media, 2001.

Stroustrup, Bjarne. *The C++ Programming Language.* 3d ed. Reading, Mass.: Addison-Wesley, 1997.

Tannenbaum, Andrew, and Albert S. Woodhull. *Operating Systems: Design and Implementation.* 2d ed. Upper Saddle River, N.J.: Prentice-Hall, 1997.

Vince, John. *Essential Virtual Reality Fast: How to Understand the Techniques and Potential of Virtual Reality.* New York: Springer-Verlag, 1998.

Weiss, M.A. *Algorithms, Data Structures, and Problem Solving with C++.* Reading, Mass.: Addison-Wesley, 1997.

White, Ron. *How Computers Work.* Millennium Ed. Indianapolis, In.: Que, 1999.

Wirth, N. *Algorithms + Data Structures = Programs.* Upper Saddle River, N.J.: Prentice-Hall, 1976.

Zwicky, Elizabeth [and others]. *Building Internet Firewalls.* 2d ed. Sebastopol, Calif.: O'Reilly, 2000.

THE BIG PICTURE (AND EMERGING TRENDS)

The final selection of titles looks at social, cultural, and philosophical aspects of the computer field, as well as visions of the future.

Berners-Lee, Tim, and Mark Fischetti. *Weaving the Web.* San Francisco: HarperSanFrancisco, 1999.

Brooks, Michael, ed. *Quantum Computing and Communications.* New York: Springer-Verlag, 1999.

Brooks, Rodney A. *Flesh and Machines: How Robots Will Change Us.* New York: Pantheon Books, 2002.

Center for Strategic and International Studies. *Cybercrime, Cyberterrorism, Cyberwarfare: Averting an Electronic Waterloo.* Washington, D.C.: CSIS Press, 1998.

Dertouzos, Michael. *What Will Be: How the New World of Information Will Change Our Lives.* Harper San Francisco, 1997.

———. The Unfinished Revolution: Human-Centered Computers and What They Can Do For Us. New York: HarperBusiness, 2001.

DiBona, Chris, Sam Ockman, and Mark Stone, eds. *Open Sources: Voices from the Open Source Revolution.* Sebastopol, Calif.: O'Reilly, 1999.

Drexler, K. Eric. *Engines of Creation.* Garden City, N.Y.: Anchor Press/Doubleday, 1986.

Dreyfus, Hubert. *What Computers Can't Do: A Critique of Artificial Reason.* New York: Harper and Row, 1972.

———. What Computers Still Can't Do. Cambridge, Mass.: MIT Press, 1992.

Feigenbaum, E. A., and J. Feldman, eds. *Computers and Thought.* New York: McGraw-Hill, 1963.

Garfinkel, Simson, and Deborah Russell. *Database Nation: The Death of Privacy in the 21st Century.* Sebastopol, Calif.: O'Reilly, 2001.

Gibson, W. *Neuromancer.* New York: Ace Books, 1984.

Gleick, J. *Chaos: The Making of New Science.* New York: Viking, 1987.

Gilder, George. *Telecosm: How Infinite Bandwidth Will Revolutionize Our World.* New York: Free Press, 2000.

Henderson, Harry. *Privacy in the Information Age* (Library in a Book). New York: Facts On File, 1999.

Hunter, Richard S. *World Without Secrets: Business, Crime, and Privacy in the Age of Ubiquitous Computing.* New York: Wiley, 2002.

Kurzweil, Ray. *The Age of Spiritual Machines: When Computers Exceed Human Intelligence.* New York: Viking, 1999.

Leonard, Andrew. *Bots: The Origin of a New Species.* San Francisco: Hardwired, 1997.

Levy, Stephen. *Artificial Life: The Quest for a New Creation.* New York: Pantheon Books, 1992.

———. Crypto. New York: Viking, 2001.

———. Hackers: Heroes of the Computer Revolution. New York: Doubleday, 1984.

Minsky, Marvin. *The Society of Mind.* New York: Simon and Schuster, 1986.

Moravec, Hans. *ROBOT: Mere Machines to Transcendent Minds.* New York: Oxford University Press, 1998.

Nelson, Theodore. *Computer Lib/Dream Machines.* Rev. ed. Chicago: Hugo's Books, 1987.

Nyce, J. M., and P. Kahn. *From Memex to Hypertext: Vannevar Bush and the Mind's Machine.* Boston: Academic Press, 1991.

Papert, Seymour. *Mindstorms: Children, Computers, and Powerful Ideas.* New York: Basic Books, 1993.

Popper, Frank. *Art of the Electronic Age.* New York: Thames & Hudson, 1997.

Raymond, Eric. *The Cathedral and the Bazaar: Musings on Linux and Open Source by an Accidental Revolutionary.* Cambridge, Mass.: O'Reilly, 1999.

———. The New Hacker's Dictionary. 3d ed. Cambridge, Mass.: MIT Press, 1996.

Rheingold, Howard. *Smart Mobs: The Next Social Revolution.* Cambridge, Mass.: Perseus Books, 2002.

———. The Virtual Community: Homesteading on the Electronic Frontier. Reading, Mass.: Addison-Wesley, 1993.

Stephenson Neil. *In the Beginning Was the Command Line.* New York: Avon Books, 1999.

Stoll, Clifford. *The Cuckoo's Egg.* Garden City, N.Y.: Doubleday, 1989.

———. Silicon Snake Oil: Second Thoughts on the Information Highway. New York: Doubleday, 1995.

Stork, David G. *Hal's Legacy.* Cambridge, Mass.: MIT Press, 1996.

Turkle, Sherry. *Life on the Screen: Identity in the Age of the Internet.* New York: Simon & Schuster, 1995.

———. The Second Self: Computers and the Human Spirit. New York: Simon & Schuster, 1984.

INDEX